S0-ADH-545

MONTGOMERY COLLEGE LIBRARY
ROCKVILLE CAMPUS

WITHDRAWN FROM LIBRARY

ESSAYING THE ESSAY

ESSAYING THE ESSAY

BY

BURGES JOHNSON

Essay Index Reprint Series

 BOOKS FOR LIBRARIES PRESS
FREEPORT, NEW YORK

PR
1363
J6   R 71   5084
1970

..., Brown, and Company

Copyright © renewed 1955 by Burges Johnson

Reprinted 1970 by arrangement with
Roland P. Carreker, Jr.
Executor of the Estate of Burges Johnson

INTERNATIONAL STANDARD BOOK NUMBER:
0-8369-1965-3

LIBRARY OF CONGRESS CATALOG CARD NUMBER:
71-134103

PRINTED IN THE UNITED STATES OF AMERICA

DEDICATED TO
MANY FORMER OCCUPANTS OF PLEASANTLY
REMEMBERED CLASSROOMS AND ESPECIALLY
TO A LITTLE GROUP IN DURANGO, COLORADO

THIS book is designed for the aid and encouragement of writers whose essays are about to be written, rather than to appraise the work of those whose task is done. It is not so much about essays as about essay writing. Selection from the work of past masters has been made with training in view, and not with any idea of furnishing a textbook for those interested solely in the place the Essay occupies in literature. The author builds his suggestions to young writers upon his experience as a teacher and also as an editor; nor would he wish to draw any great distinction between the two, since either one (if he be conscientious) must exercise many of the functions of the other.

A very small part of the following material appeared first in the pages of *The Writer* magazine, and is reprinted here by permission.

CONTENTS

COLLECTION OF ESSAYS AND PARTS OF ESSAYS OF MANY KINDS

* The date of the writing of this essay.

CONTENTS   xi

CONTENTS

ESSAYING THE ESSAY

FOR TEACHERS

The following pages, set in smaller type, are addressed to instructors; students are expressly cautioned against reading them on pain of boredom. Moreover, in order to understand them students must view themselves objectively, and that is generally foreign to their natures.

OF WRITING IN GENERAL

IT should be easy to write a book about writing. One need only examine the successful writings of others, classify them under various familiar headings and look for common multiples, which would then immediately become *rules*. News writing, feature writing, short-story writing, essays, sketches, articles, — "exposition", "narration", "description", — each of these terms may provide a chapter title in some textbook on composition. But the trouble is that successful writers take malicious pleasure in breaking rules. They view their literary activity as an art rather than a science, and they will not "stay put." They persist in upsetting textbook schemes by writing things that do not classify at all; and somehow they get away with it.

But as a teacher of composition I must classify, or I shall die. At least let me say that all forms of writing are either creative or journalistic. Either they owe their impulse and their material to a well-stored mind and a vivid imagination, or else to the desire to record and appraise objective facts. In the first field I may call my writer a *poet*, and in the second a *reporter* or a *critic.* But just as I have contentedly established my two classes, someone says that my reporter is successful because of his poetic gifts, and my poet is praised for the accuracy and vividness with which he pictures his objective experiences.

Each new effort at classification brings me back to the fact that writers of every sort in every field are using but one English and using it for their own purposes well or ill; facility in the use of it, and power of control over it as a keen or delicate tool, being common measures of their greatness.

How then may one teach rules and recipes for writing? Who knows any? Many prophets wise and foolish arise who would point a way; and some deliberately false prophets. This book is offering no chart with any royal road to literary success pricked upon it. Here are only various observations of one who is still puzzling after ten years of teaching "advanced composition," and many more years of editorial work.

In any classroom devoted to the practice of creative writing there dwells a specter. Misty of outline it hovers about, not seen in clear definition by anyone, but touching with ghostly finger every task and every discussion. Its name is *Inspiration.* Young writers wait for its approval before they begin. Instructors meekly withdraw their demands at its behest. I might be most helpful to many student friends if I could exorcise this phantom, or materialize it!

Some years ago I was riding in a train with a poet, — one whose sincerity of purpose I respect and admire. This classroom ghost was bothering me much at that time, and I had been trying vainly to lay him. "Tell me," I said suddenly to my poet, "were you ever inspired?" He took the question quite calmly. "Yes," he said, "if we can agree upon a definition." Then he told me this bit out of his own personal experience. He had lived for many years, he said, in a town where more than half of the population were negroes. This had led him to speculate about them, as his mind grew more mature, and to develop some philosophy of his own as to the tragedy of their present situation, the savagery of their background, and the hope that might lie in their future. He came to feel that perhaps their one great contribution to mankind might be a spiritual gift. All of this had eventually slipped into the background of his mind.

One day as he was traveling in a Pullman a sudden flashing glimpse of that old speculation came to him, but now it was like a telegram in code. Perhaps the rhythm of the car wheels had gotten into his head; perhaps the porter came through the car. At any rate he found himself saying:

> "Then I saw the Congo creeping through the black,
> Winding through the forest with a golden track."

Where it came from he did not know. "Call it ouija-board stuff if you like," said he to me.

"Anyhow," said the poet, "I was content with my poem. It summed up in condensed fashion all my philosophizing about the negro. But if I put that couplet into type it would mean nothing whatever to those whose thoughts had not travelled the whole distance with mine. I must settle down to the plodding task of interpreting my vision. Sheer craftsmanship would then determine whether or not I could make others see what I had seen, or feel what I had felt."

So in the final outcome his poem might be but two lines of inspiration, with one hundred lines or so of interpretation. And every true poet that ever lived has the same story to tell. Let Dante testify:

". . . And then I resolved," he says in the *Vita Nuova*, "that thenceforward I would choose for the theme of my writings only the praise of this most gracious being. But when I had thought exceedingly, it seemed to me that I had taken to myself a theme which was much too lofty, so that I dared not begin; and I remained during several days in the desire of speaking, and the fear of beginning. After which it happened, as I passed one day along a path which lay beside a stream of very clear water, that there came upon me a great desire to say somewhat in rhyme; but when I began thinking how I should say it, methought that to speak of her were unseemly, unless I spoke to other ladies in the second person; which is to say, not to *any* other ladies; but only to such as are so called because they are gentle, let alone for mere womanhood. Whereupon I declare that my tongue spake as though by its own impulse, and said, 'Ladies that have intelligence in love.' These words I laid up in my mind with great gladness, conceiving to take them as my commencement. Wherefore, having returned to the city I spake of, and considered thereof during certain days, I began a poem with this beginning . . .

> "'Ladies that have intelligence in love,
> Of mine own lady I would speak with you;
> Not that I hope to count her praises through,
> But telling what I may, to ease my mind.'"

My train companion and I talked more of this matter and agreed that a gift of poetic vision was not necessarily accompanied by the power to interpret. Probably some of the worst poetry ever published may be found between the covers of church hymnals. Yet among the poems there set down are some that have demonstrated a power to stir the hearts of multitudes through successive generations. Often in those old hymns one flashing line will stand out; all of the spiritual power of the hymn is compressed into its few words. It may not be the first line or the formal title, yet men remember the hymn by that one line and forget its context. That line embodied the whole vision of the old hymn writer; then when he tried to expand and interpret he often failed in craftsmanship.

Emily Dickinson is a good example of the visionary who sets down her little glimpses of truth or beauty in the condensed forms in which they flashed into her mind, without effort to expand and interpret, probably without the ability to do so. Her poems will never be enjoyed by a multitude of readers because she never sought to reach the many. The few who enjoy will do so by reason of the fact that they are themselves supplying most of the expansion and interpretation.

To one of my time the word *Inspiration* is sure to have a scriptural association. So perhaps I can best say what I have to say by turning to the story of Moses. The Hebrew legend has it that he received his early training in the wisest court of his time. The whole body of knowledge of that day was at his disposal in

the king's palace. Then he threw in his lot with his own people
and joined the slaves in their revolt and exodus. They must
have been a hopeless crowd of ignorant brutalized laborers,
who started upon their migration utterly unequipped. According to the legend, their leader went up into a high mountain and
was there for a long time, alone with his vision of God, — in
solitary communion with truth. While he was there, the people
encamped below heard thunder and they said that it was God
talking, but they could not understand. When Moses came
down he brought with him a body of laws that stand today the
tests of practical human application, in ethics, community living,
sanitation, government.

Here were in very truth inspired writings. Three elements
have equal share in their success. First of all was the prepared
mind; just such educational preparation as was needed for
writing of that sort. Then there was a mental readiness, a
reaching out, the lonely mountain top, the period of solitude.
Moses was not waiting for inspiration to come to him, but he
climbed a hard road nine-tenths of the way to meet it. Finally
came into play the power to translate his vision into terms the
multitude would understand.

These young creative writers who prate of inspiration should
seek three things: a background of mental training, adequate
to the visions they seek; a mind receptive to flashing glimpses
of truth or beauty; and last a power to interpret.

As to the first, one classroom can give but a modicum of the
mental training they need. Any or all classrooms, outside activities, home background, all must share responsibility for that.

Second, are the visions themselves, — the flashing glimpses.
No classroom may supply them. But the atmosphere of the
school or college and the college program as a whole may encourage or discourage them. The confusion of mind that comes
from an overcrowded schedule certainly is antagonistic to them.
Lack of solitude and opportunity for quiet meditation must also
discourage them. An unsympathetic attitude of associates
toward the expression of half-formulated fancies would act as a
deterrent. A general school tendency to exalt criticism would be

harmful; not perhaps if it were constructive criticism, yet it is almost impossible to encourage the *habit* of criticism in youthful minds and not have it generally destructive.

Psychologists tell us that these "inspired" flashes are up-rushes from the subconscious mind. We know that the greater proportion of the mental work that we do is done subconsciously. Into that subliminal chamber go our unfinished tasks. Then while our conscious minds are busy with new problems, suddenly out from this other workshop flashes something more nearly complete than we had suspected we could produce. Creative writers tell us that this happens most frequently when the conscious mind is least on guard. Perhaps it has been drugged by coffee or sleep. Perhaps it is simply quiescent from fatigue. Authors, and professional orators or lecturers, find ways of deliberately harnessing this subconscious activity to each successive task. Prolific writers find it essential to set regular times for their creative writing. "I go to my desk at nine o'clock every morning," is the testimony of one of them, "whether I feel like writing or not. Even without ideas I must somehow start my pen going. In a short time some force takes control and I am producing copy." Another confesses that he has a way of calling upon this subconscious mind to pull him out of a mess. "If I have come to an *impasse* in my story, I let it go until night. Then when I am in bed and ready for sleep, with the light out, I arrange before my mind's eye the situation that is giving me trouble. Then I manage to get to sleep. In the morning I summon my characters before me and find that somehow their paths have become clear."

Every creative writer, even the most immature, knows the sensation of a conscious mind in abeyance while the hand goes writing, writing at the dictation of some inner force. Interruptions at such a moment are destructive. Distractions are a curse. But school life is crowded with interruptions and distractions. Solitude is a commodity that is always out of stock in the college shop.

There is another trouble. The subconscious mind when it takes charge of literary creation is like the ganglia that take charge of the feet when we run down stairs. Any conscious effort to guide our muscular action at such a time would retard progress. In the same way an *overdeveloped* critical sense checks creative power, and I believe that it can ultimately so fill it with confusion as to destroy it. If I knew positively that a child possessed great creative genius I should consider four years of an undergraduate college as at present conducted a dangerous risk.

Few good editors are creative writers. They may begin as writers but the focusing of the mind upon criticism has destroyed or suppressed the power. I do not believe that this is merely because a man cannot do two things well at the same time. I believe it is because the creative and the critical impulses are at war within the one mind.

There is only one thing left for my classroom in the training of the creative writer. That is, the *interpretation* of visions. This means facility; the breaking down of physical inhibitions that stand between the mind and the moving pen; mastery over words; and the acquirement of style, which is nothing more than a personal good taste in words, and may be acquired.

If these are the tasks that lie before me in my class for creative writers, I find that it differs in no way from that other classroom where my reporters or my advertisers get their training. Any kind of writing trains for any other kind of writing. This brings me to the trouble-making assertion that the task of shaping the phrases for a sonnet differs in no way or degree from the task of building a good fifty-word advertisement. The same training is needed for both, the same skill, the same care, the same reverence for the written word, the same recognition of its potentiality. Each is an effort to interpret, — in the one case a subjective experience, in the other an objective one.

OF ESSAYS IN PARTICULAR

ANY putting down of words in writing implies a reader; and a reader implies some sort of test. For you must write skillfully enough to succeed in having your way with that reader. You may wish to interest him, or at least inform him; to arouse him, or convince him; to stir his anger or his sympathy. Even your diary, if you keep such a dangerous thing, though it be locked up in the top-bureau-drawer is intended for you yourself to read at some later time. And your later self may be a most exacting reader, demanding that those old diary pages shall thrill you with the reality of the pictures or the emotions that they recall. The pleasure that comes solely from self-expression does not wholly account even for the poet. He does not try merely to express a vision or an emotion; he tries to interpret it in terms that readers other than himself will understand.

So I think we can say of writers of every sort that they have this one motive in common: a desire to have their way with some other human being. The reporter wishes to tell the readers of a certain paper about things that have just occurred; to win and to hold attention, and to recount the facts accurately and convincingly. The story-teller would entertain his readers with a fable that he has made to resemble life; and he too seeks to win and to hold attention, and to recount his fable convincingly. The editorial writer forms certain opinions about the news events of the day and then attempts to persuade his readers to accept those opinions. The essayist, like the editorial writer, philosophizes about this and that, and then seeks to interest or entertain by recounting his ideas, but without *striving* to prove, or to convince, or to convert. The advertiser, finally, either announces to others or pleads with others, according to his lights.

When I say that all writing is intended for a human reader, I am of course thinking in terms of normal people. I do not allow for those who write bits of poetry on scraps of paper and then immediately destroy them. I have heard that there are such folk, although personally I do not know any. Nor do I allow for the sort of writing that is so often done in schoolrooms. There the writer may be normal enough, but he is not writing to influence another human being; he is writing for his teacher. Here is the very meat of the trouble with teaching of writing in the schools. The teacher may be earnest enough, and able enough, but many pupils will not think of him in the classroom as a human being, but rather as a sort of cash register that rings once every time a required piece of writing is handed in. Consequently such pupils are addressing nothing at all when they write, except a sort of mechanical device and a blank sheet of paper.

If I am to pretend to "teach" writing I must first of all insist upon the right to be my natural self in the classroom, even if I have to strive unnaturally to do so! Perhaps the easiest way is to get rid of the classroom. Second, I must insist that my students be their natural selves, even if that means at first a good deal of slang or a lot of foolishness. It is possible that some are at an age when they are naturally slangy, even foolish. For I find it a common phenomenon that a student may meet me outside class, as man to man, and tell me an experience or an opinion with vividness and skill and with a liveliness of style all his own; and then when he attempts to set the same thing down in writing as a task, the result is a stilted, unlovely thing deserving no better name than "theme."

Any photographer has a similar experience. He is well acquainted with the sort of persons, men as often as women, who, when the eye of the camera is upon them, assume a facial expression they never wear at any other time, a look unknown to God or man, that might be termed their "photograph face." It is the way they think they should look in a picture. Just so, classroom style is not a natural expression but a way that students think they should write when addressing an educational system.

Anyone who can think clearly can write clearly; anyone who can think entertainingly can write entertainingly. He may not want to, it is true. It is that *wanting to* which is so important an element in the make-up of a writer. And the converse is true; one cannot write clearly unless one thinks clearly. Muddy thinking makes muddy writing.

If the whole training of a young writer were under my direction I think that first of all I should drill him in the reporting of news; simply and clearly and accurately at first, without consideration for any other quality, and then with every effort to win and hold the interest of certain audiences. Then I should train him to interview, with all that it involves. Next should come, for the first time, some expression of his own opinion, in the form of an editorial based upon the news; and then his opinion of a book or a play, in the form of a review. After all that, he should play for a time with the familiar essay.

Essays are kittle cattle. They should contain the ripened meditations of a writer. But if the writer be himself immature, his meditations on most subjects will not be ripe enough to pluck. Then, too, the essay in the hands of the young has a way of back-firing. An essayist assumes that readers will be interested to know what he thinks about life; that they will enjoy watching the wheels of his mind go 'round. He must, in a word, assume a certain egotism. But Youth sometimes does not need to assume it; Youth too often supposes that the world will listen breathlessly while he describes all of his mental reactions to a newly discovered universe. So, then, if you set him to writing essays he will revel in it; the real task will be to turn him off.

Essays, I believe, should be the by-products of an author's pen. It is only with a rare genius like Lamb, living in an age blessed with fewer authors, that they may be the whole business. In an essay one may write more nearly to please himself alone than in any other form. He may play tricks with his words, and with his reader, as Hilaire Belloc does in his essay on "And." He may be a preacher or a scientist, or he may *pretend* to be either, but if he really preaches, or if he writes a wholly objective scientific treatise, he is no essayist.

Certain things we may demand of an essayist | that he shall follow a train of thought to its conclusion, by howsoever winding a road; and that he shall point out to our minds several new ideas along the way. There is no deadlier writing put upon paper than an essay made up of trite thoughts in threadbare phrases. Then, whether his writing be grave or gay, thoughtful or foolish, I would have him reach a constructive conclusion, and stop. And if he can invent no constructive conclusion, he should stop all the sooner.

Since in a true essay the writer assumes a degree of acquaintanceship with his reader, and a consequent willingness to reveal *himself*, then it is evident that a thoughtfully written letter is likely to be as perfect an essay as one may accomplish; so, too, is a well-prepared address, for writer and reader, so to speak, must then meet face to face.

For these reasons we are likely to find among the best essays of all time those which were first planned as orations or, what is more likely, as addresses to a group of academic associates. The critical essays of Ruskin are a sufficient instance. As for letters, essayists of every age, with Cicero for a brilliant example, have found them a pleasant subterfuge, or an actual convenience when they wished to publish comments of so personal a nature as to seem out of place in any other literary form. Those bitter wits, Swift and Defoe, availed themselves of this method, and many writers since; though it was in that day when journalism began that the open letter became truly fashionable.

Though few such essay-letters are included in this collection, and those for their style rather than their form, I would urge the beginner who finds essay writing especially difficult to put his first attempts into the form of an open letter to an intimate friend.

Another whim of the essayist had its early day in the sun. Character essays, or "Characters" as they are commonly called, were but another literary mode of offering shrewd comment upon the foibles of one's fellow men. Such "attempts" far antedated Montaigne, since Theophrastus the Greek was probably not the first to amuse himself thus, and he lived three centuries before Christ.

With so many of these early forms of the essay before me as models, I find myself returning again to the question of definition. Many collections of essays have lately been assembled in book form and classified in various ways. But often, it seems to me, the compiler is embarrassed by an effort to explain the inclusion, under one general term, of literary forms so fundamentally dissimilar as Carlyle's *Nibelungenlied;* Macaulay's *Warren Hastings;* Bacon's didactic little homilies; and essays of such widely divergent character as those of Arnold, Hazlitt, Samuel Johnson, and Lamb. In an excellent collection recently published I find the following classification : (1) the gnomic or aphoristic; (2) the personal or familiar; (3) the didactic or critical. Another divides them all into subjective and objective, without attempt to explain why both are "essays." Still another [1] carries classification to an extreme, and offers these divisions : the aphoristic essay; the character essay; the classic essay; the letter essay; the short-story essay; the biographic or critical essay; the essay of the naturalists; and the familiar essay. Unquestionably the last named is most directly the descendant of the *Essais* of Montaigne, and of the writings of those supreme journalists, Lamb, Addison, and the rest who, following Bacon, borrowed the term. So effective is this familiar type of written address that it has today come into a broad kingdom. Even exact scientists are writing with an ease and intimacy of conversational style that a generation ago would have led their scientific brethren to view them with suspicion.

Perhaps the definition of an essay that Dr. Johnson formulated for his dictionary would best satisfy those teachers who have been laboring with classroom experiments : "A loose sally of the mind, an irregular, undigested piece, not a regular and orderly performance." Fortunately for the author, the purpose of this book is not criticism but suggestion; and he exercises his right to

---

[1] "The Literary Essay in English" by Sister M. Eleanore is not a compilation. It is a critical consideration of its subject, bearing such evidences of scholarliness and exhaustive research, written in so readable a style, that the author of this book has leaned heavily upon it and owes it this tribute.

frame a definition sufficient for the practical purposes of beginners in this field of writing:

Let there be an easy, natural "talking mode" so far as style is concerned, but let it be good talk; let self-revelation be one of the objectives but let there be a worthy self to reveal. "And so," as Mr. Pepys would say, "to my scrivening."

A FEW SUGGESTIONS AS TO CLASSROOM METHOD

To get results in writing that are free of that monotonous schoolroom quality, one may have to do away with the formal classroom and cease to be the formal classroom teacher.

If essays addressed solely to the teacher, written in order to meet a class requirement, evidently suffer from the lack of a stimulating audience, then some other audience must be substituted.

If *wanting to write* is an essential to good writing, as I believe it to be, then that time is not wasted which is devoted to the building up of a classroom morale, even though some of the means seem to be remote from the business of good writing.

Students should write to win the intelligent approval of the *class*, and so, if the schedule can possibly be made to permit it, read all of their work aloud. It is not fair training if the teacher select certain pieces of written work for class reading and then gives to them the interpretation of his own voice. The argument that there is not time for such student reading of all work is generally a fallacy. Shorten the assignments; there is as much training to be had from brief essays as from long ones, perhaps more. Divide the class into squads whose work is due on successive days.

It seems hardly necessary to refer to so small a matter, yet by all means do away with the traditional classroom arrangement of seats. If the seats are nailed to the floor, use another classroom, or a library, or hire a hall. The absurdity of the conventional arrangement is manifest in such a room. A student who is reading his own work aloud, if he sits in the front row has his back to the audience; if he sits in the back row, his audience has its back to him. Break up these rows and assemble the chairs informally in a circle with no distinguishing seat for the teacher.

He should consider himself a fellow worker appointed to the chairmanship, whose business it is to see that criticism gets under way, that it sticks to the point, and that it does not last too long. After these young writers have clearly realized that the quality and character of their work must satisfy an audience of their fellows, it is evident that they must be permitted to speak a language readily understood by that audience. Dignity of diction is less important than effectiveness; though the former receives its due measure of respect, if the latter is there.

In making assignments for written work make them as far ahead as possible, having them posted in some convenient place for student reference. Creative writing is a dignified labor of life not to be treated as though it were the petty business of a schoolroom. Anyone who writes for a livelihood, or for the sheer pleasure of it, knows that the germ of an idea must exist in his mind with time for the sun of contemplation to shine upon it, and the labor of reading or conversation to water it before the task of reaping is undertaken. It is not my business as a teacher to know or to care whether the student began and finished the actual writing of his essay in the few moments before class. It is my business to protest if that writing reveals no evidence of serious and prolonged contemplation of the subject. My student may have a habit of postponing the work of writing until those last moments when the compulsion of dire necessity is an aid to creation; but if he has known for the past two weeks that he is expected to set down certain ideas and philosophizings upon the subject of "Lying Abed", the activities of the intervening days may offer him suggestions now and then, and he will masticate and digest them, perhaps subconsciously.

In arranging a schedule of assignments, remember that the classroom should furnish variety, not monotony; entertainment, not boredom; and so arrange if possible a program for each classroom hour that will stimulate interest. If several brief essays are to be read, all of them on the one subject, even individual methods of treatment will not prevent satiety. It would be better to furnish variety by departure from the essay, even when it is the principal business of the classroom, and assign to one or two of the group tasks in verse, or sketches, or some other literary form in lighter vein to lend variety to the hour's program.

The following suggestions addressed to students are divided, almost arbitrarily, into ten brief sections, and each is followed by an "assignment." Any teacher may find that the order in which they are arranged does not best suit his program or his purposes. Arrange them in any convenient order. Though only ten assignments are suggested, almost any one of them may be made the business of many class days. They are offered here merely as helpful hints to teacher or student.

As to the appended collection of essays, it seems advisable to repeat here that they have not been chosen to further a study of the place and development of the essay in English literature. But they should offer many models of many styles of writing. Familiarity with them should furnish the student with a rich fund of apt quotation and allusion. Leisurely reading of them should provide topics for other essays. With such a purpose in mind the compiler has tried to include several that approach a single subject from various directions; as for instance *Riches* in Chaucer, Ecclesiastes, and Ruskin; *Women*, in T. T., Goldsmith, Gosse, and Holmes; and so on, with any variation upon these themes. A few further suggestions of the same sort will be found on page 315.

FOR STUDENTS

The following information and suggestions are set down here for the use and guidance of students. Instructors are expected to skip that which is set in large type; there is little in it of value to them, and possibly more, owing to their advancing years, which they would be unable to understand.

GETTING READY TO BEGIN

You are addressed as students in these pages because the author knows of no more satisfactory form of address. But if the term seems to make some sharp distinction between student and teacher he would have you overlook it. Say all are students, if you like, or all teachers. The important thing to remember is that in this field of creative writing teacher and student stand upon an equal footing. Perhaps one has grown taller by reason of years and experience, or perhaps not. But all stand upon the same ground. If you can but find a natural way of expressing your thoughts, any one of you, there may be some subjects or some fragments of fancy that you will put upon paper in a better fashion than any teacher ever could discover, just because they are your own.

An *essay* means an attempt, so it is a most suitable task for those inexperienced writers who are putting their pens to paper or their fingers on the keyboard in a desire to imprison certain elusive fancies. In it you must find a way of expressing *yourself*, and I suggest that you begin in the most natural way. Write as you would in a letter to an intimate friend. Modify this style by the use of common sense, of course. Perhaps the most intimate of your friends get nothing but picture postcards from you; but there are times and there are friendships which call forth from you letters that attempt to transmit your real reflections in the very way that you would talk.

If this means slang or an informality of writing that does not sound like schoolroom stuff, never mind; *talk on paper*. Then, when you see your written word, you yourself will feel inclined to doctor it up a bit. Words on paper must have a little more dignity about them than spoken words; because the latter are explained or supplemented by a smile or a tone of the voice. But words on paper must do all the work of communication.

Our business together now is the writing of essays, and before we determine what an essay is, let us decide what it is not. First of all, it is not a classroom "theme" or a "topic." You know very well what I mean. No one ever reads a "topic" for pleasure; and someone must be made to enjoy this essay of yours, even if it is that miserable being, your teacher, who is offered so little classroom writing that he can enjoy.

It is not a "topic" because most of a "topic" is not truly your own. "Topics" are made out of encyclopedias and extracts from dull treatises written by authorities who were not writing essays. "Topics" and "theses" are padded by the insertion of undigested chunks of knowledge gleaned from others. They are written to prove something; generally to prove how much you know.

An essay is not an argument in which you fight to confute or refute another. It is not a sermon, or an editorial such as you are likely to write for the school or college paper, which inevitably ends up with the phrase "Let us therefore, all strive . . ." or begins "We regret to note that . . ."

An essay is an effort to put upon paper your meditations upon a chosen subject; your own thoughts, not the thoughts of another. First of all, you must have thoughts, and it will be necessary for you to do some reading or some conversing about the subject you have chosen, and a great deal of focusing of attention upon it, in order to acquire material. There is no reason why you should not know what other people have said and thought about the subject; in fact every reason why you should. Then with that knowledge as part of your equipment you must proceed to do your own thinking.

Assignment One

Jot down in the form of notes two subjects that might serve you for essays. Note under each subject the direction your knowledge or your fancy might lead you, and toward what climax or final conclusion. If you know that others have written on these subjects, so much the better. Note down under each subject some opinion or reflection of another writer, to which you might allude. Be prepared to *talk* about either of these subjects, with your notes in mind, rather than in hand. Perhaps you may draw out from others their own reflections which will serve to extend your material.

CONSCIOUSNESS OF STYLE

In your essay it is not enough that you should have interesting thoughts about the chosen subject; you must find interesting ways of expressing those thoughts. That means *style*. It is absurd for one to say that he has no literary style, — quite as untrue as to say that he has no way of wearing his clothes. It may be a slovenly or untidy way; it may be a careless way, but it is a way of his own, and it is quite as easy to acquire a better fashion of writing as it is to acquire a tidier or more interesting way of dressing.

Some people have a natural instinct for style in dress; the combining of colors, the adjustment of lines and shapes of garment to their own height or breadth. Others have no such natural instinct, but acquire a fashion of dressing by looking at tastefully dressed people so that soon they are conscious of their own unsatisfactory habits, and overcome them.

Some people seem to have a natural taste in words. Instinctively they balance their sentences well. They have a sense of rhythm. Others who do not by instinct thus clothe their thoughts can learn to do so by observing what the well-dressed writer wears. If you are conscious of a lack of this native taste in words, begin simply. Dress up your thoughts in simple sentences. Use only those words that are yours to command.

The essay that you are about to write must be so fashioned as to interest an audience that probably includes one teacher and a number of fellow students. Write with the majority in mind. It is possible that you possess some words that only the teacher would understand. Don't use them. It is possible that you possess others which only the students would understand. Don't use them! The words and phrases which all will understand are good enough for your thoughts in this first essay of yours.

Those among you who have long enjoyed writing and have an innate good taste in the use of words are likely in a first essay to use too many. So to them, too, I would suggest an extreme simplicity of style, and they are likely to find that the simplest fashion is at the same time the most effective, even the most beautiful. If you will read a page or two selected at random from *Robinson Crusoe* or *Pilgrim's Progress*, you will find that, barring certain old-fashioned phrases which have gone out of use, there is a strength and a vigor and a charm in sentence after sentence containing scarcely a word of three syllables and even those few the common property of all, in everyday use. Those two books are written in much the same fashion as the King James version of the Bible, a diction that has never lost its power and has affected to some extent most of the writers who are able to hold our attention today. But read also, if you like, pages taken at random from Mark Twain; not his most extravagant skits, although those will do, but any pages from *Tom Sawyer* or *The Prince and the Pauper*, and *Joan of Arc*, and count the words of Latin origin with ponderous syllables. Try the experiment of reading some such pages as I have mentioned just before you settle down to the task of your own writing.

This is a fitting place to speak about your criticism of the writing of others and their comments upon your own work. Just so soon as you are sure that criticism is honest and earnest, heed it carefully and weigh it; then act upon it as you think best.   But remember that your words were written down in order to produce an effect upon the mind of a reader.   Though a criticism seems unreasonable, still it indicates that in the case of one reader at least some phrase of yours failed to have its desired effect; and that reader may be typical of many others. After weighing the evidence you may decide to let those readers go.

In offering criticism, be searching and to the point.   You are commenting upon a writer's work, not upon himself. He is not seeking praise while in the workshop, but every constructive suggestion that will help him to better his writing.   He should welcome comment as sharp as you like, so long as you are friendly.   That last makes all the difference in criticism.

Assignment Two

Write a short essay on an approved subject.   Consciously seek a simplicity of sentence structure and of diction.   Glance through several of the essays included in this book, until you find something that impresses you by reason of its simplicity and clearness of style.   Read it through thoughtfully just before you begin upon your own writing.

THE PERSONAL PRONOUN

ONCE we were taught that the use of the personal pronoun, first person singular, in formal writing was distinctly bad form. Writers, particularly young writers, struggled to find ways of evading this embarrassing proof of egotism. "One" became a threadbare substitute. "One is led to observe, with apologies for one's effrontery in asserting one's opinion, that one might travel for days and days without discovering another one comparable to this one." "You" has offered another and often an unsatisfactory substitute. There are many sentiments that I might quite properly confess as my own which I would have no right to assert were possessed by you. "You will find it impossible," writes the essayist, "to contemplate such a scene without a tremor of emotion." If you are a reader habitually impervious to tremors of emotion, this seems to be something of an accusation and you resent it. But if the essayist writes, "I find it impossible to contemplate the scene without a tremor" no one is likely to be offended, and someone might be interested. The writer might permit himself many tremors without offending the most sensitive reader.

There is a certain fascination about the "editorial we." It is a pleasant affectation. The writer knows that the reader knows that it disguises a large capital "I." Use it as a whim, if you like, but not with the notion that it is better form, or that it lessens the appearance of egotism. The editor who uses "we" in his editorial is doing so for a definite reason. He is not expressing his own private opinion. He is, at the moment of writing, the voice of his paper; he is speaking for an editorial group, and he wishes to convey this fact. He would have no right to use the first person singular unless he wished to separate himself from his associates and speak with the greater freedom of individual responsibility. He would then probably print his editorial as a "letter to the editor", splattering it with capital "I's" and signing his own name at the end.

One of the embarrassments of a first essay may be, to many, the fact that it seems to assert the importance of their own opinions, and their early training says that is not good manners. But the same is true in criticism of books or plays or pictures. If I were to ask you to write a book review for publication in some newspaper column, it would be because I sought your opinion upon that book. You need not, then, apologize for thrusting your opinion at me. If I do not want to know it, I do not need to read what you have written. Yet it is a common failing among young critics that they are over-deprecatory about their own definite views. "If you will permit me to say so," they write, "and although I may be wrong in my judgment, it seems to me, inexperienced as I am, that the book is stupid."

There is no excuse for such apologies. The reviewer who feels as humble as all that about his views should not express them. If he is going to put his judgment into type at all, then let him say positively, "This is a stupid book." Nothing compels me to believe him if I do not want to, and there is certainly no reason why I should be bored by his apologies.

So it is with the essayist. If he feels deprecatory about the expression of his ideas, perhaps it would be better for him not to express them. But if he does write down his thoughts let him suppress all of those conventional phrases which are a form of apology, such as "If I may be permitted to say," and write with honest assurance; and let him use "I" as often as impulse directs, and then cut out as many as possible in the revision!

Assignment Three

Read the selections from Montaigne included in this book. Note the space he gives to apology and form your judgment as to the sincerity of it. Is it a pose? Does he assume that the reader will so take it?

Write a newspaper editorial based upon some item of current news, but with a chatty, essay-like quality about it. Use the "editorial we." Experiment with the impersonal "one" instead of "we", and estimate the relative values of these two forms in such an essay-editorial as you have written. Now rewrite, using "I", and note whether you feel justified in sharpening your expression of opinion.

INCIDENT AND HUMAN INTEREST

WRITING is an art, and no art can be taught by recipe. A textbook that attempts to tell you just how you should organize your thoughts, and then how you should express them, would have just one good reason for existence. You might become a great writer by consciously violating every precept you found within its pages. True artists are forever discovering new ways of mixing colors, or putting them on the canvas; new ways of arranging words in sentences and sentences in paragraphs; even of doing without sentences and paragraphs altogether. The fact that some trick of the craft has become an accepted thing, a conventional mode, means that it may all the sooner cease to serve its purpose effectively; so the very instinct of the artist urges him to abandon it. But he abandons it only when he is sure he has found something better. Those usages of written English which are seldom or never abandoned remain simply because no better fashion of expressing ideas has yet been discovered.

Words die when they wear out; styles of writing change because they become threadbare with use. Nevertheless there are some suggestions of value to the beginner in this art of writing, because there are certain natural reactions of human readers that seem never to die away. For instance, mankind has always been most interested in mankind. Let your reader be as wise a man as can be found, as grave and scholarly, yet in his heart he is more interested in concrete examples than in abstractions. If your readers are average men and women, young or old, this will be many times as true. So, though you have chosen an abstract subject, you must break in upon your philosophizing with some concrete illustration or you will tire your reader overmuch.

I remember as an early lesson of editorial days, when illustrations for the magazine were to be sorted and a page lay-out planned, my wise chief would abruptly undo the work of a morning, throwing aside some beautiful picture of a scene in the Grand Canyon, let us say, and substituting for it some poorer photograph because on an overhanging rock the tiny figure of a human being was barely discernible. "Human interest!" he would exclaim; "you must find human interest. That figure in the picture helps to interpret height and depth and grandeur. It shows the littleness of man, if you will, his weakness and unimportance, if you choose to interpret it that way; but the picture is for a human reader, and that little figure helps him to read."

Suppose, then, that I am writing gravely upon *Hospitality*, discussing with all the wisdom and philosophy I possess the obligations of a host and the behavior of a guest, it will profit me much if I recall that once upon a time — so the legend runs — there was a lord of a castle who stopped all strangers passing by and made them occupy the bed in his guest-chamber. If they were too long for the bed he lopped them off, and if they were too short he had them stretched to fit it. If I allude to this it will take the place of many generalizations; and it will revive the attention of all those readers who have left in them any of a child's joy over a story. And what other readers does anyone want?

Assignment Four

Write an essay, remembering again that brevity is no disgrace. Choose some abstract idea for your subject, such as Snobbery

or Saintliness or Idleness or "Pep." Take Hospitality, if
you like. See to it that a considerable part is devoted to a
single episode, — an experience of your own or that of another,
— heard or read, — and upon that episode base your own reflections.

QUOTATION MARKS

THE question of quotation marks can always start a pretty argument among bookish people. Is good literary taste more offended by their over-use than by too great an avoidance of them? If I am reading an essay by an unknown writer and come upon some such phrase as this: *"the quality of mercy is not strained" as Shakespeare says,* I am immediately offended. In the first place I feel that the writer doubts my own elementary equipment; and secondly he implies his recent discovery of something universally recognized. So he is doubly damned. If, on the other hand, he borrows a fine compact phrase from Browning and omits those little crediting marks on the supposition that any well-read person will recognize it, has he therefore sinned because I happen to think the phrase his own? Is the fault his or mine?

I am trying to present a large question in its simplest terms. Let me attempt to carry the question further. Every author gets all his ideas from a wide variety of sources. Some creditors he has forgotten, though the idea remains. Some things he has cheerfully borrowed and reshaped to fit his own need, with never a thank-you openly expressed. Is he free of all blame, so long as he *rewords* the borrowed idea?

Has the originator of some pleasing combination of literary ideas a proprietary right in his concept once he has given it to the public? If so, does that right apply to the ideas themselves, or to his exact manner of phrasing them? If to the ideas, then a playwright should be most careful about using any one of the seventeen plots which Schiller insisted make up the total number of plot combinations. If to the ideas, then Newton might properly have objected whenever a fellow scientist based some new hypothesis upon that falling apple.

I am not foolishly attempting to answer in this small space a broad question that has for many generations been fruitful of discussion among the wisest of men. Frankly, I am trying only to stimulate that discussion anew, contributing such fuel as I may to the flames. Upon the liberal side, the extreme opinion is that there can be no proprietary right to ideas. Man's groping conceptions of Truth and Beauty become the property of mankind when he has uttered them. Patents and copyrights are merely the expedients of government to stimulate creative minds into greater activity. It seems to be the case that in Elizabethan times, when literary creation attained to great heights, such freedom was more generally recognized, and writers "lifted" whatever they needed without concealment or shame.

But there is another side to the question, which, though it does not meet the point exactly, might be injected here.

Several years ago a United States judge decided upon evidence that much of *Cyrano de Bergerac* had been stolen, and rendered a decision that kept its distinguished author from visiting our shores. How many readers are there with so strong a prejudice against stolen goods that they would refuse to read *Cyrano* and take *The Merchant Prince of Cornville* in its place? They would probably say, if the issue were brought directly before them, "Give me the best! That worthy Chicago manufacturer had his chance and failed. At least he may feel that he helped Edmond Rostand to a great achievement, and so is not without honor."

But if it is true that Edmond Rostand benefited in any degree from a reading of *The Merchant Prince*, a word of acknowledgment would have done him no harm, and at the least would have been a courteous act. Not so many years ago an American writer, not widely known at the time, made a story out of certain data that scientists had assembled. The little book had only fair success. Another writer, of greater repute, took the idea and made a story that was widely popular. The first writer complained through the press; and the second, noting the protest, answered with bland effrontery : "Yes, I used the idea. It seemed to me too good a one to waste, so I made a better story out of it. If readers disapprove, let them refuse to read my book and read his."

"A great poet may really borrow," wrote Landor; "he may condescend to an obligation at the hand of an equal or an inferior; but he forfeits his title if he borrows more than the amount of his own possessions . . . the lowlier of intellect may lay out a table in their field, at which table the highest one shall sometimes be disposed to partake; want does not compel him." "The man of genius," said Dumas, "does not steal, he conquers, and what he conquers he annexes to his empire. He makes laws for it, he peoples it with his subjects, and extends his golden scepter over it. And where is the man who, on surveying his beautiful kingdom, shall dare to assert that this or that part of his land is no part of his property?"

Literature would indeed be poverty-stricken if all the published thoughts and fancies of men in the past were not a part of the treasure of men's minds today. But there enters increasingly into the problem a question of equity. Society is more and more demanding that those who possess the power and skill of stimulating our minds through the printed word shall lay aside other occupations and devote themselves to the task. So enters the question of a livelihood and of its protection by certain general understandings.

As to the right of the great to partake of food spread by the lowly, one thinks at once of certain obligations that attend true greatness. I should not want to lose *Cyrano*, but if some humbler artist had a share in the creation, however small, I am sure that a truly great artist would not hesitate to grant good-naturedly a small share of the distinction. The greatness of Charles Reade and of Sardou as authors would have been in no wise affected by a word of credit to the humbler ones who assisted and are now forgotten. But their reputation for good sportsmanship would have been enhanced.

I have wandered from that lesser question of the distinguishing marks around a quotation. That is quite a different question; because the essayist who quotes usually does so for the very reason that he wishes the voice of another to be heard. He likes to bring to bear upon his subject the comment of another mind; preferably one greater than his own. For he gains satisfaction from an interruption which proves the two minds can for a moment run in the same channel.

As to whether or not his readers will recognize the quotation is a question for his own good judgment to decide. If they do, he has added a subtle charm to his writing; if they do not, he has lost his only excuse for quoting, and would better do without.

Assignment Five

Reach some opinion of your own upon the question of Plagiarism, and be prepared to discuss it orally or in writing. Refer again to Montaigne who has some quaint and pointed comments upon this matter.

Using one of your former essays as a basis, or in an entirely new essay, see how many apt allusions to the writings or sayings of others you can introduce. Use your own judgment as to the necessity for quotation marks, and find whether the judgment of others accords with your own.

ESSAY–BEGINNINGS

IF I wish to win a friend's attention in order to chat with him for a time, it is likely that first of all I will hint at the matter which lies in my mind. At any rate I do well to give such a hint in my writing. The title may not do it. The title may be an odd fancy intended to pique curiosity or to reveal some greater meaning after the essay is read. In the first few sentences I am sure it is well to suggest definitely what it is I want to chat about. This will serve a double purpose. It will tend to drive off those readers who are not interested in the subject. On the other hand, it will catch the attention of all those who are interested in the subject, whether or not they care about me. Then if I chat well with them I have made new friends.

The opening sentence must be simple. I do not mean that it must be brief. Long sentences can be as simple as short ones, if they are made so. But you must remember that your reader before he has begun upon your first paragraph is to some extent a sceptic. Like the man from Missouri, he has to be shown. If you beckon to him with an obscure or perplexing or uncertain gesture, he may not come to you, or worse still he will come distrustfully.

Many people like to disparage "newspaper style." The news writer's habit of using an arousing "lead" or opening sentence they are inclined to regard as "cheap." Yet I would ask you to glance through any good collection of essays; not of our present-day essayists because they may have been "poisoned" by modern journalism; but some collection of the classic essayists that would

include not only Lamb and Hazlitt and DeQuincey, but
Carlyle and Macaulay and the ponderous Dr. Johnson;
and then note the way in which they beckon to their
readers.   In fact as I glance over some of these first lines
at this moment of writing, it occurs to me that were I
again a newspaper man I should ask no greater skill in
the starting of a news-story among my reporters than is
shown by these old worthies in the beginnings of their
essays.   Read some of them as I jot them down here.
I shall give you the title of the essay and then the opening
words of it *up to the first period*, then the name of the essayist and the year when he wrote.

Of Studies — "Studies serve for delight, for ornament,
and for ability." — Francis Bacon, 1597.

Of Truth — "'What is truth?' said jesting Pilate; and
would not stay for an answer." — Francis Bacon,
1625.

Of Painting the Face — "If that which is most ancient
be best, then the face that one is borne with, is better
than it that is borrowed: Nature is more ancient than
Art, and Art is allowed to help Nature, but not to hurt
it; to mend it, but not to mar it; but this artificiall facing doth corrupt the naturall colour of it." — T. T., 1614.

Of Myself — "It is a hard and nice subject for a man to
write of himself; it grates his own heart to say anything
of disparagement, and the reader's ears to hear anything
of praise from him." — Abraham Cowley, 1688.

On London Cries — "There is nothing which more as-
tonishes a Foreigner, and frights a Country Squire,
than the Cries of London." — Joseph Addison, 1711.

Poor Relations — "A Poor Relation — is the most irrel-
evant thing in nature, — a piece of impertinent correspondence, — an odious approximation, — a haunting

conscience, — a preposterous shadow, lengthening in
the noontide of our prosperity, — an unwelcome remembrance, — a perpetually recurring mortification, — a
drain on your purse, — a more intolerable dun upon
your pride, — a drawback upon success, — a rebuke
to your rising, — a stain in your blood, — a blot on
your 'scutcheon, — a rent in your garment, — a
death's head at your banquet, — Agathocles' pot, —
a Mordecai in your gate, — a Lazarus at your door, —
a lion in your path, — a frog in your chamber, — a fly
in your ointment, — a mote in your eye, — a triumph
to your enemy, an apology to your friends, — the one
thing not needful, — the hail in harvest, — the ounce of
sour in a pound of sweet." — Charles Lamb, 1833.

On Going a Journey — "One of the pleasantest things in
the world is going a journey; but I like to go by myself." — William Hazlitt, 1822.

At Sea — "The sea was meant to be looked at from shore,
as mountains are from the plain." — James Russell
Lowell, 1864.

Of Revenge — "Revenge is a kind of wild justice; which
the more man's nature runs to, the more ought law to
weed it out." — Roger Bacon, 1625.

The Multiplication of Books — "One of the peculiarities
which distinguish the present age is the multiplication
of books." — Dr. Samuel Johnson, 1759.

A Chapter on Ears — "I have no ear." — Charles Lamb,
1821.

Milton and the Puritans — "We would speak first of the
Puritans, the most remarkable body of men, perhaps,
which the world has ever produced." — T. B. Macaulay,
1825.

Labor — "There is a perennial nobleness, and even
sacredness, in work." — Thomas Carlyle, 1843.

The Old Gentleman — "Our Old Gentleman, in order to be exclusively himself, must be either a widower or a bachelor." — Leigh Hunt, 1820.

Assignment Six

Write two or more opening paragraphs, differing as widely as possible in style and character, for some imaginary essay of your own. So phrase one of them as to stimulate your readers' interest to the highest degree.

Select any essay from the collection in this book, read it through, and then write a different beginning for it, retaining as best you can the style of the author.

THE MATTER OF MOOD

If my friend is not in the mood for it he will not enjoy the funny story I tell him, or not enjoy it as much as he might. If my friend is in a nonsensical mood it will be a waste of time to tell him how the sunset affects me, or gropingly attempt to express my theory about a life after death. There are times when one can read an essay by Stephen Leacock with full enjoyment, and times when one cannot.

So it is plain that your reader must be in a receptive mood, or be lured into such a mood, in order to have your essay successful.

Will you permit me an extravagant illustration? Suppose that you open a magazine to a story which begins *"Merciful Heavens!" she shrieked, leaping over the edge of the cliff.* There is more than a hint of dramatic tragedy here, yet in nine cases out of ten the reader of such an opening line would laugh derisively. He would be certain that the writer was either exaggerating with humorous intent, or that he did not know how to write.

Yet I can imagine that in some story which had lured you, a breathless reader, from situation to situation up to the threshold of a tragic climax, you might read that very line with no laughter in your heart, but with aroused emotions of sympathy and horror.

"Dear reader" is a phrase that I personally find annoying in any essay, and especially in one by some writer who has not yet become endeared to me for any reason. Lamb or Stevenson might use it without offense, and so might any writer who lived long ago. But a new writer of today offends me by the use of it, just as do those impudent advertisers who point a finger at me and cry out in large type, "This means You!"

Beginners frequently make this error: a bit of writing otherwise satisfactory fails utterly because some phrase in an opening paragraph assumes too soon the reader's sympathetic mood. Sometimes it is but a single grotesque word that seems to say, "This will be a humorous essay. Please do not take it seriously, but laugh with me"; and the reader ready for any mood continues with an expectant half smile upon his lips, looking for fun and twisting expressions of honest sentiment into sarcasm, and statements of fact into exaggeration, and bits of optimistic philosophy into cynicism.

A proper sympathy between writer and reader means a complete understanding. If an author assumes a personality not his own I must know that he is assuming it. Then I can believe in his sincerity, and that is essential to my enjoyment of his work. The field of painting furnishes a good example of what I mean. There are certain futuristic pictures which convey nothing to my mind just at present. But I can study them with interest and with a sincere desire to discover their message if I believe that the painter was honestly trying to convey an idea or an emotion by a medium that I do not yet comprehend. But if something leads me to suspect that he is tricking me I will turn away.

This does not mean that I would not have an essayist assume grandiloquence or fantastic humor or some personality quite remote from his own. In fact I think I love him best when he plays at pedantry or pomposity, or at any other way with words. He seems then to be taking me into the circle of his intimate friends, when he consents to lay aside for the time being that more formal dress with which his thought is usually clothed. But both of us must know that he is playing! Thus Charles Lamb poses as an antiquarian or a Chinese scholar, and Swift as a pedant, and Carlyle as a German professor who has studied the science of tailoring.

Assignment Seven

Write upon a commonplace subject drawn from our own daily life, but assume yourself to be a visitor from Mars, or from some remote country. Let your literary manner be one quite remote from your own natural one.

ON CUTTING DOWN

THE sword might be mightier than the pen if it were used as an ink eraser. The true worth of your first essay is going to depend very largely on what you cut out of it. No one can wisely dictate to another any exact method for creative work, but many beginners will find it best to write what they have to say all the way through to an ending; saying it "all in one breath" if it is short enough for that. Then let them go over it, expanding and contracting as conditions demand. When the work is complete it will be hard to say to which process it chiefly owes whatever merit it possesses; the fundamental ideas of it set down in the ardor of creation and at the dictation of the subconscious mind; or the painstaking tiresome work of revision, the polishing of phrases, the expansions and the contractions.

First of all, there are the inevitable repetitions of thought to be cut out. The earnest writer may underestimate the ability of his reader to catch an idea and so he repeats it. Perhaps he uses other phrases, but still it is a dull repetition.

Then there are adjectives, all along the way. You will be surprised to discover how few you really need in order to convey to your readers not only your general meaning, but all the finest shades of it. The other day I tried this experiment with a group of students; to say something that I wanted to say to them, something of descriptive character in at least one hundred words, using never an adjective of any sort, not even an "a" or a "the." I put the result here before you as an illustration.

Pen Magic

They faced me in semicircle, strangers to me and to one another. None had I ever seen before; nor were we likely to meet again, after summer had passed. They did not wear their personalities outwardly, like coats for all comers to admire or contemn. There are heritages of reserve that we humans all share alike.

Then they began writing. Some played with mockery or cynicism; some with tragedy and tears; some dipped into philosophizings not their own. One jibed at everything; another swam in an ocean of adjectives and with a squeal of delight submerged herself beneath its surface. Some were poets, projecting their fancies into souls of others, gropingly, it is true, and not sure of foothold. And some were Pollyannas who forced optimism, like overdoses of sugar, upon listeners who squirmed.

Not one of them, playing at authorship, cared to expose himself on paper for strangers to read and paw over. Yet bit by bit and day by day, each one began upon self-revelation, as if putting together parts of puzzles. Jibers granted glimpses of sincerity that was in them; eyes appeared, momentarily perhaps, above waves of adjectives; iconoclasts admitted they would not destroy truth; cynics would not jeer at beauty; so that, despite screens of reserve we customarily build about ourselves, when we parted not one was any more stranger to another.

Now as to adverbs: cut out all the "verys" and "exceedinglys" and "quites", and all of those harmful little words that you have used to intensify some other word. For if that other word is not strong enough for your purpose you should find another; and if it is, and just the word you want, your "very" insults it.

A most important operation upon your essay is the cutting off of its appendix. I refer to that continuation of writing after the true end has been reached. An essayist may be like an after-dinner speaker who finds it hard to sit down though he has said all he meant to say. Perhaps it is because he is groping for a more effective final phrase, a perfect "clincher", and he keeps on talking emptily from one-half of his mind, while the other half gropes for that perfect conclusion. Scrutinize your essay after it is finished and see whether it would not be better without that final paragraph or two.

Then I would consider cutting off the beginning. Save the perfect first sentence if you like and graft it on to the second paragraph and see how you like the result. The man who would jump the highest needs a preliminary run; but I have known jumpers who started too far away from the bars and wasted their effort in the running.

I have suggested that you cut off the end and cut off the beginning; now if I were cynical I would suggest that you leave out the middle and have a perfect essay; but there is indeed one other sort of cutting to do and some expansion to balance it. It is an odd fault with all inexperienced writers that they are lengthy where they should be brief and brief where they ought to be lengthy. Yet it is a natural fault. If I am writing a story and grope about in my mind to prepare a situation, struggling for some good fashion of introducing the characters and the situation, I am likely to take too many words to it. Yet it is the dullest part of the story for my reader, and the sooner we can get by all that part, the happier for us all. But then comes the dramatic moment of the story. If my readers have followed me thus far, it is because they are interested and hopeful of stirring events and a climax. I have caught their attention and I may hold it nearly as long as I will. In fact if I can draw out the "suspense" I am writing cleverly. Yet at this point I am in the heat of creation. Thoughts hurry pell-mell, and I slap them down upon paper. Here, where skillful writing demands that I shall proceed slowly, I am likely to hurry through

as though I were writing a synopsis or a sketchy outline.
This is just as true in essay writing. There are parts
of any essay which through necessity are likely to be dull.
Cut such parts to the bare bones. Then there is that
other part toward which all of the preliminary work leads;
here you may expand, here is your chance for descriptive
writing, for color, for the adjectives that you have driven
out elsewhere.

Assignment Eight

Glance through the essays included in this book, noting any
that are notably free of adjectives.

Write a sketch or fragment of essay about two hundred words
in length, using no adjectives other than the articles and relative
pronouns, and no intensifying adverbs.

Write a leisurely book-review; cut it to one-half its original
length; reduce it to a rhymed quatrain.

VOCABULARY

AN expert teacher of the deaf has written; "Like the hearing child, the deaf pupil refuses to do much thinking until he has *words*. He is actually waiting in a forlorn belated babyhood for words. And he gives weight to a great psychologist's contention that thought itself is words — inner speech. . . . To a child whose mind has been seriously hindered by his deafness, there comes a distinct awakening during such a course of lip-and-tongue training. It is like a miracle, a never-ceasing wonder to the teacher who learns to watch for it. And once it has happened, the child goes ahead with a speed before impossible to him."

If thought is inner speech, then an extension of your vocabulary means not only a greater facility in writing, but added ease, accuracy and breadth of thinking. It is worth a conscious effort rather than a mere dependence upon chance. For the vocabulary you now possess is largely the result of chance. Words that you use are the words that you have heard used, or that you have assimilated from your reading without conscious effort.

Investigators tell us that the working vocabulary of the average grammar-school graduate contains about five hundred words. The average man who does an average amount of thinking may use two thousand. But a thinker, actually testing the powers of his own brain, probably uses many more. Shakespeare found use for fifteen thousand, while a modern dictionary of the English language contains at least two hundred thousand. These statements bear a disagreeable resemblance to statistics, but they also suggest the disturbing question, "Where do I come in?"

A conscious effort to increase one's vocabulary need not be a burdensome undertaking. In fact one may gain a good deal of pleasure from it. First of all it involves paying attention to the words one reads; measuring word values, and not being satisfied merely with the general meanings they convey.

The memory of two advertisements comes to my mind now, though I saw them a good many years ago. Each one occupied costly space, so that presumably the men who wrote them weighed the value of each word carefully. The first was on a car-card in a New York City surface car. The man who wrote it did not know that "crucial" means the final test of the cross; that a crucial moment is that last instant when a man may have to decide whether or not he is willing to die for his opinions. To say "very crucial" is to insult a great word. But this advertiser wrote "Now is a very crucial time to buy white goods." The other advertisement was a great department-store's full-page announcement of a birthday anniversary. In it the copy writer boasted of the store's foresight in choosing its present central location. He described the uninviting appearance of the site when they first moved to it; "across Broadway," he wrote, "where the Broadway Tabernacle once stood, was now a perfect *hoi polloi* of brick and mortar."

Then this conscious effort calls for an interest in the derivations of words, and their histories; and there is more entertainment to be gained in this way than one might at first suspect.

Finally, there is the deliberate effort to acquire new words and practice the use of them. There are a number of well-known desk-books that any busy writer likes to have within reach. Handy dictionaries, of course; a Latin dictionary, whether or not you are a Latin scholar; a book of synonyms; even a rhyming dictionary. Roget's *Thesaurus*, by the way, is not a prehistoric animal, though I have seen a group of college students who could be made to believe that it was. Look it up in the library and gain some amusement by reading a page or two, rapidly. Thoughts need words in order to take form; and it is often true that the sight of a column of meaningful words will stir sluggish brains into action.

Assignment Nine

Make a list of ten words discovered in your essay reading that were hitherto entirely unfamiliar, or that you had never used in speech or writing. Introduce them into former essays of your own, or into new bits of composition. Introduce them so skillfully that they will not draw undue attention to themselves, to the detriment of the work they are there to do. Look up *Trench* or some other good book on word histories and write a short essay about a single word.

IMITATION OF THE MASTERS

It is not necessary for one to know the work of other essayists in order to write essays of one's own; but no craftsman ever lived who gained proficiency in his craft and was indifferent to the workmanship of his fellows, — particularly of his betters. An essay is so inevitably the expression of yourself there is no great danger that you will become a mere imitator. The danger is that you will express no one at all, not even yourself. Robert Louis Stevenson says this more than once, and I have quoted him at length on another page; and so do many other masters of style.

So I suggest, assuming that you really care about this thing, that you write your essay after first assuring yourself that you have something to say on the subject you have chosen; and that when it is written you try it out upon whatever audience is available. Then I suggest that you read something by one of these great essayists of the past, Lamb, or De Quincey, or Dr. Johnson, and that you rewrite your essay in the peculiar fashion of one of them, imitating his mannerisms, and for the moment making his personality your own. See then whether your audience can guess whose style it is that you have borrowed.

Two results may come of this experiment. One is the discovery that you really had not enough to say of your own to put into this other fashion of writing. The other is that, having as yet no formed style of your own, this effort to assume the personality of another will lead you to assert yourself.

I have referred to "mannerisms" as something apart from style. Perhaps they are not wholly apart, and yet one thinks of them as coming from a writer's "box of tricks" rather than from within himself. Kipling's "but that is another story" and *Crusoe's* "of which in its place"; Bunyan's "Now I saw in my dream"; Chesterton's inverted aphorisms; and a dozen tricks of as many current writers which you will readily think of for yourselves; these things it is amusing to discover and appraise, — and imitate for practice's sake.

Differences in diction, on the other hand, arise from more fundamental causes. Oliver Wendell Holmes was a physician. His special experience as a technician introduces into his literary vocabulary many words that enrich it and help him to define all ideas with greater nicety. In the few paragraphs from *The Autocrat* included in this book there are a dozen words or phrases to prove his possession of the physician's viewpoint.

Perhaps it is in the building of sentences that actual differences of *style* are most marked. The student of style will find it well worth his while to hunt out one or two essays from the pen of Henry James and consider their elaborate and involved periods; then contrasting them with the explosive, staccato sentences of certain current writers. To focus attention for a time upon these literary ways of others is sure to bring about a healthy self-consciousness when one goes about his own writing business.

Assignment Ten

This assignment is adequately suggested in the preceding paragraphs. Take an essay already written and attempt to clothe its thoughts in a dress habitually worn by some well-known writer, and then see whether your readers can guess the original owner of the garment.   Do not confine your choice of models to the essay-ists.   Play with dialect, if you like, or fables ancient and modern. Several present-day writers of fiction carry about with them full boxes of tricks.   Keep your own ideas but borrow their tricks, for the purposes of this experiment.

HISTORY OF THE ESSAY

By deliberate intent I have left to the last some word about the place of the essay in literature: its first appearance; its development as a form of prose writing; and the famous writers who have used it for their various purposes. I have postponed this matter because it seems to me least important in this book. The essay is above all a *natural* way of writing. If you could discover it in part for yourselves, by saying what you have to say in that fashion which is most natural to you, I should feel that you were in a way to become essayists. While you are making these trials, rather than before, I should want you to see how other men have written in this "essay" fashion. After you have made your own first attempts, and after you have gained some enjoyment from the essays of others, it may really interest you to learn some of the more academic facts.

Michel de Montaigne, a Frenchman, in 1580 published two volumes of *Essais*. There is no record of the use of the word in such a connection before. They were brief prose *attempts, trials, experiments,* in the expression of his own personal views on certain subjects. It is not fair to say that no writers before him had ever written in a conversational informal style with frank revelation of personality. But up to that time published writings had in general been of a more formal character; they were more often the positive assertions of revealed truth in philosophy or religion designed to exhaust the subject. chosen.

Francis Bacon, considered to be the wisest Englishman of his time, and one of the wisest in the whole list of England's men of letters, borrowed this word essay from Montaigne, turning it into English and using it as a title for some short prose experiments of his own.   It was in 1625 that he published his *Essays: or Counsels, Civil and Moral.*   Many other books he wrote on far weightier subjects, but of them all I dare say that this alone is read today for pleasure.

Here again it is necessary to admit that Bacon's Essays were not the first English writings to possess the essay quality, so hard to define yet so easy to recognize.   Men before him had introduced into one fragment or another of their writings the frank expression of personality in a conversational style.   One might even call Chaucer's *Old Wive's Tale* a fair example.   But with Francis Bacon it became a definite form, seized upon soon by many others who as writers rejoiced at this release from a traditional formality.

Sir Thomas Browne, in his *Religio Medici;* Abraham Cowley, in *Several Discourses By Way of Essays;* Sir William Temple in *Miscellanea;* Daniel DeFoe in his *Weekly Review of the Affairs of France;* here is a sort of apostolic succession which brought the form down from Bacon to Steele.   It was in 1709 that Richard Steele published his *Tatler,* abandoning it a little later in favor of *The Spectator,* with Joseph Addison as an associate.   In these early magazines the essay found its kingdom. With their limited space, and an editorial policy that called for timely comment upon men and things, they were the stimulators of brilliant essays from many pens; and one periodical after another appeared, to stir competition. Dr. Johnson published his *Rambler,* and then *The Idler;* Goldsmith edited the *Citizen of the World.*   In 1802 *The*

Edinburgh Review was born; in 1809 *The Quarterly Review;* and in 1817 *Blackwood's Magazine.* With the coming of these reviews came the essays of Lamb, De-Quincy, Hazlett, Macaulay, and a host of others.

The selection of essays reprinted here is necessarily limited. I do not pretend that they are the best, or even fairly representative of all the best. In choosing them, I have tried to do this: to include some that are important historically, since they helped to create the essay form; to include others chiefly because they will serve to introduce to you several writers whose work you may be induced to investigate further. One or two are included because they exhibit a marked peculiarity of style; and others for no better reason than that the compiler happens personally to like them.

There are many essay anthologies in existence, and I hope that you will not be dependent upon any single one. A great many sensible people, and chief among them Mr. Robert Frost the poet (if I report him justly), consider anthologies of any sort pernicious things. In offering a very small fragment of any author's work, they are fair neither to writer nor to reader. What then would Mr. Frost say to this collection which gives not only so brief a glimpse into any essayist's writings, but even includes fragments of essays. I can urge in answer that these are placed before you not as a hasty survey of writers, but as examples of style. If in any essay here you catch a glimpse of a personality that attracts you, then seek out one of that writer's own books, and get to know him better. This voluntary effort you owe not so much to the author as to yourself!

A COLLECTION OF ESSAYS AND PARTS OF ESSAYS OF MANY KINDS

together with a few fragments
of other writing chosen because
they serve to suggest an
essay style

"Whenever I read a book or a passage that particularly pleased me, in which a thing was said or an effect rendered with propriety, in which there was either some conspicuous force or some happy distinction in the style, I must sit down at once and set myself to ape that quality. . . . I have thus played the sedulous ape to Hazlett, to Lamb, to Wordsworth, to Sir Thomas Browne, to De Foe, to Hawthorne, to Montaigne, to Baudelaire, and to Obermann. . . . That, like it or not, is the way to learn to write; whether I have profited or not, that is the way. It was so Keats learned, and there was never a finer temperament for literature than Keats's; it was so, if we could trace it out, that all men have learned; and that is why a revival of letters is always accompanied or heralded by a cast back to earlier and fresher models. Perhaps I hear someone cry out: But this is not the way to be original! It is not; nor is there any way but to be born so. Nor yet, if you are born original, is there anything in this training that shall clip the wings of your originality."

— ROBERT LOUIS STEVENSON

From *A College Magazine* (see p. 239).

In writing an essay today one will not go far wrong if he follows the fashion of Michel de Montaigne. Yet it was as long ago as 1580 that he dared depart from the formal literary manners of the age, and put forth a collection of informal meditative "attempts", in which he made "myselfe . . . the grounde-worke of my booke." The extracts here included are of course translations and must lose somewhat of the personality of the writer. Yet John Florio who put them into English soon after Montaigne's death did a piece of work that no one has bettered in three hundred years. It is his translation that Shakespeare knew.

A PREFACE TO HIS ESSAYS

By Michel de Montaigne. Translated by John Florio

Reader, loe here a well-meaning Booke. It doth at the first entrance forwarne thee, that in contriving the same I have proposed unto myselfe no other than a familiar and private end; I have no respect or consideration at all, either to thy service or to my glory; my forces are not capable of any such desseigne. I have vowed the same to the particular commodity of my kinsfolks and friends; to the end, that losing me (which they are likely to doe ere long), they may therein find some lineaments of my conditions and humours, and by that meanes reserve more whole, and more lively foster the knowledge and acquaintance they have had of me. Had my intention beene to forstal and purchase the world's opinion and favour, I would surely have adorned myselfe more quaintly, or kept a more grave and solemne march. I desire therein to be delineated in mine owne genuine, simple, and ordinarie fashion, without contention, art or study; for it is myselfe I pourtray. My imperfections shall therein be read to the life, and my naturall forme discerned, so farreforth as publike reverence hath permitted me. For if my fortune had beene to have lived among those nations which yet are said to live under the sweet liberty of Nature's first and uncorrupted lawes, I assure thee, I would most willingly have pourtrayed myselfe fully and naked. Thus, gentle Reader, myselfe am the groundworke of my booke; it is then no reason thou shouldest employ thy time about so frivolous and vaine a subject.

Therefore farewell.

From Montaigne.

OF BOOKES (*Incomplete*)

By Michel de Montaigne

I MAKE no doubt but it shall often befall me to speake of things which are better, and with more truth, handled by such as are their crafts-masters. Here is simply an essay of my natural faculties, and no whit of those I have acquired. And he that shall tax me with ignorance shall have no great victory at my hands; for hardly could I give others reasons for my discourses that give none unto my selfe, and am not well satisfied with them. He that shall make search after knowledge, let him seek it where it is: there is nothing I professe lesse. These are but my fantasies by which I endevour not to make things known, but my selfe. They may haply one day be knowne unto me, or have bin at other times, according as fortune hath brought me where they were declared or manifested. But I remember them no more. And if I be a man of some

reading, yet I am a man of no remembering, I conceive no
certainty, except it bee to give notice how farr the knowledge I have of it doth now reach. . . . Knowledge and
truth may be in us without judgement, and we may have
judgement without them; yea, the acknowledgement of
ignorance is one of the best and surest testimonies of judgement that I can finde. I have no other sergeant of band
to marshall my rapsodies than fortune. And looke how
my humours or conceites present themselves, so I shuffle
them up. Sometimes they prease out thicke and three
fold, and other times they come out languishing one by
one. I will have my naturall and ordinarie pace seeme
as loose and as shuffling as it is. As I am, so I goe on
plodding. And besides, these are matters that a man may
not be ignorant of, and rashly and casually to speake of
them. I would wish to have a more perfect understanding
of things, but I will not purchase it so deare as it cost.
My intention is to passe the remainder of my life quietly
and not laboriously, in rest and not in care. There is
nothing I will trouble or vex myselfe about, no not for
science it selfe, what esteeme soever it be of. I doe not
search and tosse over books but for an honester recreation
to please, and pastime to delight myselfe; or if I studie,
I only endevour to find out the knowledge that teacheth
or handleth the knowledge of my selfe, and which may
instruct me how to die well and how to live well.

> Has meus ad metas sudet oportet equus
> My horse must sweating runne,
> That this goale may be wonne.

If in reading I fortune to meet with any difficult points,
I fret not my selfe about them, but after I have given them
a charge or two, I leave them as I found them. Should
I earnestly plod upon them, I should lose both time and

my selfe, for I have a skipping wit.   What I see not at the
first view, I shall lesse see it if I opinionate my selfe upon
it.   I doe nothing without blithnesse; and an over obsti-
nate continuation and plodding contention doth dazle,
dul, and wearie the same : my sight is thereby confounded
and diminished.   I must therefore withdraw it, and at
fittes goe to it againe.   Even as to judge well of the lustre
of scarlet we are taught to cast our eyes over it, in running
over by divers glances, sodaine glimpses and reiterated
reprisings.   If one booke seeme tedious unto me I take
another, which I follow not with any earnestnesse, except
it be at such houres as I am idle, or that I am weary with
doing nothing.   I am not greatly affected to new books,
because ancient Authors are, in my judgement, more full
and pithy : nor am I much addicted to Greeke books, for-
asmuch as my understanding cannot well rid his worke
with a childish and apprentise intelligence.   Amongst
moderne bookes meerly pleasant, I esteeme Bocace his
Decameron, Rabelais, and the kisses of John the Second
(if they may be placed under this title), worth the paines-
taking to read them.   As for Amadis and such like trash
of writings they had never the credit so much as to allure
my youth to delight in them.   This I will say more, either
boldly or rashly, that this old and heavie-pased minde of
mine will no more be pleased with Aristotle, or tickled with
good Ovid : his facility and quaint inventions, which heretofore have so ravished me, they can now a days scarcely
entertaine me.   I speake my minde freely of all things,
yea, of such as peradventure exceed my sufficiencie, and
that no way I hold to be of my jurisdiction.   What my
conceit is of them is told also to manifest the proportion of
my insight, and not the measure of things. . . .
    Loe here then, concerning this kinde of subjects, what
Authors please me best: As for my other lesson, which

somewhat more mixeth profit with pleasure, whereby I
learne to range my opinions and addresse my conditions,
the Bookes that serve me thereunto are Plutarke (since
he spake French) and Seneca; both have this excellent
commodity for my humour, that the knowledge I seeke
in them is there so scatteringly and loosely handled, that
whosoever readeth them is not tied to plod long upon them,
whereof I am uncapable. And so are Plutarkes little
workes and Senecas Epistles, which are the best and most
profitable parts of their writings. It is no great matter to
draw mee to them, and I leave them where I list. . . .
As for Cicero, of all his works, those that treat of Philoso-
phie (namely morall) are they which best serve my turne,
and square with my intent. But boldly to confess the
truth (for, since the bars of impudencie were broken downe,
all curbing is taken away), his manner of writing seemeth
verie tedious unto me, as doth all such like stuffe. For his
prefaces, definitions, divisions, and Etymologies consume
the greatest part of his works; whatsoever quick, wittie,
and pithie conceit is in him is surcharged and confounded
by those his long and far-fetchd preambles. If I bestow
but one hour in reading them, which is much for me, and
let me call to minde what substance or juice I have drawne
from him, for the most part I find nothing but wind and
ostentation in him; for he is not yet come to the arguments which make for his purpose, and reasons that properly concerne the knot or pith I seek after. . . . I like
those discourses that give the first charge to the strongest
part of the doubt; his are but flourishes, and languish
everywhere. They are good for schooles, at the barre,
or for Orators and Preachers, where we may slumber;
and though we wake a quarter of an houre after, we may
finde and trace him soone enough. Such a manner of
speech is fit for those judges that a man would corrupt by

hooke or crooke, by right or wrong, or for children or the
common people, unto whom a man must tell all, and see
what the event would be.   I would not have a man go
about and labour by circumlocutions to induce and winne
me to attention, and that (as our Heralds or Criers do)
they shall ring out their words : Now heare me, now listen,
or ho-yes.   The Romanes in their religion were wont to
say, "Hoc age"; which in ours we say "Sursum corda."
They are so many lost words for me.   I come readie
prepared from my house.   I neede no allurement nor
sauce, my stomacke is good enough to digest raw meat :
And whereas with these preparatives and flourishes, or
preambles, they thinke to sharpen my taste or stir my
stomacke, they cloy and make it wallowish. . . .   As
for Cicero, I am of the common judgement, that besides
learning there was no exquisite eloquence in him : He
was a good citizen of an honest, gentle nature, as are
commonly fat and burly men; for so was he : But to
speake truly of him, full of ambitious vanity and remisse
niceness.   And I know not well how to excuse him, in that
he deemed his Poesie worthy to be published.   It is no
great imperfection to make bad verses, but it is an imperfection in him that he never perceived how unworthy they
were of the glorie of his name.   Concerning his eloquence,
it is beyond all comparison, and I verily beleeve that none
shall ever equall it.

OF THE INSTITUTION AND EDUCATION OF CHILDREN (*Incomplete*)

BY MICHEL DE MONTAIGNE

I NEVER knew father, how crooked and deformed soever
his sonne were, that would either altogether cast him off,
or not acknowledge him for his owne ; and yet (unlesse he

be meerely besotted or blinded in his affection) it may not
be said, but he plainly perceiveth his defects, and hath a
feeling of his imperfections.   But so it is, he is his owne.
So it is in my selfe.   I see better than any man else, that
what I have set downe is nought but the fond imaginations
of him who in his youth hath tasted nothing but the paring,
and seen but the superficies of true learning; whereof he
hath retained but a generall and shapelesse forme: a
smacke of everything in generall, but nothing to the purpose in particular: After the French manner.   To be
short, I know there is an art of Phisicke; a course of
lawes; foure parts of the Mathematikes; and I am not
altogether ignorant what they tend unto.   And perhaps
I also know the scope and drift of Sciences in generall to
be for the service of our life.   But to wade further, or
that ever I tired my selfe with plodding upon Aristotle
(the Monarch of our modern doctrine) or obstinately continued in search of any one science; I confess I never did it.
Nor is there any one art whereof I am able so much as to
draw the first lineaments.   And there is no scholler (be he
of the lowest forme) that may not repute himselfe wiser
than I, who am not able to oppose him in his first lesson:
and if I be forced to it, I am constrained verie imperti-
nently to draw in matter from some generall discourse,
whereby I examine, and give a guesse at his naturall judgement: a lesson as much unknowne to them as theirs is to
me.   I have not dealt or had commerce with any excellent
booke, except Plutarke or Seneca, from whom (as the
Danaides) I draw my water, uncessantly filling, and as
fast emptying; some thing whereof I fasten to this paper,
but to my selfe nothing at all.   And touching bookes:
Historie is my chiefe studie.   Poesie my only delight, to
which I am particularly affected: for as Cleanthes said,
that as the voice being forciblie pent in the narrow gullet

of a trumpet, at last issueth forth more strong and shriller, so me seemes, that a sentence cunningly and closely couched in measure-keeping Poesie, darts it selfe forth more furiously, and wounds me even to the quicke. And concerning the naturall faculties that are in me (whereof behold here an essay), I perceive them to faint under their owne burthen; my conceits and my judgement march but uncertaine, and as it were groping, staggering and stumbling at every rush: And when I have gone as far as I can, I have no whit pleased my selfe; for the further I saile the more land I descrie, and that so dimmed with fogges, and overcast with clouds, that my sight is so weakned, I cannot distinguish the same. And then undertaking to speake indifferently of all that presents itselfe unto my fantasie, and having nothing but mine own naturall meanes to imploy therein, if it be my hap (as commonly it is) among good Authors, to light upon those verie places which I have undertaken to treat off, as even now I did in Plutarke, reading his discourse of the power of imagination, wherein in regard of those wise men, I acknowledge myselfe so weake and so poore, so dull and grose-headed, as I am forced both to pittie and disdaine my selfe, yet I am pleased with this, that my opinions have often the grace to jump with theirs, and that I follow them a loofe-off, and thereby possesse at least, that which all other men have not; which is, that I know the utmost difference betweene them and my selfe: all which notwithstanding, I suffer my inventions to run abroad, as weake and faint as I have produced them, without bungling and botching the faults which this comparison hath discovered to me in them. A man had need have a strong backe, to undertake to march foot to foot with these kind of men. The indiscreet writers of our age, amidst their triviall compositions, intermingle and wrest in whole sentences taken from ancient Authors, supposing by such filching-theft to purchase honour and reputation to themselves, doe cleane contrarie. For, this infinite varietie and dissemblance of lustres, makes a face so wan, so il-favored, and so uglie, in respect of theirs, that they lose much more than gaine thereby. These were two contrarie humours: The Philosopher Chrisippus was wont to foist-in amongst his bookes, not only whole sentences and other long-long discourses, but whole bookes of other Authors, as in one, he brought in Euripides his Medea. And Opollodorus was wont to say of him, that if one should draw from out his bookes what he had stolne from others, his paper would remain blanke. Whereas Epicurus cleane contrarie to him in three hundred volumes he left behind him, had not made use of one allegation. . . . To reprove mine owne faults in others, seemes to me no more unsufferable than to reprehend (as I doe often) those of others in my selfe. They ought to be accused every where, and have all places of Sanctuarie taken from them : yet do I know how over boldly, at all times I adventure to equall my selfe unto my filchings, and to march hand in hand with them; not without a fond hardie hope, that I may perhaps be able to bleare the eyes of the Judges from discerning them. But it is as much for the benefit of my application, as for the good of mine invention and force. And I doe not furiously front, and bodie to bodie wrestle with those old champions : it is but by flights, advantages, and false offers I seek to come within them, and if I can, to give them a fall. I do not rashly take them about the necke, I doe but touch them, nor doe I go so far as by my bargaine I would seeme to doe; could I but keepe even with them, I should then be an honest man ; for I seeke not to venture on them, but where they are strongest. To doe as I have seen some, that is, to shroud themselves under other armes, not daring so much as to show their fingers ends unarmed, and to botch up all their works (as it is an easie matter in a common subject, namely for the wiser sort) with ancient inventions, here and there hudled up together. And in those who endeavoured to hide what they have filced from others, and make it their owne, it is first a minifest note of injustice, then a plaine argument of cowardlinesse; who having nothing of any worth in themselves to make show of, will yet under the countenance of others sufficiencie goe about to make a faire offer: Moreover (oh great foolishnesse) to seek by such cosening tricks to forestall the ignorant approbation of the common sort, nothing fearing to discover their ignorance to men of understanding (whose praise only is of value) who will soone trace out such borrowed ware. As for me, there is nothing I will doe lesse. I never speake of others, but that I may the more speake of my selfe. . . . For, howsoever, these are but my humors and opinions, and I deliver them but to show what my conceit is, and not what ought to be beleeved. Wherein I ayme at nothing but to display my selfe, who peradventure (if a new prentiship change me) shall be another tomorrow.

That man who has been called the wisest of Englishmen, to whom so many have attributed the writing of Shakespeare's plays, borrowed Montaigne's title of "essays", and his brevity of form, but little of his informality of manner. Bacon's essays are formal, didactic, moralizing discourses; yet they pointed a way out of far more ponderous styles of prose into an easier fashion of intimate discourse. In at least one of them, given here only in part, he seems to allow his "owne genuine, simple, and ordinarie" self to appear.

OF TRAVEL

By Francis Bacon

TRAVEL, in the younger sort, is a part of education; in the elder, a part of experience. He that travelleth into a country before he hath some entrance into the language, goeth to school, and not to travel. That young men travel under some tutor, or grave servant, I allow well; so that he be such a one that hath the language and hath been in the country before; whereby he may be able to tell them what things are worthy to be seen in the country where they go; what acquaintances they are to seek; what exercises or discipline the place yieldeth. For else young men shall go hooded, and look abroad little. It is a strange thing that in sea-voyages, where there is nothing to be seen but sky and sea, men should make diaries, but in land-travel, wherein so much is to be observed, for the most part they omit it; as if chance were fitter to be registered than observation. Let diaries, therefore, be brought in use. The things to be seen and observed are:

the courts of princes, specially when they give audience to ambassadors; the courts of justice, while they sit and hear causes, and so of consistories ecclesiastic; the churches and monasteries, with the monuments which are therein extant; the walls and fortifications of cities and towns, and so the havens and harbours; antiquities and ruins; libraries; colleges, disputations, and lectures, where any are; shipping and navies; houses and gardens of state and pleasure, near great cities; armories; arsenals; magazines; exchanges; burses; warehouses; exercises of horsemanship, fencing, training of soldiers, and the like; comedies, such whereunto the better sort of persons do resort; treasuries of jewels and robes; cabinets and rarities; and, to conclude, whatsoever is memorable in the places where they go. After all which the tutors or servants ought to make diligent enquiry. As for triumphs, masques, feasts, weddings, funerals, capital executions, and such shews, men need not to be put in mind of them: yet are they not to be neglected. If you will have a young man to put his travel into a little room, and in short time to gather much, this you must do. First, as was said, he must have some entrance into the language, before he goeth. Then he must have such a servant, or tutor, as knoweth the country, as was likewise said. Let him carry with him also some card or book describing the country where he travelleth; which will be a good key to his enquiry. Let him keep also a diary. Let him not stay long in one city or town; more or less as the place deserveth, but not long: nay, when he stayeth in one city or town, let him change his lodging from one end and part of the town to another; which is a great adamant of acquaintance. Let him sequester himself from the company of his countrymen, and diet in such places where there is good company of the nation where he travelleth. Let him, upon his removes from one place to another, procure recommendation to some person of quality residing in the place whither he removeth; that he may use his favour in those things he desireth to see or know. Thus he may abridge his travel with much profit. As for the acquaintance which is to be sought in travel; that which is most of all profitable is acquaintance with the secretaries and employed men of ambassadors; for so in travelling in one country he shall suck the experience of many. Let him also see and visit eminent persons in all kinds, which are of great name abroad; that he may be able to tell how the life agreeth with the fame. For quarrels, they are with care and discretion to be avoided: they are commonly for mistresses, healths, place, and words. And let a man beware how he keepeth company with choleric and quarrelsome persons; for they will engage him into their own quarrels. When a traveller returneth home, let him not leave the countries where he hath travelled altogether behind him, but maintain a correspondence by letters with those of his acquaintance which are of most worth. And let his travel appear rather in his discourse than in his apparel or gesture; and in his discourse, let him be rather advised in his answers than forwards to tell stories; and let it appear that he doth not change his country manners for those of foreign parts, but only prick in some flowers of that he hath learned abroad into the customs of his own country.

OF STUDIES

By Francis Bacon

Studies serve for *delight*, for *ornament*, and for *ability*. Their chief use for delight is in privateness and retiring; for ornament, is in discourse; and for ability, is in the judgement and disposition of business. For expert men can execute, and perhaps judge of particulars, one by one; but the general counsels, and the plots and marshalling of affairs, come best from those that are learned. To spend too much time in studies is sloth; to use them too much for ornament is affectation; to make judgement wholly by their rules is the humour of the scholar. They perfect nature, and are perfected by experience; for natural abilities are like natural plants, that need proyning by study; and studies themselves do give forth directions too much at large, except they be bounded in by experience. Crafty men contemn studies; simple men admire them; and wise men use them: for they teach not their own use; but that is a wisdom without them and above them, won by observation. Read not to contradict and confute; nor to believe and take for granted; nor to find talk and discourse; but to weigh and consider. *Some books are to be tasted, others to be swallowed, and some few to be chewed and digested:* that is, some books are to be read only in parts; others to be read, but not curiously; and some few to be read wholly, and with diligence and attention. Some books also may be read by deputy, and extracts made of them by others; but that would be only in the less important arguments, and the meaner sort of books; else distilled books are like common distilled waters, flashy things. Reading maketh a full man; conference a ready man; and writing an exact man. And therefore, if a man write little, he had need have a great memory; if he confer little, he had need have a present wit; and if he read little, he had need have much cunning, to seem to know that he doth not. Histories make men wise; poets witty; the mathematics subtile; natural philosophy deep; morals grave; logic and rhetoric able to contend. *Abeunt studia in mores.* Nay, there is no stone or impediment in the wit, but may be wrought out by fit studies: like as diseases of the body may have appropriate exercises. Bowling is good for the stone and reins; shooting for the lungs and breast; gentle walking for the stomach; riding for the head; and the like. So if a man's wit be wandering, let him study the mathematics; for in demonstrations, if his wit be called away never so little, he must begin again: if his wit be not apt to distinguish or find differences, let him study the schoolmen; for they are *cymini sectores:* if he be not apt to beat over matters, and to call one thing to prove and illustrate another, let him study the lawyers' cases: so every defect of the mind may have a special receipt.

OF GARDENS (*Incomplete*)

By Francis Bacon

God Almighty first planted a garden. And indeed it is the purest of human pleasures. It is the greatest refreshment to the spirits of man; without which, buildings and palaces are but gross handyworks: and a man shall ever see that when ages grow to civility and elegancy, men come to build stately sooner than to garden finely; as if gardening were the greater perfection. I do hold it, in the royal ordering of gardens, there ought to be gardens for all the months in the year; in which, severally, things of beauty may then be in season. For December and January and the latter part of November, you must take such things as are green all winter: holly; ivy; bays; juniper; cypress-trees; yew; pine-apple-trees; fir-trees; rosemary; lavender; periwinkle, the white, the purple, and the blue; germander; flags; orange-trees, lemon-trees, and myrtles, if they be stoved; and sweet marjoram, warm set. There followeth, for the latter part of January

and February, the mezereon-tree, which then blossoms;
crocus vernus, both the yellow and the gray; primroses;
anemones; the early tulippa; hyacinthus orientalis;
chamaïris; fritillaria. For March, there come violets,
specially the single blue, which are the earliest; the yellow
daffodil; the daisy; the almond-tree in blossom; the
peach-tree in blossom; the cornelian-tree in blossom;
sweet briar. In April follow the double white violet;
the wall-flower; the stock-gillyflower; the cowslip;
flower-delices, and lilies of all natures; rosemary flowers;
the tulippa; the double piony; the pale daffadil; the
French honeysuckle; the cherry-tree in blossom; the
dammasin and plum-trees in blossom; the white-thorn
in leaf; the lilac-tree. In May and June come pinks of all
sorts, specially the blush pink; roses of all kinds, except
the musk, which comes later; honeysuckles; strawberries;
bugloss; columbine; the French marygold; flos Afri-
canus; cherry-tree in fruit; ribes; figs in fruit; rasps;
vine flowers; lavender in flower; the sweet satyrian, with
the white flower; herba muscaria; lilium convallium;
the apple-tree in blossom. In July come gillyflowers of
all varieties; musk-roses; the lime-tree in blossom;
early pears and plums in fruit; ginitings; quadlins. In
August come plums of all sorts in fruit; pears; apricocks;
berberries; filberds; musk-melons; monkshoods, of all
colours. In September come grapes; apples; poppies of
all colours; peaches; melocotones; nectarines; cornel-
ians; wardens; quinces. In October and the beginning
of November come services; medlars, bullises; roses
cut or removed to come late; hollyokes; and such like.
These particulars are for the climate of London; but my
meaning is perceived, that you may have *ver perpetuum*,
as the place affords.

And because the breath of flowers is far sweeter in the

air (where it comes and goes, like the warbling of music) than in the hand, therefore nothing is more fit for that delight, than to know what be the flowers and plants that do best perfume the air. Roses, damask and red, are fast flowers of their smells; so that you may walk by a whole row of them, and find nothing of their sweetness; yea, though it be in a morning's dew. Bays likewise yield no smell as they grow. Rosemary little; nor sweet marjoram. That which above all others yields the sweetest smell in the air, is the violet; specially the white double violet, which comes twice a year; about the middle of April, and about Bartholomewtide. Next to that is the musk-rose. Then the strawberry-leaves dying, which [yield] a most excellent cordial smell. Then the flower of the vines; it is a little dust, like the dust of a bent, which grows upon the cluster in the first coming forth. Then sweet-briar. Then wall-flowers, which are very delightful to be set under a parlour or lower chamber window. Then pinks and gillyflowers, specially the matted pink and clove gillyflower. Then the flowers of the lime-tree. Then the honeysuckles, so they be somewhat afar off. Of bean flowers I speak not, because they are field flowers. But those which perfume the air most delightfully, not passed by as the rest, but being trodden upon and crushed, are three: that is, burnet, wild thyme, and water-mints. Therefore you are to set whole alleys of them, to have the pleasure when you walk or tread. . . .

Three examples are here introduced of earlier English writing, because in each case the author has offered a glimpse of his "owne genuine selfe": Caxton, the great printer, writing in 1485 a preface to his edition of Morte d'Arthur; Geoffrey Chaucer in 1386 speaking his mind through the mouth of Dame Riches, in the "Tale of Melibeus"; and Shakespeare speaking through "Hamlet."

A PRINTER'S PROLOGUE

By WILLIAM CAXTON

AFTER that I had accomplished and finished divers histories, as well of contemplation as of other historical and worldly acts of great conquerors and princes, and also of certain books of ensamples and doctrine, many noble and divers gentlemen of this realm of England, came and demanded me, many and ofttimes, why that I did not cause to be imprinted the noble history of the Sancgreal, and of the most renowned Christian king, first and chief of the three best Christian and worthy, King Arthur, which ought most to be remembered among us Englishmen, before all other Christian kings; for it is notoriously known, through the universal world, that there be nine worthy and the best that ever were, that is, to wit, three Paynims, three Jews, and three Christian men. As for the Paynims, they were before the Incarnation of Christ, which were named, the first, Hector of Troy, of whom the history is common, both in ballad and in prose; the second, Alexander the Great; and the third, Julius Cæsar, Emperor of Rome, of which the histories be well known and had.

And as for the three Jews, which also were before the Incarnation of our Lord, of whom the first was Duke Joshua, which brought the children of Israel into the land of behest; the second was David, King of Jerusalem; and the third Judas Maccabeus. Of these three, the Bible rehearseth all their noble histories and acts. And, since the said Incarnation, have been three noble Christian men, stalled and admitted through the universal world, into the number of the nine best and worthy: of whom was first, the noble Arthur, whose noble acts I purpose to write in this present book here following; the second was Charlemagne, or Charles the Great, of whom the history is had in many places, both in French and in English; and the third, and last, was Godfrey of Boulogne, of whose acts and life I made a book unto the excellent prince and king, of noble memory, King Edward the Fourth.

The said noble gentlemen instantly required me for to imprint the history of the said noble king and conqueror, King Arthur, and of his knights, with the history of the Sancgreal, and of the death and ending of the said Arthur, affirming that I ought rather to imprint his acts and noble feats, than of Godfrey of Boulogne, or any of the other eight, considering that he was a man born within this realm, and king and emperor of the same; and that there be in French divers and many noble volumes of his acts, and also of his knights. To whom I have answered, that divers men hold opinion that there was no such Arthur, and that all such books as he made of him be but feigned and fables, because that some chronicles make of him no mention, nor remember him nothing, nor of his knights. Whereto they answered, and one in especial said, that in him that should say or think that there was never such a king called Arthur, might well be aretted great folly and blindness; for he said there were many evidences to the contrary. First ye may see his sepulchre in the monastery of Glastonbury. And also in Policroni-con, in the fifth book, the sixth chapter, and in the seventh book, the twenty-third chapter, where his body was buried, and after found, and translated into the said monastery. Ye shall see also in the History of Bochas, in his book *De Casu Principum*, part of his noble acts, and also of his fall. Also Galfridus, in his British book, recounteth his life. And in divers places of England, many remembrances be yet of him, and shall remain perpetually of him, and also of his knights. First, in the Abbey of Westminster, at St. Edward's shrine, remaineth the print of his seal in red wax closed in beryl, in which is written — "Patricius Arthurus Britanniæ, Galliæ, Germaniæ, Daciæ Imperator." Item in the castle of Dover ye may see Sir Gawaine's skull, and Cradok's mantle: at Winchester, the Round Table: in other places Sir Launcelot's sword, and many other things. Then all these things considered, there can no man reasonably gainsay but that there was a king of this land named Arthur: for in all the places, Christian and heathen, he is reputed and taken for one of the nine worthies, and the first of the three Christian men. And also he is more spoken beyond the sea, and more books made of his noble acts, than there be in England, as well in Dutch, Italian, Spanish, and Greek, as in French. And yet of record, remaineth in witness of him in Wales, in the town of Camelot, the great stones, and the marvellous works of iron lying under the ground, and royal vaults, which divers now living have seen. Wherefore it is a great marvel why that he is no more renowned in his own country, save only it accordeth to the word of God, which saith, that no man is accepted for a prophet in his own country. Then all things aforesaid alleged, I could not well deny but that there was such a noble king named

Arthur, and reputed for one of the nine worthies, and
first and chief of the Christian men.   And many noble
volumes be made of him and of his noble knights in French,
which I have seen and read beyond the sea, which be
not had in our maternal tongue.   But in Welsh be many,
and also in French, and some in English, but nowhere nigh
all.   Wherefore, such as have late been drawn out briefly
into English, I have, after the simple cunning that God
hath sent me, under the favour and correction of all noble
lords and gentlemen enprised to imprint a book of the
noble histories of the said King Arthur, and of certain of
his knights after a copy unto me delivered; which copy
Sir Thomas Malory did take out of certain books of French,
and reduced it into English.   And I, according to my
copy, have down set it in print, to the intent that noble men
may see and learn the noble acts of chivalry, the gentle and
virtuous deeds that some knights used in those days, by
which they came to honour, and how they that were
vicious were punished, and oft put to shame and rebuke;
humbly beseeching all noble lords and ladies, with all
other estates of what state or degree they be of, that
shall see and read in this present book and work, that
they take the good and honest acts in their remembrance, and follow the same.   Wherein they shall find
many joyous and pleasant histories, and the noble and
renowned acts of humanity, gentleness, and chivalry.   For,
herein may be seen noble chivalry, courtesy, humanity,
friendliness, hardiness, love, friendship, cowardice, murder,
hate, virtue, and sin.   Do after the good, and leave the evil,
and it shall bring you unto good fame and renown.   And,
for to pass the time, this book shall be pleasant to read in,
but for to give faith and belief that all is true that is
contained herein, ye be at your own liberty.   But all is
written for our doctrine, and for to beware that we fall not

to vice nor sin, but to exercise and follow virtue, by the which we may come and attain to good fame and renown in this life, and after this short and transitory life to come unto everlasting bliss in heaven; the which He grant us that reigneth in heaven, the blessed Trinity. Amen.

DAME PRUDENCE ON RICHES
(from the "Tale of Melibeus")

By Geoffrey Chaucer

WHEN Prudence had heard her husband avaunt himself of his riches and of his money, dispreising the power of his adversaries, she spake and said in this wise: Certes, dear sir, I grant you that ye ben rich and mighty, and that riches ben good to 'em that han well ygetten 'em, and that well can usen 'em; for, right as the body of a man may not liven withouten soul, no more may it liven withouten temporal goods, and by riches may a man get him great friends; and therefore saith Pamphilus: If a neatherd's daughter be rich, she may chese of a thousand men which she wol take to her husband; for of a thousand men one wol not forsaken her ne refusen her. And this Pamphilus saith also: If thou be right happy, that is to sayn, if thou be right rich, thou shalt find a great number of fellows and friends; and if thy fortune change, that thou wax poor, farewell friendship and fellowship, for thou shalt be all alone withouten any company, but if it be the company of poor folk. And yet saith this Pamphilus, moreover, that they that ben bond and thrall of linage shuln be made worthy and noble by riches. And right so as by riches there comen many goods, right so by poverty come there many harms and evils; and therefore clepeth Cassiodore, poverty the mother of ruin, that is to sayn, the mother of overthrowing or falling down;

and therefore saith Piers Alphonse: One of the greatest
adversities of the world is when a free man by kind, or of
birth, is constrained by poverty to eaten the alms of his
enemy.   And the same saith Innocent in one of his books;
he saith that sorrowful and mishappy is the condition of
a poor beggar, for if he ax not his meat he dieth of hunger,
and if he ax he dieth for shame; and algates necessity
constraineth him to ax; and therefore saith Solomon:
That better it is to die than for to have such poverty; and,
as the same Solomon saith: Better it is to die of bitter
death, than for to liven in such wise.   By these reasons
that I have said unto you, and by many other reasons that
I could say, I grant you that riches ben good to 'em that
well geten 'em and to him that well usen tho' riches; and
therefore wol I shew you how ye shulen behave you in
gathering of your riches, and in what manner ye shulen
usen 'em.

First, ye shuln geten 'em withouten great desire, by
good leisure, sokingly, and not over hastily, for a man that
is too desiring to get riches abandoneth him first to theft
and to all other evils; and therefore saith Solomon:
He that hasteth him too busily to wax rich, he shall be
non innocent: he saith also, that the riches that hastily
cometh to a man, soon and lightly goeth and passeth from
a man, but that riches that cometh little and little, waxeth
alway and multiplieth.   And, sir, ye shuln get riches by
your wit and by your travail, unto your profit, and that
withouten wrong or harm doing to any other person; for
the law saith: There maketh no man himself rich, if he
do harm to another wight; that is to say, that Nature
defendeth and forbiddeth by right, that no man make himself rich unto the harm of another person.   And Tullius
saith: That no sorrow, ne no dread of death, ne nothing
that may fall unto a man, is so muckle agains nature as

a man to increase his own profit to harm of another man. And though the great men and the mighty men geten riches more lightly than thou, yet shalt thou not ben idle ne slow to do thy profit, for thou shalt in all wise flee idleness; for Solomon saith : That idleness teacheth a man to do many evils; and the same Solomon saith : That he that travaileth and busieth himself to tillen his lond, shall eat bread, but he that is idle, and casteth him to no business ne occupation, shall fall into poverty, and die for hunger. And he that is idle and slow can never find convenable time for to do his profit; for there is a versifier saith, that the idle man excuseth him in winter because of the great cold, and in summer then by encheson of the heat. For these causes, saith Caton, waketh and inclineth you not over muckle to sleep, for over muckle rest nourisheth and causeth many vices; and therefore saith St. Jerome: Doeth some good deeds, that the devil, which is our enemy, ne find you not unoccupied, for the devil he taketh not lightly unto his werking such as he findeth occupied in good werks.

Then thus in getting riches ye musten flee idleness; and afterward ye shuln usen the riches which ye han geten by your wit and by your travail, in such manner, than men hold you not too scarce, ne too sparing, ne fool-large, that is to say, over large a spender; for right as men blamen an avaricious man because of his scarcity and chinchery, in the same wise he is to blame that spendeth over largely; and therefore saith Caton: Use (saith he) the riches that thou hast ygeten in such manner, that men have no matter ne cause to call thee nother wretch ne chinch, for it is a great shame to a man to have a poor heart and a rich purse; he saith also : The goods that thou hast ygeten, use 'em by measure, that is to sayn, spend measureably, for they that folily wasten and despenden the goods that they han, when they han no more proper of 'eir own, that they shapen 'em to take the goods of another man. I say, then, that ye shuln flee avarice, using your riches in such manner, that men sayen not that your riches been buried, but that ye have 'em in your might and in your wielding; for a wise man reproveth the avaricious man, and saith thus in two verse: Whereto and why burieth a man his goods by his great avarice, and knoweth well that needs must he die, for death is the end of every man as in this present life? And for what cause or encheson joineth he him, or knitteth he him so fast unto his goods, that all his wits mowen not disseveren him or departen him fro his goods, and knoweth well, or ought to know, that when he is dead he shall nothing bear with him out of this world? and therefore saith St. Augustine, that the avaricious man is likened unto hell, that the more it swalloweth the more desire it hath to swallow and devour. And as well as he wold eschew to be called an avaricious man or an chinch, as well should ye keep you and govern you in such wise, that men call you not fool-large; therefore, saith Tullius: The goods of thine house ne should not ben hid ne kept so close, but that they might ben opened by pity and debonnairety, that is to sayen, to give 'em part that han great need; ne they goods shoulden not ben so open to be every man's goods.

Afterward, in getting of your riches, and in using of 'em, ye shuln alway have three things in your heart, that is to say, our Lord God, conscience, and good name. First ye shuln have God in your heart, and for no riches ye shuln do nothing which may in any manner displease God that is your creator and maker; for, after the word of Solomon, it is better to have a little good, with love of God, than to have muckle good and lese the love of his

Lord God; and the prophet saith, that better it is to ben
a good man and have little good and treasure, than to
be holden a shrew and have great riches.   And yet I say
furthermore, that ye shulden always do your business to
get your riches, so that ye get 'em with a good conscience.
And the apostle saith, that there nis thing in this world,
of which we shulden have so great joy, as when our
conscience beareth us good witness; and the wise man
saith: The substance of a man is full good when sin is
not in a man's conscience.   Afterward, in getting of your
riches and in using of 'em, ye must have great business
and great diligence that your good name be alway kept
and conserved; for Solomon saith, that better it is and
more it availeth a man to have a good name than for to
have great riches; and therefore he saith in another place:
Do great diligence (saith he) in keeping of thy friends and
of thy good name, for it shall longer abide with thee than
any treasure, be it never so precious; and certainly he
should not be called a gentleman that, after God and good
conscience all things left, ne doth his diligence and business to keepen his good name; and Cassiodore saith,
that it is a sign of a gentle heart, when a man loveth
and desireth to have a good name.   And therefore saith
Seint Augustyn, that ther ben two thinges that ben
necessarie and needful; and that is good conscience and
good loos; that is to sayn, good conscience in thin oughne
persone in-ward, and good loos of thin neghebor out-ward.
And he that trusteth him so muckle in his good conscience,
that he despiseth or setteth at nought his good name or
los, and recketh not though he kept not his good name,
n'is but a cruel churl.

HAMLET'S ADVICE TO THE PLAYERS

By William Shakespeare

Speak the speech, I pray you, as I pronounced it to you, trippingly on the tongue : but if you mouth it, as many of your players do, I had as lief the town-crier spoke my lines. Nor do not saw the air too much with your hand, thus ; but use all gently, for in the very torrent, tempest, and, as I may say, whirlwind of your passion, you must acquire and beget a temperance that may give it smoothness. O, it offends me to the soul to hear a robustious periwig-pated fellow tear a passion to tatters, to very rags, to split the ears of the groundlings, who, for the most part, are capable of nothing but inexplicable dumb-shows and noise : I would have such a fellow whipped for o'erdoing Termagant ; it out-herods Herod : pray you, avoid it. Be not too tame neither, but let your own discretion be your tutor : suit the action to the word, the word to the action ; with this special observance, that you o'erstep not the modesty of nature : for anything so overdone is from the purpose of playing, whose end, both at the first and now, was and is, to hold, as 't were, the mirror up to nature ; to show virtue her own feature, scorn her own image, and the very age and body of the time his form and pressure. Now this overdone or come tardy off, though it make the unskilful laugh, cannot but make the judicious grieve ; the censure of the which one must in your allowance o'erweigh a whole theatre of others. O, there be players that I have seen play, and heard others praise, and that highly, not to speak it profanely, that neither having the accent of Christians nor the gait of Christian, pagan, nor man, have so strutted and bellowed, that I have thought some of nature's journeymen had made men, and not made them well, they imitated humanity so abominably. O, reform

it altogether.   And let those that play your clowns speak
no more than is set down for them : for there be of them
that will themselves laugh, to set on some quantity of
barren spectators to laugh too, though in the mean time
some necessary question of the play be then to be considered : that's villainous, and shows a most pitiful ambition in the fool that uses it.

*Whatever identity was hidden behind the initials " T. T."
may have been known to friends and neighbors in 1614;
but today only a few essays remain to tell us all we know of
that nameless personality.   The following extract from one
of them is included here, both because it offers a good example
of early essay style, and because it presents a point of view
of possible use to a present-day writer.*

OF PAINTING THE FACE (*Incomplete*)

By T. T.

IF that which is most ancient be best, then the face
that one is borne with, is better than it that is borrowed :
Nature is more ancient than Art, and Art is allowed to
help Nature, but not to hurt it; to mend it, but not to
mar it; for perfection, but not for perdition : but this
artificiall facing doth corrupt the naturall colour of it.
Indeed God hath given a man oil for his countenance, as
He hath done wine for his heart, to refresh and cheere it;
but this is by reflection and not by plaister-worke; by
comforting, and not by dawbing and covering; by mend-
ing and helping the naturall colour, and not by marring
or hiding it with an artificiall lit.   What a miserable vanity
is it a man or woman beholding in a glasse their borrowed
face, their bought complexion, to please themselves with
a face that is not their owne?   And what is the cause they
paint?   Without doubt nothing but pride of heart, dis-
daining to bee behind their neighbour, discontentment with
the worke of God, and vaine glory, or a foolish affectation
of the praise of men.   This kind of people are very hypo-

crites, seeming one thing and being another, desiring
to bee that in show which they cannot be in substance,
and coveting to be judged that, they are not : They are
very grosse Deceivers; for they study to delude men with
shewes, seeking hereby to bee counted more lovely creatures than they are, affecting that men should account
that naturall, which is but artificiall.   I may truly say they
are deceivers of themselves; for if they thinke they doe
well to paint, they are deceived; if they think it honest
and just to beguile men, and to make them account them
more delicate and amiable, than they are in truth, they
are deceived; if they thinke it meete that that should bee
counted God's worke, which is their owne, they are deceived. . . .   To bee murdered of another is not a sin in
him that is murdered; but for a man to be deceived in
what he is forbidden, is a sinne; it were better to bee
murdered, than so to be deceived : For there the body is
but killed, but here the soule herself is endangered.   Now,
how unhappy is the danger, how grievous is the sin, when
a man is merely of himself indangered ?   It is a misery
of miseries for a man to bee slaine with his owne sword,
with his owne hand, and long of his owne will : Besides,
this painting is very scandalous, and of ill report; for
any man therefore to use it, is to thwart the precept of the
Holy Ghost in Saint Paul, who saith unto the Phillippians
in this wise, Whatsoever things are true (but a painted
face is a false face) whatsoever things are venerable (but
who esteems a painted face venerable ?) whatsoever things
are just (but will any man of judgement say, that to paint
the face is a point of justice ?   Who dare say it is according
to the will of God which is the rule of justice ? . . .

Painting is an enemy of blushing, which is vertues colour.
And indeed how unworthy are they to bee credited in
things of moment, that are so false in their haire, or colour,

over which age, and sicknesse, and many accidents doe tyrannize; yea and where their deceipt is easily discerned? And whereas the passions and conditions of a man, and his age, is something discovered by the face, this painting hindereth a mans judgement herein, so that if they were as well able to colour the eyes, as they are their haire and faces, a man could discerne little or nothing in such kind of people. In briefe, these painters are sometimes injurious to those, that are naturally faire and lovely, and no painters; partly, in that these are thought sometimes to bee painted, because of the common use of painting; and partly, in that these artificial creatures steal away the praise from the naturall beauty by reason of their Art, when it is not espyed, whereas were it not for their cunning, they would not bee deemed equall to the other. It is great pity that this outlandish vanity is in so much request and practise with us, as it is.

Here are a few early "character" essays. The first has more of the chatty quality of later essayists than was common in this type of writing or in this writer's time. (Fuller's writings are full of humorous comment, and Charles Lamb read them with delight.) Thomas Dekker is another character writer who overstepped the limits of that type and wrote much that lives today as apt quotation. Following Dekker is a classic forerunner of the "character" in seventeenth century English literature. Theophrastus the Greek lived and wrote about three centuries before Christ.

THE GOOD SCHOOLMASTER

BY THOMAS FULLER

THERE is scarce any profession in the commonwealth more necessary, which is so slightly performed. The reasons whereof I conceive to be these: First, young scholars make this calling their refuge; yea, perchance, before they have taken any degree in the university, commence schoolmasters in the country, as if nothing else were required to set up this profession but only a rod and a ferula. Secondly, others who are able, use it only as a passage to better preferment, to patch the rents in their present fortune, till they can provide a new one, and betake themselves to some more gainful calling. Thirdly, they are disheartened from doing their best with the miserable reward which in some places they receive, being masters to their children and slaves to their parents.

Fourthly, being grown rich, they grow negligent, and scorn to touch the school but by the proxy of the usher. But see how well our schoolmaster behaves himself.

His genius inclines him with delight to his profession. Some men had as well be schoolboys as schoolmasters, to be tied to the school, as Cooper's Dictionary and Scapula's Lexicon are chained to the desk therein; and though great scholars, and skilful in other arts, are bunglers in this. But God, of His goodness, hath fitted several men for several callings, that the necessity of Church and State, in all conditions, may be provided for. So that he who beholds the fabric thereof, may say, God hewed out the stone, and appointed it to lie in this very place, for it would fit none other so well, and here it doth most excellent. And thus God mouldeth some for a schoolmaster's life, undertaking it with desire and delight, and discharging it with dexterity and happy success.

He studieth his scholars' natures as carefully as they their books; and ranks their dispositions into several forms. And though it may seem difficult for him in a great school to descend to all particulars, yet experienced schoolmasters may quickly make a grammar of boys' natures, and reduce them all — saving some few exceptions — to these general rules:

1. Those that are ingenious and industrious. The conjunction of two such planets in a youth presage much good unto him. To such a lad a frown may be a whipping, and a whipping a death; yea, where their master whips them once, shame whips them all the week after. Such natures he useth with all gentleness.

2. Those that are ingenious and idle. These think with the hare in the fable, that running with snails — so they count the rest of their schoolfellows — they shall come soon enough to the post, though sleeping a good while before

their starting. Oh, a good rod would finely take them napping.

3. Those that are dull and diligent. Wines, the stronger they be, the more lees they have when they are new. Many boys are muddy-headed till they be clarified with age, and such afterwards prove the best. Bristol diamonds are both bright, and squared, and pointed by nature, and yet are soft and worthless; whereas orient ones in India are rough and rugged naturally. Hard, rugged, and dull natures of youth, acquit themselves afterwards the jewels of the country, and therefore their dulness at first is to be borne with, if they be diligent. That schoolmaster deserves to be beaten himself who beats nature in a boy for a fault. And I question whether all the whipping in the world can make their parts which are naturally sluggish rise one minute before the hour nature hath appointed.

4. Those that are invincibly dull, and negligent also. Correction may reform the latter, not amend the former. All the whetting in the world can never set a razor's edge on that which hath no steel in it. Such boys he consigneth over to other professions. Shipwrights and boat-makers will choose those crooked pieces of timber which other carpenters refuse. Those may make excellent merchants and mechanics which will not serve for scholars.

He is able, diligent, and methodical in his teachng; not leading them rather a circle than forwards. He minces his precepts for children to swallow, hanging clogs on the nimbleness of his own soul, that his scholars may go along with him.

He is and will be known to be an absolute monarch in his school. If cockering mothers proffer him money to purchase their sons' exemption from his rod — to live, as it were, in a peculiar, out of their master's jurisdiction

— with disdain he refuseth it, and scorns the late custom in some places of commuting whipping into money, and ransoming boys from the rod at a set price. If he hath a stubborn youth, correction-proof, he debaseth not his authority by contesting with him, but fairly, if he can, puts him away before his obstinacy hath infected others.

He is moderate in inflicting deserved correction. Many a schoolmaster better answereth the name *paidotribes* than *paidagogos*, rather tearing his scholars' flesh with whipping than giving them good education. No wonder if his scholars hate the muses, being presented unto them in the shape of fiends and furies.

Such an Orbilius mars more scholars than he makes. Their tyranny hath caused many tongues to stammer which spake plain by nature, and whose stuttering at first was nothing else but fears quavering on their speech at their master's presence; and whose mauling them about their heads hath dulled those who in quickness exceeded their master.

He makes his school free to him who sues to him *in formâ pauperis*. And surely learning is the greatest alms that can be given. But he is a beast who, because the poor scholar cannot pay him his wages, pays the scholar in his whipping; rather are diligent lads to be encouraged with all excitements to learning. This minds me of what I have heard concerning Mr. Bust, that worthy late schoolmaster of Eton, who would never suffer any wandering begging scholar — such as justly the statute hath ranked in the fore-front of rogues — to come into his school, but would thrust him out with earnestness — however privately charitable unto him — lest his schoolboys should be disheartened from their books, by seeing some scholars after their studying in the university preferred to beggary.

He spoils not a good school to make thereof a bad college, therein to teach his scholars logic. For, besides that logic may have an action of trespass against grammar for encroaching on her liberties, syllogisms are solecisms taught in the school, and oftentimes they are forced afterwards in the university to unlearn the fumbling skill they had before.

Out of his school he is no way pedantical in carriage or discourse; contenting himself to be rich in Latin, though he doth not gingle with it in every company wherein he comes.

To conclude, let this, amongst other motives, make schoolmasters careful in their place — that the eminences of their scholars have commended the memories of their schoolmasters to posterity, who, otherwise in obscurity, had altogether been forgotten. Who had ever heard of R. Bond, in Lancashire, but for the breeding of learned Ascham, his scholar? or of Hartgrave, in Brundly School, in the same county, but because he was the first did teach worthy Dr. Whitaker? Nor do I honour the memory of Mulcaster for anything so much as his scholar, that gulf of learning, Bishop Andrews. This made the Athenians, the day before the great feast of Theseus, their founder, to sacrifice a ram to the memory of Conidas, his schoolmaster, that first instructed him.

OF WINTER

By Thomas Dekker

WINTER, the sworne enemie to summer, the friend to none but colliers and woodmongers: the frostbitten churl that hangs his nose still over the fire: the dog that bites fruits, and the devil that cuts down trees, the unconscionable binder up of vintners' faggots, and the only consumer

of burnt sack and sugar : This cousin to Death, father to
sickness, and brother to old age, shall not show his hoary
bald-pate in this climate of ours (according to our usual
computation) upon the twelfth day of December, at the
first entering of the sun into the first minute of the sign
Capricorn, when the said Sun shall be at his greatest south
declination from the equinoctial line, and so forth, with
much more such stuff than any mere Englishman can
understand — no, my countrymen, never beat the bush so
long to find out Winter, where he lies, like a beggar shiver-
ing with cold, but take these from me as certain and most
infallible rules, know when Winter plums are ripe and
ready to be gathered.

When Charity blows her nails and is ready to starve,
yet not so much as a watchman will lend her a flap of his
frieze gown to keep her warm : when tradesmen shut up
shops, by reason their frozen-hearted creditors go about
to nip them with beggary : when the price of sea-coal
riseth, and the price of men's labour falleth : when every
chimney casts out smoke, but scarce any door opens to
cast so much as a maribone to a dog to gnaw ; when beasts
die for want of fodder in the field, and men are ready to
famish for want of food in the city ; when the first word
that a wench speaks at your coming into the room in a
morning is, "Prithee send for some faggots," and the
best comfort a sawyer beats you withal is to say, "What
will you give me?"; when gluttons blow their pottage to
cool them; and Prentices blow their nails to heat them;
and lastly when the Thames is covered over with ice and
men's hearts caked over and crusted with cruelty : Then
mayest thou or any man be bold to swear it is winter.

CHARACTERS OF THEOPHRASTUS

TRANSLATED BY CHARLES E. BENNETT AND
WILLIAM A. HAMMOND

THE TACTLESS MAN

TACTLESSNESS is the faculty of hitting a moment that is
unpleasant to the persons concerned. The tactless man
is the sort of person who selects a man's busy hour to go
and confer with him. He serenades his sweetheart when
she has a fever. If an acquaintance has just lost bail-
money on a friend, he hunts him up and asks him to be
his surety. After a verdict has been rendered he appears
at the trial to give evidence. At a wedding where he is
a guest he declaims against womankind.

When a friend has just finished a long journey he invites
him to go for a walk. He has a faculty for fetching a
higher bidder for an article after it has been sold; and in
a group of companions he gets up and explains from the
beginning a story which the others have just heard and
have completely understood. He is anxious to give himself the trouble to do what nobody wants done, and yet
what nobody likes to decline.

When men are in the midst of religious offerings and are
making outlay of money, he goes to collect his interest.
If he happens to be standing by when a slave is flogged,
he tells the story of how he once flogged a slave who then
went away and hanged himself. If he is arbitrator in a
dispute, he sets both contestants by the ears just at the
moment when they are ready to settle their differences.
When he wants to dance he takes a partner who is not yet
merry.

THE BORE

We may define a bore as a man who cannot refrain from
talking. A bore is the sort of fellow who, the moment you

open your mouth, tells you that your remarks are idle, that he knows all about it, and if you'll only listen, you'll soon find out. As you attempt to make answer, he suddenly breaks in with such interruptions as: "Don't forget what you were about to say" — "That reminds me" — "What an admirable thing talk is!" — "But, as I omitted to mention" — "You grasp the idea at once" — "I was watching this long time to see whether you would come to the same conclusion as myself." In phrases like this he's so fertile that the person who happens to meet him cannot even open his mouth to speak.

When he has vanquished a few stray victims here and there, his next move is to advance upon whole companies and put them to flight in the midst of their occupations. He goes upon the wrestling ground or into the schools, and prevents the boys from making progress with their lessons, so incessant is his talk with the teachers and the wrestling-masters.

If you say you are going home, he's pretty sure to come along and escort you to your house.

Whenever he learns the day set for the session of the Assembly he noises it diligently abroad, and recalls Demosthenes's famous bout with Aeschines in the archonship of Aristophon. He mentions, too, his own humble effort on a certain occasion, and the approval which it won among the people. As he rattles on he launches invectives against the masses, in such fashion that his audience either becomes oblivious or begins to doze, or else melts away in the midst of his harangue.

When he's on a jury he's an obstacle to reaching a verdict, when he's in the theatre he prevents attention to the play; at a feast he hinders eating, remarking that silence is too much of an effort, that his tongue is hung in the middle, and that he couldn't keep still, even though he should seem a worse chatterer than a magpie; and when he's made a butt by his own children, he submits, — when in their desire to go to sleep they say, "Papa, tell us something, in order that sleep may come."

Abraham Cowley seems to be, more than any one other, the forerunner of Lamb, both in spirit and in style. Lamb gives him unstinted praise; and many of his essays deserve rereading today not merely as literary curiosities but for their vitality and charm.

OF MYSELF

By Abraham Cowley

It is a hard and nice subject for a man to write of himself; it grates his own heart to say anything of disparagement, and the reader's ears to hear anything of praise from him. There is no danger from me of offending him in this kind; neither my mind, nor my body, nor my fortune, allow me any materials for that vanity. It is sufficient, for my own contentment, that they have preserved me from being scandalous, or remarkable on the defective side. But besides that, I shall here speak of myself only in relation to the subject of these precedent discourses, and shall be likelier thereby to fall into the contempt, than rise up to the estimation of most people. As far as my memory can return back into my past life, before I knew or was capable of guessing what the world, or glories, or business of it were, the natural affections of my soul gave a secret bent of aversion from them, as some plants are said to turn away from others, by an antipathy imperceptible to themselves, and inscrutable to man's understanding. Even when I was a very young boy at school, instead of running about on holidays, and playing with my fellows, I was wont to steal from them, and walk into

the fields, either alone with a book, or with some one
companion, if I could find any of the same temper.   I was
then, too, so much an enemy to constraint, that my
masters could never prevail on me, by any persuasions or
encouragements, to learn, without book, the common rules
of grammar, in which they dispensed with me alone, because they found I made a shift to do the usual exercise
out of my own reading and observation.   That I was then
of the same mind as I am now — which, I confess, I wonder
at myself — may appear at the latter end of an ode which
I made when I was but thirteen years old, and which was
then printed, with many other verses.   The beginning of
it is boyish; but of this part which I here set down, if a
very little were corrected, I should hardly now be much
ashamed.

> This only grant me, that my means may lie
> Too low for envy, for contempt too high.
>> Some honour I would have,
> Not from great deeds, but good alone;
> Th' unknown are better than ill-known.
>> Rumour can ope the grave;
> Acquaintance I would have; but when 't depends
> Not on the number, but the choice of friends.
>
> Books should, not business, entertain the light,
> And sleep, as undisturbed as death, the night.
>> My house a cottage, more
> Than palace, and should fitting be
> For all my use, no luxury.
> My garden painted o'er
> With Nature's hand, not Art's; and pleasures yield,
> Horace might envy in his Sabine field.
>
> Thus would I double my life's fading space,
> For he that runs it well, twice runs his race.

>   And in this true delight,
>   These unbought sports, that happy state,
>   I would not fear nor wish my fate,
>   But boldly say each night,
>   To-morrow let thy sun his beams display,
>   Or in clouds hide them; I have lived to-day.

You may see by it I was even then acquainted with the
poets, for the conclusion is taken out of Horace; and perhaps it was the immature and immoderate love of them
which stamped first, or rather engraved, the characters in
me. They were like letters cut in the bark of a young
tree, which, with the tree, still grow proportionably. But
how this love came to be produced in me so early, is a
hard question: I believe I can tell the particular little
chance that filled my head first with such chimes of verse,
as have never since left ringing there: for I remember
when I began to read, and take some pleasure in it, there
was wont to lie in my mother's parlour — I know not by
what accident, for she herself never in her life read any
book but of devotion — but there was wont to lie Spenser's
works; this I happened to fall upon, and was infinitely
delighted with the stories of the knights, and giants, and
monsters, and brave houses, which I found everywhere
there — though my understanding had little to do with all
this — and by degrees, with the tinkling of the rhyme, and
dance of the numbers; so that I think I had read him all
over before I was twelve years old. With these affections
of mind, and my heart wholly set upon letters, I went to
the university; but was soon torn from thence by that
public violent storm, which would suffer nothing to stand
where it did, but rooted up every plant, even from the
princely cedars, to me, the hyssop. Yet I had as good
fortune as could have befallen me in such a tempest; for
I was cast by it into the family of one of the best persons,

and into the court of one of the best princesses in the world. Now, though I was here engaged in ways most contrary to the original design of my life; that is, into much company, and no small business, and into a daily sight of greatness, both militant and triumphant — for that was the state then of the English and the French courts — yet all this was so far from altering my opinion, that it only added the confirmation of reason to that which was before but natural inclination. I saw plainly all the paint of that kind of life, the nearer I came to it; and that beauty which I did not fall in love with, when, for aught I knew, it was real, was not like to bewitch or entice me when I saw it was adulterate. I met with several great persons, whom I liked very well, but could not perceive that any part of their greatness was to be liked or desired, no more than I would be glad or content to be in a storm, though I saw many ships which rid safely and bravely in it. A storm would not agree with my stomach, if it did with my courage; though I was in a crowd of as good company as could be found anywhere, though I was in business of great and honourable trust, though I eat at the best table, and enjoyed the best conveniences for present subsistence that ought to be desired by a man of my condition, in banishment and public distresses; yet I could not abstain from renewing my old school-boy's wish, in a copy of verses to the same effect:

Well, then, I now do plainly see
This busy world and I shall ne'er agree, &c.

And I never then proposed to myself any other advantage from his majesty's happy restoration, but the getting into some moderately convenient retreat in the country, which I thought in that case I might easily have compassed, as well as some others, who, with no greater probabilities or pretences, have arrived to extraordinary fortunes. But I had before written a shrewd prophecy against myself, and I think Apollo inspired me in the truth, though not in the elegance of it —

> Thou neither great at court, nor in the war,
> Nor at the Exchange shalt be, nor at the wrangling bar;
> Content thyself with the small barren praise
> Which thy neglected verse does raise, &c.

However, by the failing of the forces which I had expected, I did not quit the design which I had resolved on; I cast myself into it a *corpus perditum*, without making capitulations, or taking counsel of fortune. But God laughs at man, who says to his soul, Take thy ease: I met presently not only with many little incumbrances and impediments, but with so much sickness — a new misfortune to me — as would have spoiled the happiness of an emperor as well as mine. Yet I do neither repent nor alter my course; *Non ego perfidum dixi sacramentum.* Nothing shall separate me from a mistress which I have loved so long, and have now at last married; though she neither has brought me a rich portion, nor lived yet so quietly with me as I hoped from her.

> *Nec vos dulcissima mundi*
> *Nomina, vos musæ, libertas, otia, libri,*
> *Hortique, sylvæque, animâ remanente relinquam.*

> Nor by me e'er shall you,
> You of all names the sweetest and the best,
> You muses, books, and liberty, and rest;
> You gardens, fields, and woods forsaken be,
> As long as life itself forsakes not me.

The "King James version" of the Bible has done more than any one book, or than many books, to determine a standard of English style. In selecting out of so rich a treasure, three fragments have been chosen that are in themselves detached essays; and each contributes to a discussion that might be chosen today by some experimenting essayist. The virtue of silence is touched upon by other writers in this collection; and so is "Riches." Yet St. James speaks to us across a time-chasm of much more than a thousand years; while the second writer, perhaps King Solomon himself, may have written more than two thousand years ago, or more than three; and the third even longer ago. Yet we quote them today in reflecting upon our own affairs. Only one change has been made from the phraseology of the translators of 1611 and that is to substitute for "vexation of spirit", a later translator's "striving after wind."

THE TONGUE

AN ESSAY FROM THE EPISTLE OF ST. JAMES, ACCORDING TO THE "KING JAMES VERSION"

MY brethren, . . . in many things we all stumble. If any man stumble not in word, the same is a perfect man, and able also to bridle the whole body. Behold, we put bits in the horses' mouths, that they may obey us; and we turn about their whole body. Behold also the ships, which though they be so great, and are driven of fierce winds, yet are they turned about with a very small rudder, whithersoever the steersman listeth. Even so the tongue is a little member, and boasteth great things. Behold, how great a matter a little fire kindleth! And the tongue is a fire, a world of iniquity; so is the tongue among our members, that it defileth the whole body, and setteth on fire the course of nature; and it is set on fire by hell.   For every kind of beasts, and of birds, and of serpents, and of things in the sea, is tamed, and hath been tamed of mankind: but the tongue can no man tame; it is an unruly evil, full of deadly poison.   Therewith bless we God, even the Father; and therewith curse we men, which are made after the similitude of God.   Out of the same mouth proceedeth blessing and cursing.   My brethren, these things ought not so to be.   Doth a fountain send forth at the same time sweet water and bitter?   Can the fig tree, my brethren, bear olive berries? either a vine, figs? so can no fountain yield both salt water and fresh.

THE VANITY OF RICHES

FROM ECCLESIASTES

I THE Preacher was king over Israel in Jerusalem.   And I gave my heart to seek and search out by wisdom concerning all things that are done under heaven: this sore travail hath God given to the sons of man to be exercised therewith.   I have seen all the works that are done under the sun; and, behold, all is vanity and a striving after wind.   That which is crooked cannot be made straight; and that which is wanting cannot be numbered.   I communed with mine own heart, saying, Lo, I am come to great estate, and have gotten more wisdom than all they that have been before me in Jerusalem; yea, my heart had great experience of wisdom and knowledge.   And I gave my heart to know wisdom, and to know madness and folly; I perceived that this also is a striving after wind.   For in much wisdom is much grief; and he that increaseth knowledge increaseth sorrow.

I said in mine heart, Go to, now, I will prove thee with mirth, therefore enjoy pleasure; and, behold, this also was vanity. I said of laughter, It is mad; and of mirth, What doeth it? I sought in mine heart to give myself unto wine, yet acquainting mine heart with wisdom; and to lay hold on folly, till I might see what was that good for the sons of men, which they should do under the heaven all the days of their life. I made me great works; I builded me houses; I planted me vineyards; I made me gardens and orchards, and I planted trees in them of all kind of fruits; I made me pools of water, to water therewith the wood that bringeth forth trees; I got me servants and maidens, and had servants born in my house; also I had great possessions of great and small cattle above all that were in Jerusalem before me; I gathered me also silver and gold, and the peculiar treasure of kings and of the provinces; I gat me men singers and women singers, and the delights of the sons of men, as musical instruments, and that of all sorts. So I was great, and increased more than all that were before me in Jerusalem; also my wisdom remained with me. And whatsoever mine eyes desired I kept not from them, I withheld not my heart from any joy; for my heart rejoiced in all my labour; and this was my portion of all my labour. Then I looked on all the works that my hands had wrought, and on the labour that I had laboured to do; and behold, all was vanity and a striving after wind, and there was no profit under the sun.

And I turned myself to behold wisdom, and madness, and folly; for what can the man do that cometh after the king? even that which hath been already done. Then I saw that wisdom excelleth folly, as far as light excelleth darkness. The wise man's eyes are in his head; but the fool walketh in darkness; and I myself perceived also that one event happeneth to them all. Then said I in my heart, As it happeneth to the fool, so it happeneth even to me; and why was I then more wise? Then I said in my heart that this also is vanity. For there is no remembrance of the wise more than of the fool for ever; seeing that which now is in the days to come shall all be forgotten. And how dieth the wise man? as the fool. Therefore I hated life, because the work that is wrought under the sun is grievous unto me; for all is vanity and a striving after wind.

Yea, I hated all my labour which I had taken under the sun; because I should leave it unto the man that shall be after me. And who knoweth whether he shall be a wise man or a fool? yet shall he have rule over all my labour wherein I have laboured; and wherein I have shewed myself wise under the sun. This also is vanity. Therefore I went about to cause my heart to despair of all the labour which I took under the sun. For there is a man whose labour is in wisdom, and in knowledge, and in equity; yet to a man that hath not laboured therein shall he leave it for his portion. This also is vanity and a great evil. For what hath man of all his labour, and of the vexation of his heart, wherein he hath laboured under the sun? For all his days are sorrows, and his travail grief; yea, his heart taketh not rest in the night; This is also vanity.

There is nothing better for a man, than that he should eat and drink, and that he should make his soul enjoy good in his labour. This also I saw, that it was from the hand of God. For who can eat, or who else can hasten unto it, more than I? For God giveth to a man that is good in his sight wisdom, and knowledge, and joy; but to the sinner he giveth travail, to gather and to heap up, that he may give to him that is good before God. This also is vanity and a striving after wind.

A HOUSE OF ONE'S OWN

FROM ECCLESIASTICUS

THE chief thing for life is water, and bread, and a garment, and a house to cover shame. Better is the life of a poor man under a shelter of logs, than sumptuous fare in another man's house. With little or with much, be well satisfied. It is a miserable life to go from house to house; and where thou art a sojourner, thou shalt not dare to open thy mouth. Thou shalt entertain, and give to drink, and have no thanks; and besides this thou shalt hear bitter words.

> Come higher, thou sojourner,
>   Furnish a table,
> And if thou hast aught in thy hand,
>   Feed me with it.
>
> Go forth, thou sojourner,
>   From the face of honour;
> My brother is come to be my guest;
>   I have need of my house.

These things are grievous to a man of understanding — the upbraiding of house-room, and the reproaching of the money-lender.

John Bunyan was an essayist, and some fragment of one of his essays might have been included here. But it is "Pilgrim's Progress" that will cause him to be remembered and held in veneration long after all his other writings are forgotten. Here again is an example of the pure English of the King James version of the Bible. So a fragment has been taken almost at random, as a model for style and diction.

THE SLOUGH OF DESPOND

An Extract from Pilgrim's Progress by John Bunyan

Now I saw in my dream that, just as they had ended this talk, they drew near to a very miry slough that was in the midst of the plain; and they being heedless did both fall suddenly into the bog. The name of the slough was Despond. Here, therefore, they wallowed for a time, being grievously bedaubed with the dirt; and Christian, because of the burden that was on his back, began to sink in the mire.

Then said Pliable, "Ah! neighbor Christian, where are you now?"

"Truly," said Christian, "I do not know."

At that Pliable began to be offended, and angrily said to his fellow, "Is this the happiness you have told me all this while of? If we have such ill speed at our first setting out, what may we expect 'twixt this and our journey's end? May I get out again with my life, you shall possess the brave country alone for me." And with that he gave a desperate struggle or two, and got out of the mire on that side of the slough which was next to his own house; so away he went, and Christian saw him no more.

Wherefore Christian was left to tumble in the Slough of Despond alone; but still he endeavoured to struggle to that side of the slough that was farthest from his own house, and next to the wicket-gate: the which he did, but could not get out because of the burden that was upon his back. But I beheld, in my dream, that a man came to him whose name was Help, and asked him, What he did there?

"Sir," said Christian, "I was bid to go this way by a man called Evangelist, who directed me also to yonder gate, that I might escape the wrath to come; and as I was going thither, I fell in here."

"But why did you not look for the steps?"

"Fear followed me so hard, that I fled the next way, and fell in."

Then said he, "Give me thy hand." So he gave him his hand, and he drew him out, and set him upon the sound ground, and bid him go on his way.

Then I stepped to him that plucked him out, and said, "Sir, wherefore, since over this place is the way from the city of Destruction to yonder gate, is it that this plat is not mended, that poor travellers might go thither with more security?" And he said unto me, "This miry slough is such a place as cannot be mended; it is the descent whither the scum and filth that attends conviction for sin doth continually run; and therefore it is called the Slough of Despond. For still, as the sinner awakened about his lost condition, there ariseth in his soul many fears and doubts, and discouraging apprehensions, which all of them get together, and settle in this place: and this is the reason of the badness of this ground.

"It is not the pleasure of the king that this place should

remain so bad; his labourers also have, by the directions
of his majesty's surveyors, been for above this sixteen
hundred years employed about this patch of ground, if
perhaps it might have been mended: yea, and to my
knowledge," said he, "here have been swallowed up at
least twenty thousand cart-loads, yea millions, of wholesome instructions, that have, at all seasons, been brought
from all places of the king's dominions (and they that can
tell say they are the best materials to make good ground of
the place), if so be it might have been mended; but it is
the Slough of Despond still, and so will be, when they have
done what they can."

Defoe was not only an occasional essayist himself, but the editor of a review which helped to establish the essay-form in English literature. As in the case of Bunyan, an extract has been chosen at random from that one of his books which has the greatest vitality, and has had the greatest influence upon later writers. Note the sentence structure, and the paucity of adjectives.

INTERVENTION OF PROVIDENCE

Extract from Robinson Crusoe by Daniel Defoe (1719)

During this time, I made my rounds in the woods for game every day, when the rain permitted me, and made frequent discoveries in these walks, of something or other to my advantage; particularly, I found a kind of wild pigeons, who build, not as wood-pigeons, in a tree, but rather as house-pigeons in the holes of the rocks; and, taking some young ones, I endeavored to breed them up tame, and did so; but when they grew older, they flew all away; which, perhaps, was, at first, for want of feeding them, for I had nothing to give them; however, I frequently found their nests, and got their young ones, which were very good meat. And now, in the managing my household affairs, I found myself wanting in many things, which I thought at first it was impossible for me to make; as indeed, as to some of them, it was: for instance, I could never make a cask to be hooped. I had a small runlet or two, as I observed before; but I could never arrive at the capacity of making one by them, though I spent many

weeks about it; I could neither put in the heads, nor
join the staves so true to one another as to make them
hold water; so I gave that also over. In the next place, I
was at a great loss for candle; so that as soon as it was
dark, which was generally by seven o'clock, I was obliged
to go to bed. I remembered the lump of bees-wax with
which I made candles in my African adventure; but I
had none of that now: the only remedy I had was, that
when I had killed a goat, I saved the tallow; and with a
little dish made of clay, which I baked in the sun, to which
I added a wick of some oakum, I made me a lamp; and
this gave me light, though not a clear steady light like a
candle. In the middle of all my labours it happened,
that in rummaging my things, I found a little bag; which,
as I hinted before, had been filled with corn, for the feeding of poultry; not for this voyage, but before, as I suppose, when the ship came from Lisbon. What little
remainder of corn had been in the bag was all devoured
by the rats, and I saw nothing in the bag but husks and
dust; and being willing to have the bag for some other
use (I think it was to put powder in, when I divided it for
fear of the lightning, or some such use) I shook the husks
of corn out of it, on one side of my fortification, under the
rock.

It was a little before the great rain just now mentioned,
that I threw this stuff away; taking no notice of anything,
and not so much as remembering that I had thrown anything there; when, about a month after, I saw some few
stalks of something green, shooting out of the ground,
which I fancied might be some plant I had not seen;
but I was surprised, and perfectly astonished, when, after
a little longer time, I saw about ten or twelve ears come
out, which were perfect green barley, of the same kind as
our European, nay, as our English barley.

It is impossible to express the astonishment and confusion of my thoughts on this occasion. I had hitherto acted upon no religious foundation at all; indeed, I had very few notions of religion in my head, nor had entertained any sense of any things that had befallen me, otherwise than as chance, or, as we lightly say, what pleases God; without so much as inquiring into the end of Providence in these things or his order in governing events in the world. But after I saw barley grow there, in a climate which I knew was not proper for corn, and especially as I knew not how it came there, it startled me strangely; and I began to suggest, that God had miraculously caused this grain to grow without any help of seed sown, and that it was so directed purely for my sustenance, on that wild miserable place.

This touched my heart a little, and brought tears out of my eyes; and I began to bless myself that such a prodigy of nature should happen upon my account: and this was the more strange to me, because I saw near it still, all along by the side of the rock, some other straggling stalks, which proved to be stalks of rice, and which I knew, because I had seen it grow in Africa, when I was ashore there.

I not only thought these the pure productions of Providence for my support, but, not doubting that there was more in the place I went over all that part of the island where I had been before, searching in every corner, and under every rock, for more of it; but I could not find any. At last it occurred to my thoughts, that I had shook out a bag of chicken's-meat in that place, and then the wonder began to cease; and I must confess, my religious thankfulness to God's providence began to abate too, upon the discovering that all this was nothing but what was common; though I ought to have been as thankful for so strange and unforseen a providence, as if it had been miraculous; for it was really the work of Providence, as to me, that should order or appoint that ten or twelve grains of corn should remain unspoiled, when the rats had destroyed all the rest, as if it had been dropped from heaven; as also, that I should throw it out in that particular place, where, it being in the shade of a high rock, it sprang up immediately; whereas, if I had thrown it anywhere else, at that time, it would have been burned up and destroyed.

I carefully saved the ears of this corn, you may be sure, in their season, which was about the end of June; and, laying up every corn, I resolved to sow them all again; hoping, in time, to have some quantity sufficient to supply me with bread. But it was not till the fourth year that I could allow myself the least grain of this corn to eat, and even then but sparingly, as I shall show afterwards in its order; for I lost all that I sowed the first season, by not observing the proper time; as I sowed just before the dry season, so that it never came up at all, at least not as it would have done; of which in its place.

Pope and Swift are here grouped together, because in outstanding fashion they resorted to keen and biting satire in their writings. Both were essayists, though both are better remembered for writing in other fields.

THE GRAND ELIXIR

By Alexander Pope

THERE is an oblique way of Reproof, which takes off from the Sharpness of it; and an Address in Flattery, which makes it agreeable though never so gross : But of all Flatterers, the most skilful is he who can do what you like, without saying any thing which argues you do it for his Sake; the most winning Circumstance in the World being the Conformity of Manners. I speak of this as a Practice necessary in gaining People of Sense, who are not yet given up to Self-Conceit; those who are far gone in admiration of themselves need not be treated with so much Delicacy. The following Letter puts this Matter in a pleasant and uncommon Light : The Author of it attacks this Vice with an Air of Compliance, and alarms us against it by exhorting us to it.

To the GUARDIAN

"SIR,

"As you profess to encourage all those who any way contribute to the Publick Good, I flatter my self I may claim your Countenance and Protection. I am by profession a Mad Doctor, but of a peculiar Kind, not of those whose Aim it is to remove Phrenzies, but one who makes it my Business to confer an agreeable Madness on my

Fellow-Creatures, for their mutual Delight and Benefit. Since it is agreed by the Philosophers, that Happiness and Misery consist chiefly in the Imagination, nothing is more necessary to Mankind in general than this pleasing Delirium, which renders every one satisfied with himself, and persuades him that all others are equally so.

"I have for several Years, both at home and abroad, made this Science my particular Study, which I may venture to say I have improved in almost all the Courts of *Europe;* and have reduced it into so safe and easie a Method, as to practise it on both Sexes, of what Disposition, Age or Quality soever, with Success. What enables me to perform this great Work, is the Use of my *Obsequium Catholicon*, or the *Grand Elixir*, to support the Spirits of human Nature. This Remedy is of the most grateful Flavour in the World, and agrees with all Tastes whatever. 'T is delicate to the Senses, delightful in the Operation, may be taken at all Hours without Confinement, and is as properly given at a Ball or Play-house as in a private Chamber. It restores and vivifies the most dejected Minds, corrects and extracts all that is painful in the knowledge of a Man's self. One Dose of it will instantly disperse it self through the whole Animal System, dissipate the first Motions of Distrust so as never to return, and so exhilerate the Brain and rarifie the Gloom of Reflection, as to give the Patients a new flow of Spirits, a Vivacity of Behaviour, and a pleasing Dependence upon their own Capacities.

"LET a Person be never so far gone, I advise him not to despair; even though he has been troubled many Years with restless Reflections, which by long Neglect have hardened into settled Consideration. Those that have been stung with Satyr may here find a certain Antidote, which infallibly disperses all the Remains of Poison that

has been left in the Understanding by bad Cures. It forti-
fies the Heart against the Rancour of Pamphlets, the
Inveteracy of Epigrams, and the Mortification of Lam-
poons ; as has been often experienced by several Persons of
both Sexes, during the Seasons of *Tunbridge* and the *Bath.*

"I could, as farther Instances of my Success, produce
Certificates and Testimonials from the Favourites and
Ghostly Fathers of the most eminent Princes of *Europe;*
but shall content my self with the Mention of a few Cures,
which I have performed by this my *Grand Universal
Restorative,* during the Practice of one Month only since
I came to this City."

Cures in the Month of February, 1713

"*GEORGE SPONDEE,* Esq.; Poet, and Inmate of the
Parish of St. *Paul's Covent-Garden,* fell into violent Fits
of the Spleen upon a thin Third Night. He had been
frighted into a Vertigo by the Sound of Cat-calls on the
First Day ; and the frequent Hissings on the Second made
him unable to endure the bare Pronunciation of the Letter
S. I searched into the Causes of his Distemper ; and by
the Prescription of a Dose of my *Obsequium,* prepared
Secundum Artem, recovered him to his Natural State of
Madness. I cast in at proper Intervals the Words, *Ill
Taste of the Town, Envy of Cliticks, bad Performance of the
Actors,* and the like. He is so perfectly cured that he has
promised to bring another Play upon the State next
Winter.

"A Lady of professed Virtue, of the Parish of St.
James's Westminster, who hath desired her Name may
be concealed, having taken Offence at a Phrase of double
Meaning in Conversation, undiscovered by any other in
the Company, suddenly fell into a cold Fit of Modesty.
Upon a right Application of Praise of her Virtue, I threw

the Lady into an agreeable waking Dream, settled the Fermentation of her Blood into a warm Charity, so as to make her look with Patience on the very Gentleman that offended.

"*HILARIA*, of the Parish of St. *Giles's in the Fields*, a Coquet of long Practice, was by the Reprimand of an old Maiden reduced to look grave in Company, and deny her self the Play of the Fan. In short, she was brought to such Melancholy Circumstances, that she would sometimes unawares fall into Devotion at Church. I advis'd her to take a few *innocent Freedoms with occasional Kisses* prescribed her the *Exercise of the Eyes*, and immediately raised her to her former State of Life. She on a sudden recovered her Dimples, furled her Fan, threw round her Glances, and for these two *Sundays* last past has not once been seen in an attentive Posture. This the Church-Wardens are ready to attest upon Oath.

"*ANDREW TERROR*, of the *Middle-Temple*, *Mohock*, was almost induced by an aged Bencher of the same House to leave off bright Conversation, and pore over *Cook upon Littleton*. He was so ill that his Hat began to flap, and he was seen one Day in the last Term at *Westminster-Hall*. This Patient had quite lost his Spirit of Contradiction; I, by the Distillation of a few of my vivifying Drops in his Ear, drew him from his Lethargy, and restored him to his usual vivacious Misunderstanding. He is at present very easie in his Condition.

"I will not dwell upon the Recital of the innumerable Cures I have performed within Twenty Days last past; but rather proceed to exhort all Persons, of whatever Age, Complexion or Quality, to take as soon as possible of this my intellectual Oyl; which applied at the Ear seizes all the Senses with a most agreeable Transport, and discovers its Effects, not only to the Satisfaction of the Patient, but all who converse with, attend upon, or any way relate to him or her that receives the kindly Infection. It is often administered by Chamber-Maids, Valets, or any the most ignorant Domestick; it being one peculiar Excellence of this my Oyl, that 't is most prevalent, the more unskilful the Person is or appears who applies it. It is absolutely necessary for Ladies to take a Dose of it just before they take Coach to go a visiting.

"BUT I offend the Publick, as *Horace* said, when I trespass on any of your Time. Give me leave then, Mr. *Ironside*, to make you a Present of a Drachm or two of my Oyl; though I have Cause to fear my Prescriptions will not have the Effect upon you I could wish : Therefore I do not endeavour to bribe you in my Favour by the Present of my Oyl, but wholly depend upon your Publick Spirit and Generosity; which, I hope, will recommend to the World the useful Endeavours of,

"*SIR,*
"*Your most Obedient, most Faithful, most Devoted, most Humble Servant and Admirer,*
                              "GNATHO.

" ** Beware of Counterfeits, for such are abroad.
"*N. B.* I teach the *Arcana* of my Art at reasonable Rates to Gentlemen of the Universities, who desire to be qualified for writing Dedications; and to young Lovers and Fortune-hunters, to be paid at the Day of Marriage. I instruct Persons of bright Capacities to flatter others, and those of the meanest to flatter themselves.

"I was the first Inventor of Pocket Looking-Glasses."

A MEDITATION UPON A BROOMSTICK, ACCORDING TO THE STYLE AND MANNER OF THE HON. ROBERT BOYLE'S MEDITATIONS

By Jonathan Swift

THIS single stick, which you now behold ingloriously lying in that neglected corner, I once knew in a flourishing state in a forest; it was full of sap, full of leaves, and full of boughs; but now in vain does the busy art of man pretend to vie with nature, by tying that withered bundle of twigs to its sapless trunk; it is now at best but the reverse of what it was, a tree turned upside down, the branches on the earth, and the root in the air; it is now handled by every dirty wench, condemned to do her drudgery, and, by a capricious kind of fate, destined to make her things clean, and be nasty itself; at length, worn out to the stumps in the service of the maids, it is either thrown out of doors, or condemned to the last use of kindling a fire. When I beheld this, I sighed, and said within myself: Surely mortal man is a broomstick! nature sent him into the world strong and lusty, in a thriving condition, wearing his own hair on his head, the proper branches of this reasoning vegetable, until the axe of intemperance has lopped off his green boughs, and left him a withered trunk; he then flies to art, and puts on a periwig, valuing himself upon an unnatural bundle of hairs, all covered with powder, that never grew on his head; but now should this our broomstick pretend to enter the scene, proud of those birchen spoils it never bore, and all covered with dust, though the sweepings of the finest lady's chamber, we should be apt to ridicule and despise its vanity. Partial judges that we are of our own excellences, and other men's defaults!

But a broomstick, perhaps you will say, is an emblem

of a tree standing on its head: and pray, what is man but a topsy-turvy creature, his animal faculties perpetually mounted on his rational, his head where his heels should be — grovelling on the earth! and yet, with all his faults, he sets up to be a universal reformer and corrector of abuses, a remover of grievances; rakes into every slut's corner of nature, bringing hidden corruptions to the light, and raises a mighty dust where there was none before, sharing deeply all the while in the very same pollutions he pretends to sweep away. His last days are spent in slavery to women, and generally the least deserving; till, worn to the stumps, like his brother-besom, he is either kicked out of doors, or made use of to kindle flames for others to warm themselves by.

THE ART OF POLITICAL LYING (*Incomplete*)

BY JONATHAN SWIFT

WE are told the devil is the father of lies, and was a liar from the beginning; so that, beyond contradiction, the invention is old: and, which is more, his first Essay of it was purely political, employed in undermining the authority of his prince, and seducing a third part of the subjects from their obedience: for which he was driven down from heaven, where (as Milton expresses it) he had been viceroy of a great western province; and forced to exercise his talent in inferior regions among other fallen spirits, poor or deluded men, whom he still daily tempts to his own sin, and will ever do so, till he be chained in the bottomless pit.

But although the devil be the father of lies, he seems, like other great inventors, to have lost much of his reputation by the continual improvements that have been made upon him.

Who first reduced lying into an art, and adapted it to
politics, is not so clear from history, although I have made
some diligent inquiries. I shall therefore consider it only
according to the modern system, as it has been cultivated
these twenty years past in the southern part of our own
island.

The poets tell us that, after the giants were overthrown
by the gods, the earth in revenge produced her last offspring, which was Fame. And the fable is thus inter-
preted: that when tumults and seditions are quieted,
rumours and false reports are plentifully spread through a
nation. So that, by this account, lying is the last relief
of a routed, earth-born, rebellious party in a state. But
here the moderns have made great additions, applying this
art to the gaining of power and preserving it, as well as
revenging themselves after they have lost it; as the same
instruments are made use of by animals to feed themselves when they are hungry, and to bite those that tread
upon them.

But the same genealogy cannot always be admitted for
political lying; I shall therefore desire to refine upon it,
by adding some circumstances of its birth and parents. A
political lie is sometimes born out of a discarded statesman's head, and thence delivered to be nursed and dandled
by the rabble. Sometimes it is produced a monster, and
licked into shape: at other times it comes into the world
completely formed, and is spoiled in the licking. It is
often born an infant in the regular way, and requires time
to mature it; and often it sees the light in its full growth,
but dwindles away by degrees. Sometimes it is of noble
birth, and sometimes the spawn of a stock-jobber. . . . I
know a lie that now disturbs half the kingdom with its
noise, [of] which, although too proud and great at present
to own its parents, I can remember its whisperhood. To

conclude the nativity of this monster; when it comes into the world without a sting it is still-born; and whenever it loses its sting it dies.

No wonder if an infant so miraculous in its birth should be destined for great adventures; and accordingly we see it has been the guardian spirit of a prevailing party for almost twenty years. It can conquer kingdoms without fighting, and sometimes with the loss of a battle. It gives and resumes employments; can sink a mountain to a mole-hill, and raise a mole-hill to a mountain; has presided for many years at committees of elections; can wash a black-moor white; make a saint of an atheist, and a patriot of a profligate; can furnish foreign ministers with intelligence, and raise or let fall the credit of the nation. This goddess flies with a huge looking-glass in her hands, to dazzle the crowd, and make them see, according as she turns it, their ruin in their interest, and their interest in their ruin. In this glass you will behold your best friends, clad in coats powdered with *fleurs de lis* and triple crowns; their girdles hung round with chains, and beads, and wooden shoes; and your worst enemies adorned with the ensigns of liberty, property, indulgence, moderation, and a cornu-copia in their hands. Her large wings, like those of a flying-fish, are of no use but while they are moist; she therefore dips them in mud, and, soaring aloft, scatters it in the eyes of the multitude, flying with great swiftness; but at every turn is forced to stoop in dirty ways for new supplies.

I have been sometimes thinking, if a man had the art of the second sight for seeing lies, as they have in Scotland for seeing spirits, how admirably he might entertain him-self in this town, by observing the different shapes, sizes, and colours of those swarms of lies which buzz about the heads of some people, like flies about a horse's ears in

summer; or those legions hovering every afternoon in
Exchange-alley, enough to darken the air; or over a club
of discontented grandees, and thence sent down in cargoes
to be scattered at elections.

There is one essential point wherein a political liar differs
from others of the faculty, that he ought to have but a
short memory, which is necessary according to the various
occasions he meets with every hour of differing from himself and swearing to both sides of a contradiction, as he
finds the persons disposed with whom he has to deal. In
describing the virtues and vices of mankind, it is convenient, upon every article, to have some eminent person
in our eye, from whom we copy our description. I have
strictly observed this rule, and my imagination this
minute represents before me a certain great man famous
for this talent, to the constant practice of which he owes
his twenty years' reputation of the most skilful head in
England for the management of nice affairs. The superiority of his genius consists in nothing else but an inex-
haustible fund of political lies, which he plentifully dis-
tributes every minute he speaks, and by an unparalleled
generosity forgets, and consequently contradicts, the next
half-hour. He never yet considered whether any proposition were true or false, but whether it were convenient for
the present minute or company to affirm or deny it; so
that, if you think fit to refine upon him by interpreting
everything he says, as we do dreams, by the contrary,
you are still to seek, and will find yourself equally deceived
whether you believe or not: the only remedy is to suppose
that you have heard some inarticulate sounds, without
any meaning at all; and besides, that will take off the
horror you might be apt to conceive at the oaths wherewith
he perpetually tags both ends of every proposition; although, at the same time, I think he cannot with any

justice be taxed with perjury when he invokes God and Christ, because he has often fairly given public notice to the world that he believes in neither.

Some people may think that such an accomplishment as this can be of no great use to the owner, or his party, after it has been often practised and is become notorious; but they are widely mistaken. Few lies carry the inventor's mark, and the most prostitute enemy to truth may spread a thousand without being known for the author: besides, as the vilest writer has his readers, so the greatest liar has his believers; and it often happens that, if a lie be believed only for an hour, it has done its work, and there is no farther occasion for it. Falsehood flies, and truth comes limping after it, so that when men come to be undeceived it is too late; the jest is over, and the tale has had its effect: like a man who has thought of a good repartee when the discourse is changed or the company parted; or like a physician who has found out an infallible medicine after the patient is dead. . . .

Steele and Addison — two names that are closely associated in the minds of all readers of belles-lettres. *They were friends, born in the same year, and associated as editors and as authors. "Dick" Steele first edited* The Tatler *which gave English writers an added incentive to use the essay style and form. Abandoning* The Tatler, *he and Addison brought out* The Spectator, *and among many "Spectator papers" gave to the world Sir Roger de Coverly.*

JACK LIZARD (*Incomplete*)

By Richard Steele

JACK LIZARD was about Fifteen when he was first entered in the University, and being a Youth of a great deal of Fire, and a more than ordinary Application to his Studies, it gave his Conversation a very particular Turn. He had too much Spirit to hold his Tongue in Company; but at the same time so little Acquaintance with the World, that he did not know how to talk like other People.

AFTER a Year and half's stay at the University, he came down among us to pass away a Month or two in the Country. The first Night after his Arrival, as we were at Supper, we were all of us very much improved by *Jack's* Table-Talk. He told us, upon the Appearance of a Dish of Wild-Fowl, that according to the Opinion of some natural Philosophers they might be lately come from the Moon. Upon which the *Sparkler* bursting out into a Laugh, he insulted her with several Questions relating to the Bigness and Distance of the Moon and

Stars; and after every Interrogatory would be winking
upon me, and smiling at his Sister's Ignorance. *Jack*
gained his Point; for the Mother was pleased, and all
the Servants stared at the Learning of their young Master.
Jack was so encouraged at this Success, that for the first
Week he dealt wholly in Paradoxes. It was a common
Jest with him to pinch one of his Sister's Lap-Dogs, and
afterwards prove he could not feel it. When the Girls
were sorting a Set of Knots, he would demonstrate to
them that all the Ribbands were of the same Colour;
or rather, says *Jack*, of no Colour at all. My Lady *Lizard*
her self, though she was not a little pleas'd with her Son's
Improvements, was one Day almost angry with him; for
having accidently burnt her Fingers as she was lighting
the Lamp for her Tea-pot; in the midst of her Anguish,
Jack laid hold of the Opportunity to instruct her that
there was no such thing as Heat in Fire. In short, no Day
pass'd over our Heads, in which *Jack* did not imagine he
made the whole Family wiser than they were before.

THAT part of his Conversation which gave me the most
Pain, was what pass'd among those Country Gentlemen
that came to visit us. On such Occasions *Jack* usually
took upon him to be the Mouth of the Company; and
thinking himself obliged to be very merry, would entertain
us with a great many odd Sayings and Absurdities of their
College-Cook. I found this Fellow had made a very strong
Impression upon *Jack's* Imagination; which he never considered was not the Case of the rest of the Company,
'till after many repeated Tryals he found that his Stories
seldom made any Body laugh but himself.

I all this while looked upon *Jack* as a young Tree shooting out into Blossoms before its Time; the Redundancy
of which, though it was a little unseasonable, seemed to
foretel an uncommon Fruitfulness.

IN order to wear out the vein of Pedantry which ran through his Conversation, I took him out with me one Evening, and first of all insinuated to him this Rule, which I had my self learned from a very great Author, *To think with the Wise, but talk with the Vulgar. Jack's* good Sense soon made him reflect that he had often exposed himself to the Laughter of the Ignorant by a contrary Behaviour; upon which he told me, that he would take Care for the future to keep his Notions to himself, and converse in the common received Sentiments of Mankind. He at the same time desired me to give him any other Rules of Conversation which I thought might be for his Improvement. I told him I would think of it; and accordingly, as I have a particular Affection for the young Man, I gave him next Morning the following Rules in Writing, which may perhaps have contributed to make him the agreeable Man he now is.

THE Faculty of interchanging our Thoughts with one another, or what we express by the Word *Conversation*, has always been represented by Moral Writers as one of the noblest Privileges of Reason, and which more particularly sets Mankind above the Brute Part of the Creation.

THOUGH nothing so much gains upon the Affections as this *Extempore Eloquence*, which we have constantly Occasion for, and are obliged to practice every Day, we very rarely meet with any who excel in it.

THE Conversation of most Men is disagreeable, not so much for Want of Wit and Learning, as of Good-breeding and Discretion.

IF you resolve to please, never speak to gratifie any particular Vanity or Passion of your own, but always with a Design either to divert or inform the Company. A Man who only aims at one of these, is always easie in his Discourse. He is never out of Humour at being interrupted, because he considers that those who hear him are the best Judges whether what he was saying could either divert or inform them.

A modest Person seldom fails to gain the Good-Will of those he converses with, because no body envies a Man, who does not appear to be pleased with himself.

WE should talk extreamly little of our selves. Indeed what can we say? It would be as imprudent to discover our Faults, as ridiculous to count over our fancied Virtues. Our private and domestick Affairs are no less improper to be introduced in Conversation. What does it concern the Company how many Horses you keep in your Stables? Or whether your Servant is most Knave or Fool?

A man may equally affront the Company he is in, by engrossing all the Talk, or observing a contemptuous Silence.

BEFORE you tell a Story it may be generally not amiss to draw a short Character, and give the Company a true Idea of the principal Persons concerned in it. The Beauty of most things consisting not so much in their being said or done, as in their being said or done by such a particular Person, or on such a particular Occasion.

NOTWITHSTANDING all the Advantages of Youth, few young People please in Conversation; the Reason is, that want of Experience makes them positive, and what they say is rather with a Design to please themselves than any one else. . . .

    *   *   *   *   *   *   *

NOTHING is more silly than the Pleasure some People take in what they call *speaking their Minds*. A Man of this Make will say a rude thing for the meer Pleasure of saying it, when an opposite Behaviour, full as Innocent, might have preserved his Friend, or made his Fortune.

IT is not impossible for a Man to form to himself as exquisite a Pleasure in complying with the Humour and Sentiments of others, as of bringing others over to his own; since 't is the certain Sign of a Superior Genius, that can take and become whatever Dress it pleases.

I shall only add, that besides what I have here said, there is something which can never be learnt but in the Company of the Polite. The Virtues of Men are catching as well as their Vices, and your own Observations added to these, will soon discover what it is that commands Attention in one Man and makes you tired and displeased with the Discourse of another.

SIR ROGER AT CHURCH

By Joseph Addison

I am always very well pleased with a Country *Sunday;* and think, if keeping holy the Seventh Day were only a human Institution, it would be the best Method that could have been thought of for the polishing and civilizing of Mankind. It is certain the Country-People would soon degenerate into a kind of Savages and Barbarians, were there not such frequent Returns of a stated Time, in which the whole Village meet together with their best Faces, and in their cleanliest Habits, to converse with one another upon indifferent Subjects, hear their Duties explained to them, and join together in Adoration of the Supreme Being. *Sunday* clears away the Rust of the whole Week, not only as it refreshes in their Minds the Notions of Religion, but as it puts both the Sexes upon appearing in their most agreeable Forms, and exerting all such Qualities as are apt to give them a Figure in the Eye of the Village. A Country-Fellow distinguishes himself as much in the *Churchyard*, as a Citizen does upon the *Change;*

the whole Parish-Politicks being generally discuss'd in that Place either after Sermon or before the Bell rings.

My Friend Sir ROGER being a good Churchman, has beautified the Inside of his Church with several Texts of his own chusing: He has likewise given a handsome Pulpit-Cloth, and railed in the Communion-Table at his own Expence. He has often told me, that at his coming to his Estate he found his Parishioners very irregular; and that in order to make them kneel and join in the Responses, he gave every one of them a Hassock and a Common-prayer Book: and at the same Time employed an itinerant Singing-Master, who goes about the Country for that Purpose, to instruct them rightly in the Tunes of the Psalms; upon which they now very much value themselves, and indeed out-do most of the Country Churches that I have ever heard.

As Sir ROGER is Landlord to the whole Congregation, he keeps them in very good Order, and will suffer no Body to sleep in it besides himself; for if by Chance he has been surprized into a short Nap at Sermon, upon recovering out of it he stands up and looks about him, and if he sees any Body else nodding, either wakes them himself, or sends his Servants to them. Several other of the old Knight's Particularities break out upon these Occasions: Sometimes he will be lengthening out a Verse in the Singing-Psalms, half a Minute after the rest of the Congregation have done with it; sometimes, when he is pleased with the Matter of his Devotion, he pronounces *Amen* three or four times to the same Prayer; and sometimes stands up when every Body else is upon their Knees, to count the Congregation, or see if any of his Tenants are missing.

I was yesterday very much surprized to hear my old Friend, in the Midst of the Service, calling out to one

John Matthews to mind what he was about, and not dis-
turb the Congregation. This *John Matthews* it seems is
remarkable for being an idle Fellow, and at that Time
was kicking his Heels for his Diversion. This Authority
of the Knight, though exerted in that odd Manner which
accompanies him in all Circumstances of Life, has a very
good Effect upon the Parish, who are not polite enough
to see anything ridiculous in his Behaviour; besides that,
the general good Sense and Worthiness of his Character
make his friends observe these little Singularities as Foils
that rather set off than blemish his good Qualities.

As soon as the Sermon is finished, no Body presumes
to stir till Sir ROGER is gone out of the Church. The
Knight walks down from his Seat in the Chancel between
a double Row of his Tenants, that stand bowing to him
on each Side; and every now and then enquires how such
an one's Wife, or Mother, or Son, or Father do whom he
does not see at Church; which is understood as a secret
Reprimand to the Person that is absent.

The Chaplain has often told me, that upon a Catechiz-
ing-day, when Sir ROGER has been pleased with a Boy that
answers well, he has ordered a Bible to be given him
next Day for his Encouragement; and sometimes accompanies it with a Flitch of Bacon to his Mother. Sir
ROGER has likewise added five Pounds a Year to the
Clerk's Place; and that he may encourage the young
Fellows to make themselves perfect in the Church-Service,
has promised upon the Death of the present Incumbent,
who is very old, to bestow it according to Merit.

The fair Understanding between Sir ROGER and his
Chaplain, and their mutual Concurrence in doing Good, is
the more remarkable, because the very next Village is
famous for the Differences and Contentions that rise
between the Parson and the 'Squire, who live in a per-

petual State of War. The Parson is always preaching at
the 'Squire, and the 'Squire to be revenged on the Parson
never comes to Church. The 'Squire has made all his
Tenants Atheists and Tithe-Stealers; while the Parson
instructs them every *Sunday* in the Dignity of his Order,
and insinuates to them in almost every Sermon, that he
is a better Man than his Patron. In short, Matters are
come to such an Extremity, that the 'Squire has not said
his Prayers either in publick or private this half Year;
and that the Parson threatens him, if he does not mend his
Manners, to pray for him in the Face of the whole Congregation.

Feuds of this Nature, though too frequent in the
Country, are very fatal to the ordinary People; who are
so used to be dazled with Riches, that they pay as much
Deference to the Understanding of a Man of an Estate,
as of a Man of Learning; and are very hardly brought
to regard any Truth, how important soever it may be, that
is preached to them, when they know there are several
Men of five hundred a Year who do not believe it.

WITCHES

By JOSEPH ADDISON

THERE are some Opinions in which a Man should stand
Neuter, without engaging his Assent to one side or the
other. Such a hovering Faith as this, which refuses to
settle upon any Determination, is absolutely necessary
in a Mind that is careful to avoid Errors and Prepasses-
sions. When the Arguments press equally on both sides in
Matters that are indifferent to us, the safest Method is to
give up ourselves to neither.

It is with this Temper of Mind that I consider the Subject of Witchcraft. When I hear the Relations that

are made from all Parts of the World, not only from *Norway* and *Lapland*, from the *East* and *West Indies*, but from every particular Nation in *Europe*, I cannot forbear thinking that there is such an Intercourse and Commerce with Evil Spirits, as that which we express by the Name of Witchcraft. But when I consider that the ignorant and credulous Parts of the World abound most in these Relations, and that the Persons among us who are supposed to engage in such an Infernal Commerce are People of a weak Understanding and crazed Imagination, and at the same time reflect upon the many Impostures and Delusions of this Nature that have been detected in all Ages, I endeavour to suspend my Belief till I hear more certain Accounts than any which have yet come to my Knowledge. In short, when I consider the Question, Whether there are such Persons in the World as those we call Witches? my Mind is divided between the two opposite Opinions; or rather (to speak my Thoughts freely) I believe in general that there is, and has been such a thing as Witchcraft; but at the same time can give no Credit to any Particular Instance of it.

I am engaged in this Speculation, by some Occurrences that I met with Yesterday, which I shall give my Reader an Account of at large. As I was walking with my Friend Sir ROGER by the side of one of his Woods, an old Woman applied her self to me for my Charity. Her Dress and Figure put me in mind of the following Description in *Otway*.

> In a close Lane as I pursu'd my Journey,
> I spy'd a wrinkled Hag, with Age grown double,
> Picking dry Sticks, and mumbling to her self.
> Her Eyes with scalding Rheum were gall'd and red;
> Cold Palsy shook her Head: her Hands seem'd wither'd;
> And on her crooked Shoulders had she wrapp'd

The tatter'd Remnants of an old striped Hanging,
Which serv'd to keep her Carcass from the Cold:
So there was nothing of a-piece about her.
Her lower Weeds were all o'er coarsely patch'd
With diff'rent-colour'd Rags, black, red, white, yellow,
And seem'd to speak Variety of Wretchedness.

As I was musing on this Description, and comparing
it with the Object before me, the Knight told me, that this
very old Woman had the Reputation of a Witch all over
the Country, that her Lips were observed to be always in
Motion, and that there was not a Switch about her House
which her Neighbours did not believe had carried her
several hundreds of Miles. If she chanced to stumble,
they always found Sticks or Straws that lay in the Figure
of a Cross before her. If she made any Mistake at
Church, and cryed *Amen* in a wrong Place, they never
failed to conclude that she was saying her Prayers backwards. There was not a Maid in the Parish that would
take a Pin of her, though she should offer a Bag of Money
with it. She goes by the name of *Moll White*, and has
made the Country ring with several imaginary Exploits
which are palmed upon her. If the Dairy Maid does not
make her Butter come so soon as she would have it, *Moll
White* is at the bottom of the Churn. If a Horse sweats
in the Stable, *Moll White* has been upon his Back. If a
Hare makes an unexpected Escape from the Hounds, the
Huntsman curses *Moll White*. Nay, (says Sir ROGER) I
have known the Master of the Pack, upon such an Occasion, send one of his Servants to see if *Moll White* had
been out that Morning.

This Account raised my Curiosity so far, that I begged
my Friend Sir ROGER to go with me into her Hovel, which
stood in a solitary Corner under the side of the Wood.
Upon our first entering Sir ROGER winked to me, and

pointed at something that stood behind the Door, which upon looking that way I found to be an old Broomstaff. At the same time he whispered me in the Ear to take notice of a Tabby Cat that sat in the Chimney-Corner, which, as the old Knight told me, lay under as bad a Report as *Moll White* her self; for besides that *Moll* is said often to accompany her in the same Shape, the Cat is reported to have spoken twice or thrice in her Life, and to have played several Pranks above the Capacity of an ordinary Cat.

I was secretly concerned to see Human Nature in so much Wretchedness and Disgrace, but at the same time could not forbear smiling to hear Sir ROGER, who is a little puzzled about the old Woman, advising her as a Justice of the Peace to avoid all Communication with the Devil, and never to hurt any of her Neighbours' Cattle. We concluded our Visit with a Bounty, which was very acceptable.

In our Return home Sir ROGER told me, that old *Moll* had been often brought before him for making Children spit Pins, and giving Maids the Night-Mare; and that the Country People would be tossing her into a Pond and trying Experiments with her every Day, if it was not for him and his Chaplain.

I have since found, upon Enquiry, that Sir ROGER was several times staggered with the Reports that had been brought him concerning this old Woman, and would frequently have bound her over to the County Sessions, had not his Chaplain with much ado perswaded him to the contrary.

I have been the more particular in this Account, because I hear there is scarce a Village in *England* that has not a *Moll White* in it. When an old Woman begins to doat, and grow chargeable to a Parish, she is generally turned into a Witch, and fills the whole Country with extravagant

Fancies, imaginary Distempers, and terrifying Dreams. In the meantime the poor Wretch that is the innocent Occasion of so many Evils begins to be frighted at herself, and sometimes confesses secret Commerce and Familiarities that her Imagination forms in a delirious old Age. This frequently cuts off Charity from the greatest Objects of Compassion, and inspires People with a Malevolence towards those poor decrepid Parts of our Species, in whom Human Nature is defaced by Infirmity and Dotage.

Oliver Goldsmith, "Poor Noll", was born the year before Steele died, and died the year before Lamb was born. He must stand alone in this brief collection for many friends and associates of his time. But the student of style will do well to contrast his simplicity with the ponderosity of Dr. Samuel Johnson, who spoke so contemptuously of essays and yet felt constrained to attempt them himself.

OLD MAIDS AND BACHELORS

By Oliver Goldsmith

LATELY in company with my friend in black, whose conversation is now both my amusement and instruction, I could not avoid observing the great numbers of old bachelors and maiden ladies with which this city seems to be over-run. "Sure marriage," said I, "is not sufficiently encouraged, or we should never behold such crowds of battered beaux and decayed coquettes still attempting to drive a trade they have been so long unfit for, and swarming upon the gaiety of the age. I behold an old bachelor in the most contemptible light, as an animal that lives upon the common stock, without contributing his share: he is a beast of prey, and the laws should make use of as many stratagems, and as much force to drive the reluctant savage into the toils, as the Indians when they hunt the rhinoceros. The mob should be permitted to halloo after him, boys might play tricks on him with impunity, every well-bred company should laugh at him, and if, when turned of sixty, he offered to make love, his

mistress might spit in his face, or, what would be perhaps
a greater punishment, should fairly grant the favour.

"As for old maids," continued I, "they should not be
treated with so much severity, because I suppose none
would be so if they could. No lady in her senses would
choose to make a subordinate figure at christenings and
lyings-in, when she might be the principal herself; nor
curry favour with a sister-in-law, when she might command an husband; nor toil in preparing custards, when
she might lie a-bed and give directions how they ought to
be made; nor stifle all her sensations in demure formality,
when she might with matrimonial freedom shake her
acquaintance by the hand, and wink at a double entendre.
No lady could be so very silly as to live single, if she could
help it. I consider an unmarried lady declining into
the vale of years, as one of those charming countries bor-
dering on China that lies waste for want of proper inhabitants. We are not to accuse the country, but the
ignorance of its neighbours, who are insensible of its
beauties, though at liberty to enter and cultivate the soil."

"Indeed, sir," replied my companion, "you are very
little acquainted with the English ladies, to think they
are old maids against their will. I dare venture to affirm,
that you can hardly select one of them all but has had
frequent offers of marriage, which either pride or avarice
has not made her reject. Instead of thinking it a disgrace,
they take every occasion to boast of their former cruelty;
a soldier does not exult more when he counts over the
wounds he has received, than a female veteran when she
relates the wounds she has formerly given: exhaustless
when she begins a narrative of the former death-dealing
power of her eyes. She tells of the knight in gold lace,
who died with a single frown, and never rose again till —
he was married to his maid; of the squire, who being

cruelly denied, in a rage flew to the window, and lifting up the sash, threw himself in an agony — into his arm chair; of the parson who, crossed in love, resolutely swallowed opium, which banished the stings of despised love by — making him sleep. In short, she talks over her former losses with pleasure, and, like some tradesmen, finds some consolation in the many bankruptcies she has suffered.

"For this reason, whenever I see a superannuated beauty still unmarried, I tacitly accuse her either of pride, avarice, coquetry, or affectation. There's Miss Jenny Tinderbox, I once remember her to have had some beauty, and a moderate fortune. Her elder sister happened to marry a man of quality, and this seemed as a statute of virginity against poor Jane. Because there was one lucky hit in the family, she was resolved not to disgrace it by introducing a tradesman. By thus rejecting her equals, and neglected or despised by her superiors, she now acts in the capacity of tutoress to her sister's children, and undergoes the drudgery of three servants, without receiving the wages of one.

"Miss Squeeze was a pawnbroker's daughter; her father had early taught her that money was a very good thing, and left her a moderate fortune at his death. She was so perfectly sensible of the value of what she had got, that she was resolved never to part with a farthing without an equality on the part of her suitor : she thus refused several offers made her by people who wanted to better themselves, as the saying is ; and grew old and ill-natured, without ever considering that she should have made an abatement in her pretensions, from her face being pale, and marked with the small-pox.

"Lady Betty Tempest, on the contrary, had beauty, with fortune and family. But fond of conquest, she passed from triumph to triumph; she had read plays and romances, and there had learned that a plain man of common sense was no better than a fool: such she refused, and sighed only for the gay, giddy, inconstant, and thoughtless; after she had thus rejected hundreds who liked her, and sighed for hundreds who despised her, she found herself insensibly deserted: at present she is company only for her aunts and cousins, and sometimes makes one in a country-dance, with only one of the chairs for a partner, casts off round a joint-stool, and sets to a corner-cupboard. In a word, she is treated with civil contempt from every quarter, and placed, like a piece of old-fashioned lumber, merely to fill up a corner.

"But Sophronia, the sagacious Sophronia, how shall I mention her? She was taught to love Greek, and hate the men from her very infancy: she has rejected fine gentlemen because they were not pedants, and pedants because they were not fine gentlemen; her exquisite sensibility has taught her to discover every fault in every lover, and her inflexible justice has prevented her pardoning them: thus she rejected several offers, till the wrinkles of age had overtaken her; and now, without one good feature in her face, she talks incessantly of the beauties of the mind."

Charles Lamb, the prince of essayists, has brought inspiration and stimulus to every true essayist since his day. Perhaps it may be true that those essays which most perfectly reveal the personality of the writer will most successfully retain vitality through the centuries, because human nature changes so slightly. Any one of Lamb's chosen topics offers its challenge to the beginner nowadays, and its style sets a worthy standard. Selection is too difficult. One may choose at random.

OLD CHINA

By Charles Lamb

I HAVE an almost feminine partiality for old china. When I go to see any great house, I enquire for the china-closet, and next for the picture gallery. I cannot defend the order of preference, but by saying, that we have all some taste or other, of too ancient a date to admit of our remembering distinctly that it was an acquired one. I can call to mind the first play, and the first exhibition, that I was taken to; but I am not conscious of a time when china jars and saucers were introduced into my imagination.

I had no repugnance then — why should I now have? — to those little, lawless, azure-tinctured grotesques, that under the notion of men and women, float about, uncircumscribed by any element, in that world before perspective — a china tea-cup.

I like to see my old friends — whom distance cannot diminish — figuring up in the air (so they appear to our

optics), yet on *terra firma* still — for so we must in courtesy interpret that speck of deeper blue, — which the
decorous artist, to prevent absurdity, had made to spring
up beneath their sandals.

I love the men with women's faces, and the women, if
possible, with still more womanish expressions.

Here is a young and courtly Mandarin, handing tea to
a lady from a salver — two miles off. See how distance
seems to set off respect! And here the same lady, or
another — for likeness is identity on tea-cups — is stepping
into a little fairy boat, moored on the hither side of this
calm garden river, with a dainty mincing foot, which in a
right angle of incidence (as angles go in our world) must
infallibly land her in the midst of a flowery mead — a
furlong off on the other side of the same strange stream!

Farther on — if far or near can be predicated of their
world — see horses, trees, pagodas, dancing the hays.

Here — a cow and rabbit couchant, and co-extensive —
so objects show, seen through the lucid atmosphere of
fine Cathay.

I was pointing out to my cousin last evening, over our
Hyson, (which we are old fashioned enough to drink un-
mixed still of an afternoon) some of these *speciosa miracula*
upon a set of extraordinary old blue china (a recent purchase) which we were now for the first time using; and
could not help remarking, how favourable circumstances
had been to us of late years, that we could afford to please
the eye sometimes with trifles of this sort — when a passing
sentiment seemed to overshade the brows of my companion. I am quick at detecting these summer clouds in
Bridget.

"I wish the good old times would come again," she
said, "when we were not quite so rich. I do not mean,
that I want to be poor; but there was a middle state" —

so she was pleased to ramble on, — "in which I am sure
we were a great deal happier. A purchase is but a purchase, now that you have money enough and to spare.
Formerly it used to be a triumph. When we coveted a
cheap luxury (and, O ! how much ado I had to get you to
consent in those times !) — we were used to have a debate
two or three days before, and to weigh the *for* and *against*,
and think what we might spare it out of, and what saving
we could hit upon, that should be an equivalent. A thing
was worth buying then, when we felt the money that we
paid for it."

"Do you remember the brown suit, which you made to
hang upon you, till all your friends cried shame upon you,
it grew so thread-bare — and all because of that folio
Beaumont and Fletcher, which you dragged home late at
night from Barker's in Covent Garden? Do you remember how we eyed it for weeks before we could make
up our minds to the purchase, and had not come to a
determination till it was near ten o'clock of the Saturday
night, when you set off from Islington, fearing you should
be too late — and when the old bookseller with some
grumbling opened his shop, and by the twinkling taper
(for he was setting bedwards) lighted out the relic from his
dusty treasures — and when you lugged it home, wishing it
were twice as cumbersome — and when you presented it to
me — and when we were exploring the perfectness of it
(*collating* you called it) — and while I was repairing some
of the loose leaves with paste, which your impatience
would not suffer to be left till daybreak — was there no
pleasure in being a poor man? or can those neat black
clothes which you wear now, and are so careful to keep
brushed, since we have become rich and finical, give you
half the honest vanity, with which you flaunted it about
in that overworn suit — your old corbeau — for four or

five weeks longer than you should have done, to pacify
your conscience for the mighty sum of fifteen — or sixteen
shillings was it ? — a great affair we thought it then —
which you had lavished on the old folio. Now you can
afford to buy any book that pleases you, but I do not see
that you ever bring me home any nice old purchases now."

"When you came home with twenty apologies for laying
out a less number of shillings upon that print after Lion-
ardo, which we christened the 'Lady Blanch;' when you
looked at the purchase, and thought of the money —
and thought of the money, and looked again at the picture
— was there no pleasure in being a poor man? Now, you
have nothing to do but to walk into Colnaghi's, and buy
a wilderness of Lionardos. Yet do you?"

"Then, do you remember our pleasant walks to Enfield,
and Potter's Bar, and Waltham, when we had a holyday —
holydays, and all other fun, are gone, now we are rich —
and the little hand-basket in which I used to deposit our
day's fare of savoury cold lamb and salad — and how you
would pry about at noon-tide for some decent house,
where we might go in, and produce our store — only paying
for the ale that you must call for — and speculate upon the
looks of the landlady, and whether she was likely to allow
us a table-cloth — and wish for such another honest
hostess, as Izaak Walton has described many a one on the
pleasant banks of the Lea, when he went a fishing — and
sometimes they would prove obliging enough, and sometimes they would look grudgingly upon us — but we had
cheerful looks still for one another, and would eat our
plain food savorily, scarcely grudging Piscator his Trout
Hall? Now, — when we go out a day's pleasuring, which
is seldom moreover, we *ride* part of the way — and go into
a fine inn, and order the best of dinners, never debating the
expense — which, after all, never has half the relish of

those chance country snaps, when we were at the mercy of uncertain usage, and a precarious welcome."

"You are too proud to see a play anywhere now but in the pit. Do you remember where it was we used to sit, when we saw the Battle of Hexham, and the Surrender of Calais, and Bannister and Mrs. Bland in the Children in the Wood — when we squeezed out our shillings a-piece to sit three or four times in a season in the one-shilling gallery — where you felt all the time that you ought not to have brought me — and more strongly I felt obligation to you for having brought me — and the pleasure was the better for a little shame — and when the curtain drew up, what cared we for our place in the house, or what mattered it where we were sitting, when our thoughts were with Rosalind in Arden, or with Viola at the Court of Illyria? You used to say, that the Gallery was the best place of all for enjoying a play socially — that the relish of such exhibitions must be in proportion to the infrequency of going — that the company we met there, not being in general readers of plays, were obliged to attend the more, and did attend, to what was going on, on the stage — because a word lost would have been a chasm, which it was impossible for them to fill up. With such reflections we consoled our pride then — and I appeal to you, whether, as a woman, I met generally with less attention and accommodation, than I have done since in more expensive situations in the house? The getting in indeed, and the crowding up those inconvenient staircases, was bad enough, — but there was still a law of civility to woman recognised to quite as great an extent as we ever found in the other passages — and how a little difficulty overcome heightened the snug seat, and the play, afterwards. Now we can only pay our money and walk in. You cannot see, you say, in the galleries now. I am sure we saw, and heard too, well enough then — but sight, and all, I think, is gone with our poverty."

"There was pleasure in eating strawberries, before they became quite common — in the first dish of peas, while they were yet dear — to have them for a nice supper, a treat. What treat can we have now? If we were to treat ourselves now — that is, to have dainties a little above our means, it would be selfish and wicked. It is very little more that we allow ourselves beyond what the actual poor can get at, that makes what I call a treat — when two people living together, as we have done, now and then indulge themselves in a cheap luxury, which both like; while each apologises, and is willing to take both halves of the blame to his single share. I see no harm in people making much of themselves in that sense of the word. It may give them a hint how to make much of others. But now — what I mean by the word — we never do make much of ourselves. None but the poor can do it. I do not mean the veriest poor of all, but persons as we were, just above poverty."

"I know what you were going to say, that it is mighty pleasant at the end of the year to make all meet, — and much ado we used to have every Thirty-first Night of December to account for our exceedings — many a long face did you make over your puzzled accounts, and in contriving to make it out how we had spent so much — or that we had not spent so much — or that it was impossible we should spend so much next year — and still we found our slender capital decreasing — but then, betwixt ways, and projects, and compromises of one sort or another, and talk of curtailing this charge, and doing without that for the future — and the hope that youth brings, and laughing spirits (in which you were never poor till now) we pocketed up our loss, and in conclusion, with 'lusty brimmers' (as you used to quote it out of *hearty cheerful Mr. Cotton*, as you called him), we used to welcome in the 'coming guest.' Now we have no reckoning at all at the end of the old year — no flattering promises about the new year doing better for us."

Bridget is so sparing of her speech on most occasions, that when she gets into a rhetorical vein, I am careful how I interrupt it. I could not help, however, smiling at the phantom of wealth which her dear imagination had conjured up out of a clear income of a poor — hundred pounds a year. "It is true we were happier when we were poorer, but we were also younger, my cousin. I am afraid we must put up with the excess, for if we were to shake the superflux into the sea, we should not much mend ourselves. That we had much to struggle with, as we grew up together, we have reason to be most thankful. It strengthened, and knit our compact closer. We could never have been what we have been to each other, if we had always had the sufficiency which you now complain of. The resisting power — those natural dilations of the youthful spirit, which circumstances cannot straighten — with us are long since passed away. Competence to age is supplementary youth, a sorry supplement indeed, but I fear the best that is to be had. We must ride, where we formerly walked: live better, and lie softer — and shall be wise to do so — than we had means to do in those good old days you speak of. Yet could those days return — could you and I once more walk our thirty miles a-day — could Bannister and Mrs. Bland again be young, and you and I be young to see them — could the good old one-shilling gallery days return — they are dreams, my cousin, now — but could you and I at this moment, instead of this quiet argument, by our well-carpeted fire-side, sitting on this luxurious sofa — be once more struggling up those inconvenient stair cases, pushed about, and squeezed, and elbowed by the poorest rabble or poor gallery scramblers — could I once more hear those anxious shrieks of yours — and the delicious *Thank God, we are safe*, which always followed when the topmost stair, conquered, let in the first light of the whole cheerful theatre down beneath us — I know not the fathom line that ever touched a descent so deep as I would be willing to bury more wealth in than Crœsus had, or the great Jew R—— is supposed to have, to purchase it. And now do just look at that merry little Chinese waiter holding an umbrella, big enough for a bed-tester, over the head of that pretty insipid half-Madonaish chit of a lady in that very blue summer house."

POPULAR FALLACIES

By Charles Lamb

III. THAT WE SHOULD RISE WITH THE LARK

At what precise minute that little airy musician doffs his night gear, and prepares to tune up his unseasonable matins, we are not naturalists enough to determine. But for a mere human gentleman — that has no orchestra business to call him from his warm bed to such preposterous exercises — we take ten, or half after ten (eleven, of course, during this Christmas solstice), to be the very earliest hour, at which he can begin to think of abandoning his pillow. We think of it, we say; for to do it in earnest, requires another half-hour's good consideration. Not but there are pretty sun-risings, as we are told, and such like gawds, abroad in the world, in summer time especially, some hours before what we have assigned; which a gentleman may see, as they say, only for getting up. But, having been tempted, once or twice, in earlier life, to assist at those

ceremonies, we confess our curiosity abated. We are no
longer ambitious of being the sun's courtiers, to attend at
his morning levees. We hold the good hours of the dawn
too sacred to waste them upon such observances; which
have in them, besides, something Pagan and Persic. To
say truth, we never anticipated our usual hour, or got up
with the sun (as 't is called), to go a journey, or upon a
foolish whole day's pleasuring, but we suffered for it all
the long hours after in listlessness and headaches; Nature
herself sufficiently declaring her sense of our presumption
in aspiring to regulate our frail waking courses by the
measures of that celestial and sleepless traveller. We deny
not that there is something sprightly and vigorous, at the
outset especially, in these break-of-day excursions. It is
flattering to get the start of a lazy world; to conquer death
by proxy in his image. But the seeds of sleep and mor-
tality are in us; and we pay usually in strange qualms
before night falls, the penalty of the unnatural inversion.
Therefore, while the busy part of mankind are fast
huddling on their clothes, are already up and about their
occupations, content to have swallowed their sleep by
wholesale; we choose to linger a-bed, and digest our
dreams. It is the very time to recombine the wandering
images, which night in a confused mass presented; to
snatch them from forgetfulness; to shape, and mould
them. Some people have no good of their dreams. Like
fast feeders, they gulp them too grossly, to taste them
curiously. We love to chew the cud of a foregone vision;
to collect the scattered rays of a brighter phantasm, or act
over again, with firmer nerves, the sadder nocturnal
tragedies; to drag into day-light a struggling and half-
vanishing night-mare; to handle and examine the terrors,
or the airy solaces. We have too much respect for these
spiritual communications, to let them go so lightly. We

are not so stupid, or so careless, as that Imperial forgetter of his dreams, that we should need a seer to remind us of the form of them. They seem to us to have as much significance as our waking concerns; or rather to import us more nearly, as more nearly we approach by years to the shadowy world, whither we are hastening. We-have shaken hands with the world's business; we have done with it; we have discharged ourself of it. Why should we get up? we have neither suit to solicit, nor affairs to manage. The drama has shut in upon us at the fourth act. We have nothing here to expect, but in a short time a sick bed, and a dismissal. We delight to anticipate death by such shadows as night affords. We are already half acquainted with ghosts. We were never much in the world. Disappointment early struck a dark veil between us and its dazzling illusions. Our spirits showed grey before our hairs. The mighty changes of the world already appear as but the vain stuff out of which dramas are composed. We have asked no more of life than what the mimic images in play-houses present us with. Even those types have waxed fainter. Our clock appears to have struck. We are SUPERANNUATED. In this dearth of mundane satisfaction, we contract politic alliances with shadows. It is good to have friends at court. The abstracted media of dreams seem no ill introduction to that spiritual presence, upon which, in no long time, we expect to be thrown. We are trying to know a little of the usages of that colony; to learn the language, and the faces we shall meet with there, that we may be less awkward at our first coming among them. We willingly call a phantom our fellow, as knowing we shall soon be of their dark companionship. Therefore, we cherish dreams. We try to spell in them the alphabet of the invisible world; and think we know already, how it shall be with us. Those uncouth shapes, which, while we clung to flesh and blood, affrighted us, have become familiar. We feel attenuated into their meagre essences, and have given the hand of half-way approach to incorporeal being. We once thought life to be something; but it has unaccountably fallen from us before its time. Therefore we choose to dally with visions. The sun has no purposes of ours to light us to. Why should we get up?

THE TWO RACES OF MEN

By Charles Lamb

The human species, according to the best theory I can form of it, is composed of two distinct races, *the men who borrow and the men who lend.* To these two original diversities may be reduced all those impertinent classifications of Gothic and Celtic tribes, white men, black men, red men. All the dwellers upon earth, "Parthians, and Medes, and Elamites," flock hither, and do naturally fall in with one or other of these primary distinctions. The infinite superiority of the former, which I chose to designate as the great race, is discernible in their figure, port, and a certain instinctive sovereignty. The latter are born degraded. "He shall serve his brethren." There is something in the air of one of this cast, lean and suspicious; contrasting with the open, trusting, generous manners of the other.

Observe who have been the greatest borrowers of all ages — Alcibiades — Falstaff — Sir Richard Steele — our late incomparable Brinsley — what a family likeness in all four!

What a careless, even deportment hath your borrower! What rosy gills! What a beautiful reliance on Providence doth he manifest — taking no more thought than lilies!

What contempt for money — accounting it (yours and mine especially) no better than dross! What a liberal compounding of those pedantic distinctions of *meum* and *tuum!* or rather, what a noble simplification of language (beyond Tooke), resolving these supposed opposites into one clear, intelligible pronoun adjective! What near approaches doth he make to the primitive community — to the extent of one half of the principle at least!

He is the true taxer who "calleth all the world up to be taxed;" and the distance is as vast between him and one of us, as subsisted between the Augustan Majesty and the poorest obolary Jew that paid his tribute-pittance at Jerusalem! His extractions, too, have such a cheerful, voluntary air! So far removed from your sour parochial or state-gatherers — those inkhorn varlets, who carry their want of welcome in their faces! He cometh to you with a smile, and troubleth you with no receipt; confining himself to no set season. Every day is His Candlemas, or his feast of Holy Michael. He applieth the *lene tormentum* of a pleasant look to your purse — which to that gentle warmth expands her silken leaves, as naturally as the cloak of the traveler, for which sun and wind contended. He is the true Propontic which never ebbed. The sea which taketh handsomely at each man's hand. In vain the victim, whom he delighteth to honor, struggles with destiny; he is in the net. Lend therefore cheerfully, O man ordained to lend — that thou lose no in the end, with thy worldly penny, the reversion promised. Combine not preposterously in thine own person the penalties of Lazarus and of Dives — but, when thou seest the proper authority coming, meet it smilingly, as it were halfway. Come, a handsome sacrifice! See how light he makes of it! Strain not courtesies with a noble enemy.

Reflections like the foregoing were forced upon my mind

by the death of my old friend, Ralph Bigod, Esq., who parted this life on Wednesday evening; dying, as he had lived, without much trouble. He boasted himself a descendant from mighty ancestors of that name, who heretofore held ducal dignities in this realm. In his actions and sentiments he belied not the stock to which he pretended. Early in life he found himself invested with ample revenues; which, with that noble disinterestedness which I have noticed as inherent in men of the great race, he took almost immediate measures entirely to dissipate and bring to nothing; for there is something revolting in the idea of a king holding a private purse; and the thoughts of Bigod were all regal. Thus furnished, by the very act of disfurnishment; getting rid of the cumbersome luggage of riches, more apt (as one sings)

> To slacken virtue, and abate her edge,
> Than prompt her to do aught may merit praise,

he set forth, like some Alexander, upon his great enterprise, "Borrowing and to borrow."

In his periegesis, or triumphant progress throughout this island, it has been calculated that he laid a tythe part of the inhabitants under contribution. I reject this estimate as greatly exaggerated; but having had the honor of accompanying my friend divers time, in his perambulations about this vast city, I own I was greatly struck at first with the prodigious number of faces we met who claimed a sort of respectful acquaintance with him. He was one day so obliging as to explain the phenomenon. It seems these were his tributaries; feeders of his exchequer; gentlemen, his good friends (as he was pleased to express himself), to whom he had occasionally been beholden for a loan. Their multitudes did no way disconcert him. He rather took pride in numbering them; and, with Comus, seemed pleased to be "stocked with so fair a herd."

With such sources, it was a wonder how he contrived to keep his treasury always empty. He did it by force of an aphorism, which he had often in his mouth, that "money kept longer than three days stinks." So he made use of it while it was fresh. A good part he drank away (for he was an excellent tosspot), some he gave away, the rest he threw away, literally tossing and hurling it violently from him — as boys do burrs, or as if it had been infectious — into ponds, or ditches, or deep holes, inscrutable cavities of the earth; or he would bury it (where he would never seek it again) by a river's side under some bank, which (he would facetiously observe) paid no interest — but out away from him it must go peremptorily, as Hagar's offspring into the wilderness, while it was sweet. He never missed it. The streams were perennial which fed his fisc. When new supplies became necessary, the first person to fall in with him, friend or stranger, was sure to contribute to the deficiency. For Bigod had an undeniable way with him. He had a cheerful, open exterior, a quick jovial eye, a bald forehead, just touched with gray (*cana fides*). He anticipated no excuse, and found none. And, waiving for a while my theory as to the great race, I would put it to the most untheorizing reader, who may at times have disposable coin in his pocket, whether it is not more repugnant to the kindliness of his nature to refuse such a one as I am describing, than to say no to a poor petitionary rogue (your bastard borrower), who, by his mumping visnomy, tells you that he expects nothing better; and, therefore, whose preconceived notions and expectations you do in reality so much less chock in the refusal.

When I think of this man; his fiery glow of heart; his swell of feeling; how magnificent, how ideal he was;

how great at the midnight hour; and when I compare
with him the companions with whom I have associated
since, I grudge the saving of a few idle ducats, and think
that I am fallen into the society of lenders and little men.

To one like Elia, whose treasures are rather cased in
leather covers than closed in iron coffers, there is a class
of alienators more formidable than that which I have
touched upon; I mean your borrowers of books — those
multilators of collections, spoilers of the symmetry of
shelves, and creators of odd volumes. There is Comberbatch, matchless in his depredations.

That foul gap in the bottom shelf facing you, like a great
eyetooth knocked out — (you are now with me in my
little black study in Bloomsbury, Reader) — with the
huge Switzer-like tomes on each side (like the Guildhall
giants, in their reformed posture, guardant of nothing)
once held the tallest of my folios, *Opera Bonaventuræ*,
choice and massy divinity, to its two supporters (school
divinity also, but of a lesser caliber — Bellarmine, and
Holy Thomas), showing but as dwarfs — itself an Ascapart!
— that Comberbatch abstracted upon the faith of a theory
he holds, which is more easy, I confess, for me to suffer by
than to refute, namely, that "the title to property in a
book (my Bonaventure, for instance) is in exact ratio to
the claimant's powers of understanding and appreciating
the same." Should he go on acting upon this theory,
which of our shelves is safe?

The slight vacuum in the left-hand case — two shelves
from the ceiling — scarcely distinguishable but by the
quick eye of a loser — was whilom the commodious resting place of Browne on Urn Burial. C. will hardly allege
that he knows more about that treatise than I do, who
introduced it to him, and was indeed the first (of the moderns) to discover its beauties — but so have I known a fool-

ish lover to praise his mistress in the presence of a rival
more qualified to carry her off than himself.   Just below,
Dodsley's dramas want their fourth volume, where *Vittoria
Corombona* is.   The remainder nine are as distasteful as
Priam's refuse sons, when the Fates borrowed Hector.
Here stood the *Anatomy of Melancholy*, in sober state.
There loitered the *Complete Angler;* quiet as in life, by
some stream side.   In yonder nook, John Buncle, a
widower-volume, with "eyes closed", mourns his ravished
mate.

One justice I must do my friend, that if he sometimes,
like the sea, sweeps away a treasure, at another time,
sea-like, he throws up as rich an equivalent to match it.
I have a small under-collection of this nature (my friend's
gatherings in his various calls), picked up, he has forgotten
at what odd places, and deposited with as little memory at
mine.   I take in these orphans, the twice-deserted.   These
proselytes of the gate are welcome as the true Hebrews.
There they stand in conjunction; natives, and naturalized.
The latter seem as little disposed to inquire out their true
lineage as I am.   I charge no warehouse room for those
deodands, nor shall ever put myself to the ungentlemanly
trouble of advertising a sale of them to pay expenses.

To lose a volume to C. carries some sense and meaning
in it.   You are sure that he will make one hearty meal on
your viands, if he can give no account of the platter after
it.   But what moved thee, wayward, spiteful K. to be so
importunate to carry off with thee, in spite of tears and
adjurations to thee to forbear, the Letters of that princely
woman, the thrice noble Margaret Newcastle? — knowing
at the time, and knowing that I knew also, thou most
assuredly wouldst never turn over one leaf of the illustrious
folio — what but the mere spirit of contradiction, and
childish love of getting the better of thy friend?   Then,

worst cut of all! to transport it with thee to the Gallican
land —

Unworthy land to harbor such a sweetness,
A virtue in which all ennobling thoughts dwelt,
Pure thoughts, kind thoughts, high thoughts, her sex's wonder!

— hadst thou not thy playbooks, and books of jests and
fancies, about thee, to keep these merry, even as thou
keepest all companies with thy guips and mirthful tales?
Child of the Greenroom, it was unkindly done of thee.
They wife, too, that part-French, better-part-English-
woman! — that she could fix upon no other treatise to
bear away, in kindly token of remembering us, than the
works of Fulke Greville, Lord Book — of which no Frenchman, nor woman of France, Italy, or England, was ever
by nature constituted to comprehend a tittle! Was there
not Zimmerman on Solitude?

Reader, if haply you art blessed with a moderate collection, be shy of showing it; or if thy heart overfloweth to
lend them, lend thy books; but let it be to such a one as
S. T. C. He will return them (generally anticipating the
time appointed) with usury; enriched with annotations,
tripling their value. I have had experience. Many are
those precious MSS. of his (in matter oftentimes, and
almost in quantity not unfrequently, vying with the orig-
inals) in no very clerkly hand — legible in my Daniel; in
old Burton; in Sir Thomas Browne; and those abstruser
cogitations of the Greville, now, alas! wandering in pagan
lands. I counsel thee, shut not thy heart, nor thy library
against S. T. C.

Hazlitt and Hunt were friends who lived in Lamb's day; but they belong less to all time. Hazlitt in particular seems never to surrender so completely to the mood of the moment; there is less of bubbling humor and more readiness to adopt a conventional classic form. Exact quotations abound. Hunt is given double representation because of the subjects themselves. The beginner choosing to write upon that question of eternal and daily interest, "Getting Up", will find here and in Lamb material for apt allusion. "The Maid Servant" is a late example of that once popular form, the "character."

ON GOING A JOURNEY (*Incomplete*)

By WILLIAM HAZLITT

ONE of the pleasantest things in the world is going a journey; but I like to go by myself. I can enjoy society in a room; but out of doors, nature is company enough for me. I am then never less alone than when alone.

"The fields his study, nature was his book."

I cannot see the wit of walking and talking at the same time. When I am in the country, I wish to vegetate like the country. I am not for criticising hedge-rows and black cattle. I go out of town in order to forget the town and all that is in it. There are those who for this purpose go to watering-places, and carry the metropolis with them. I like more elbow-room, and fewer incumbrances. I like solitude, when I give myself up to it, for the sake of solitude; nor do I ask for

"—— a friend in my retreat,
Whom I may whisper solitude is sweet."

The soul of a journey is liberty, perfect liberty, to think, feel, do just as one pleases. We go a journey chiefly to be free of all impediments and of all inconveniences; to leave ourselves behind, much more to get rid of others. It is because I want a little breathing-space to muse on indifferent matters, where Contemplation

"May plume her feathers and let grow her wings,
    That in the various bustle of resort
    Were all too ruffled, and sometimes impair'd,"

that I absent myself from the town for awhile, without feeling at a loss the moment I am left by myself. Instead of a friend in a post-chaise or in a Tilbury, to exchange good things with, and vary the same stale topics over again, for once let me have a truce with impertinence. Give me the clear blue sky over my head, and the green turf beneath my feet, a winding road before me, and a three hours' march to dinner — and then to thinking! It is hard if I cannot start some game on these lone heaths. I laugh, I run, I leap, I sing for joy. From the point of yonder rolling cloud, I plunge into my past being, and revel there, as the sun-burnt Indian plunges headlong into the wave that wafts him to his native shore. Then long-forgotten things, like "sunken wrack and sumless treasuries", burst upon my eager sight, and I begin to feel, think, and be myself again. Instead of an awkward silence, broken by attempts at wit or dull common-places, mine is that undisturbed silence of the heart which alone is perfect eloquence. No one likes puns, alliterations, antitheses, argument, and analysis better than I do; but I sometimes had rather be without them. "Leave, oh, leave me to my repose!" I have just now other business in hand, which would seem idle to you, but is with me "very stuff of the conscience." Is not this wild rose sweet

without a comment?   Does not this daisy leap to my heart
set in its coat of emerald?   Yet if I were to explain to you
the circumstance that has so endeared it to me, you would
only smile.   Had I not better then keep it to myself, and
let it serve me to brood over, from here to yonder craggy
point, and from thence onward to the far-distant horizon?
I should be but bad company all that way, and therefore
prefer being alone.   I have heard it said that you may,
when the moody fit comes on, walk or ride on by yourself,
and indulge your reveries.   But this looks like a breach
of manners, a neglect of others, and you are thinking all
the time that you ought to rejoin your party.   "Out upon
such half-faced fellowship," say I.   I like to be either
entirely to myself, or entirely at the disposal of others;
to talk or be silent, to walk or sit still, to be sociable or
solitary.   I was pleased with an observation of Mr. Cob-
bett's, that "he thought it a bad French custom to drink
our wine with our meals, and that an Englishman ought
to do only one thing at a time."   So I cannot talk and
think, or indulge in melancholy musing and lively conversation by fits and starts.   "Let me have a companion
of my way," says Sterne, "were it but to remark how the
shadows lengthen as the sun declines."   It is beautifully
said : but in my opinion, this continual comparing of notes
interferes with the involuntary impression of things upon
the mind, and hurts the sentiment.   If you only hint what
you feel in a kind of dumb show, it is insipid : if you have
to explain it, it is making a toil of a pleasure.   You cannot read the book of nature, without being perpetually
put to the trouble of translating it for the benefit of others.
I am for the synthetical method on a journey, in preference
to the analytical.   I am content to lay in a stock of ideas
then, and to examine and anatomise them afterwards.   I
want to see my vague notions float like the down of the

thistle before the breeze, and not to have them entangled
in the briars and thorns of controversy. For once, I like
to have it all my own way; and this is impossible unless
you are alone, or in such company as I do not covet. I
have no objection to argue a point with any one for twenty
miles of measured road, but not for pleasure. If you
remark the scent of a beanfield crossing the road, perhaps
your fellow-traveller has no smell. If you point to a
distant object, perhaps he is short-sighted, and has to take
out his glass to look at it. There is a feeling in the air,
a tone in the colour of a cloud which hits your fancy, but
the effect of which you are unable to account for. There is
then no sympathy, but an uneasy craving after it, and a
dissatisfaction which pursues you on the way, and in the
end probably produces ill humour. Now I never quarrel
with myself, and take all my own conclusions for granted
till I find it necessary to defend them against objections.
It is not merely that you may not be of accord on the
objects and circumstances that present themselves before
you — these may recall a number of objects, and lead to
associations too delicate and refined to be possibly com-
municated to others. Yet these I love to cherish, and
sometimes still fondly clutch them, when I can escape
from the throng to do so. To give way to our feelings,
before company, seems extravagance or affectation; and
on the other hand, to have to unravel this mystery of our
being at every turn, and to make others take an equal
interest in it (otherwise the end is not answered) is a task
to which few are competent. We must "give it an understanding, but no tongue." My old friend C——, however,
could do both. He could go on in the most delightful
explanatory way over hill and dale, a summer's day, and
convert a landscape into a didactic poem or a Pindaric
ode. "He talked far above singing." If I could so

clothe my ideas in sounding and flowing words, I might perhaps wish to have some one with me to admire the swelling theme; or I could be more content, were it possible for me still to hear his echoing voice in the woods of All-Foxden. They had "that fine madness in them which our first poets had;" and if they could have been caught by some rare instrument, would have breathed such strains as the following.

"—— Here be woods as green
As any, air likewise as fresh and sweet
As when smooth Zephyrus plays on the fleet
Face of the curled stream, with flow'rs as many
As the young spring gives, and as choice as any;
Here be all new delights, cool streams and wells,
Arbours o'ergrown with woodbine, caves and dells;
Choose where thou wilt, while I sit by and sing,
Or gather rushes to make many a ring
For thy long fingers; tell thee tales of love,
How the pale Phœbe, hunting in a grove,
First saw the boy Endymion, from whose eyes
She took eternal fire that never dies;
How she convey'd him softly in a sleep,
His temples bound with poppy, to the steep
Head of old Latmos, where she stoops each night,
Gilding the mountain with her brother's light,
To kiss her sweetest."——
                              FAITHFUL SHEPHERDESS.

Had I words and images at command like these, I would attempt to wake the thoughts that lie slumbering on golden ridges in the evening clouds: but at the sight of nature my fancy, poor as it is, droops and closes up its leaves, like flowers at sunset. I can make nothing out on the spot: — I must have time to collect myself. —

In general, a good thing spoils out-of-door prospects: it should be reserved for Table-talk. L —— is for this reason, I take it, the worst company in the world out of doors; because he is the best within. I grant, there is one subject on which it is pleasant to talk on a journey; and that is, what one shall have for supper when we get to our inn at night. The open air improves this sort of conversation or friendly altercation, by setting a keener edge on appetite. Every mile of the road heightens the flavour of the viands we expect at the end of it. How fine it is to enter some old town, walled and turreted just at the approach of night-fall, or to come to some straggling village, with the lights streaming through the surrounding gloom; and then after inquiring for the best entertainment that the place affords, to "take one's ease at one's inn!" These eventful moments in our lives' history are too precious, too full of solid, heart-felt happiness to be frittered and dribbled away in imperfect sympathy. I would have them all to myself, and drain them to the last drop: they will do to talk of or to write about afterwards. What a delicate speculation it is, after drinking whole goblets of tea,

"The cups that cheer, but not inebriate,"

and letting the fumes ascend into the brain, to sit considering what we shall have for supper — eggs and a rasher, a rabbit smothered in onions, or an excellent veal-cutlet! Sancho in such a situation once fixed upon cow-heel; and his choice, though he could not help it, is not to be disparaged. Then in the intervals of pictured scenery and Shandean contemplation, to catch the preparation and the stir in the kitchen — *Procul, O procul este profani!* These hours are sacred to silence and to musing, to be treasured up in the memory, and to feed the source of smiling thoughts hereafter. I would not waste them in idle talk; or if I must have the integrity of fancy broken in upon,

I would rather it were by a stranger than a friend.   A
stranger takes his hue and character from the time and
place; he is a part of the furniture and costume of an
inn.   If he is a Quaker, or from the West Riding of
Yorkshire, so much the better.   I do not even try to
sympathise with him, and he breaks no squares.   I associate nothing with my travelling companion but present
objects and passing events.   In his ignorance of me and
my affairs, I in a manner forget myself.   But a friend
reminds one of other things, rips up old grievances, and
destroys the abstraction of the scene.   He comes in un-
graciously between us and our imaginary character.
Something is dropped in the course of conversation that
gives a hint of your profession and pursuits; or from
having some one with you that knows the less sublime
portions of your history, it seems that other people do.
You are no longer a citizen of the world: but your "un-
housed free condition is put into circumscription and
confine."   The *incognito* of an inn is one of its striking
privileges — "lord of one's-self, uncumber'd with a
name." . . .
As another exception to the above reasoning, I should
not feel confident in venturing on a journey in a foreign
country without a companion.   I should want at intervals
to hear the sound of my own language.   There is an involuntary antipathy in the mind of an Englishman to
foreign manners and notions that requires the assistance
of social sympathy to carry it off.   As the distance from
home increases, this relief, which was at first a luxury,
becomes a passion and an appetite.   A person would
almost feel stifled to find himself in the deserts of Arabia
without friends and countrymen: there must be allowed
to be something in the view of Athens or old Rome that
claims the utterance of speech; and I own that the Pyra-

mids are too mighty for any simple contemplation. In
such situations, so opposite to all one's ordinary train of
ideas, one seems a species by one's-self, a limb torn off
from society, unless one can meet with instant fellowship
and support. — Yet I did not feel this want or craving
very pressing once, when I first set my foot on the laughing
shores of France. Calais was peopled with novelty and
delight. The confused, busy murmur of the place was like
oil and wine poured into my ears; nor did the mariners'
hymn, which was sung from the top of an old crazy vessel
in the harbour, as the sun went down, send an alien sound
into my soul. I only breathed the air of general humanity.
I walked over "the vine-covered hills and gay regions of
France", erect and satisfied; for the image of man was not
cast down and chained to the foot of arbitrary thrones:
I was at no loss for language, for that of all the great schools
of painting was open to me. The whole is vanished like
a shade. Pictures, heroes, glory, freedom, all are fled:
nothing remains but the Bourbons and the French people!
— There is undoubtedly a sensation in travelling into
foreign parts that is to be had nowhere else: but it is more
pleasing at the time than lasting. It is too remote from
our habitual associations to be a common topic of discourse
or reference, and, like a dream or another state of existence, does not piece into our daily modes of life. It is an
animated but a momentary hallucination. It demands an
effort to exchange our actual for our ideal identity; and
to feel the pulse of our old transports revive very keenly,
we must "jump" all our present comforts and connexions.
Our romantic and itinerant character is not to be domesti-
cated. Dr. Johnson remarked how little foreign travel
added to the facilities of conversation in those who had
been abroad. In fact, the time we have spent there is
both delightful and in one sense instructive; but it appears

to be cut out of our substantial, downright existence, and never to join kindly on to it.   We are not the same, but another, and perhaps more enviable individual, all the time we are out of our own country.   We are lost to ourselves, as well as our friends.   So the poet somewhat quaintly sings,

"Out of my country and myself I go."

Those who wish to forget painful thoughts, do well to absent themselves for a while from the ties and objects that recall them : but we can be said only to fulfill our destiny in the place that gave us birth.   I should on this account like well enough to spend the whole of my life in travelling abroad, if I could any where borrow another life to spend afterwards at home !

GETTING UP ON COLD MORNINGS

By LEIGH HUNT

AN Italian author — Giulio Cordara, a Jesuit — has written a poem upon insects, which he begins by insisting that those troublesome and abominable little animals were created for our annoyance, and that they were certainly not inhabitants of Paradise.   We of the north may dispute this piece of theology ; but on the other hand, it is clear as the snow on the house-tops, that Adam was not under the necessity of shaving ; and that when Eve walked out of her delicious bower, she did not step upon ice three inches thick.

Some people say it is a very easy thing to get up of a cold morning.   You have only, they tell you, to take this resolution ; and the thing is done.   This may be very true ; just as a boy at school has only to take a flogging, and the thing is over.   But we have not at all made up

our minds upon it ; and we find it a very pleasant exercise
to discuss the matter, candidly, before we get up. This
at least is not idling, though it may be lying. It affords
an excellent answer to those, who ask how lying in bed
can be indulged in by a reasoning being, — a rational
creature. How ? Why with the argument calmly at work
in one's head, and the clothes over one's shoulder. Oh —
it is a fine way of spending a sensible, impartial half-hour.

If these people would be more charitable, they would
get on with their argument better. But they are apt to
reason so ill, and to assert so dogmatically, that one could
wish to have them stand round one's bed of a bitter
morning, and lie before their faces. They ought to hear
both sides of the bed, the inside and out. If they cannot
entertain themselves with their own thoughts for half an
hour or so, it is not the fault of those who can. If their
will is never pulled aside by the enticing arms of imagination, so much the luckier for the stage-coachman.

Candid inquiries into one's decumbency, besides the
greater or less privileges to be allowed a man in proportion to his ability of keeping early hours, the work given
his faculties, etc., will at least concede their due merits to
such representations as the following. In the first place,
says the injured but calm appealer, I have been warm all
night, and find my system in a state perfectly suitable to
a warm-blooded animal. To get out of this state into the
cold, besides the inharmonious and uncritical abruptness
of the transition, is so unnatural to such a creature, that
the poets, refining upon the tortures of the damned, make
one of their greatest agonies consist in being suddenly
transported from heat to cold, — from fire to ice. They
are "haled" out of their "beds," says Milton, by "harpy-
footed furies," — fellows who come to call them. On my
first movement towards the anticipation of getting up, I

find that such parts of the sheets and bolster, as are exposed to the air of the room, are stone-cold.   On opening my eyes, the first thing that meets them is my own breath rolling forth, as if in the open air, like smoke out of a cottage chimney.   Think of this symptom.   Then I turn my eyes sideways and see the window all frozen over. Think of that.   Then the servant comes in.   "It is very cold this morning, is it not?" — "Very cold, Sir." — "Very cold indeed, isn't it?" — "Very cold indeed, Sir." — "More than usually so, isn't it, even for this weather?" (Here the servant's wit and good-nature are put to a considerable test, and the inquirer lies on thorns for the answer.)   "Why,   Sir . . . I   think   it   *is*."   (Good creature!   There is not a better, or more truth-telling servant going.)   "I must rise, however — get me some warm water." — Here comes a fine interval between the departure of the servant and the arrival of the hot water; during which, of course, it is of "no use" to get up.   The hot water comes.   "Is it quite hot?" — "Yes, Sir." — "Perhaps too hot for shaving: I must wait a little?" — "No, Sir; it will just do."   (There is an over-nice propriety sometimes, an officious zeal of virtue, a little troublesome.)   "Oh — the shirt — you must air my clean shirt; — linen gets very damp this weather." — "Yes, Sir." Here another delicious five minutes.   A knock at the door. "Oh, the shirt — very well.   My stockings — I think the stockings had better be aired too." — "Very well, Sir." — Here another interval.   At length everything is ready, except myself.   I now, continues our incumbent (a happy word, by the bye, for a country vicar) — I now cannot help thinking a good deal — who can? — upon the unnecessary and villainous custom of shaving: it is a thing so unmanly (here I nestle closer) — so effeminate (here I recoil from an unlucky step into the colder part of the bed.)

— No wonder that the Queen of France took part with the rebels against the degenerate King, her husband, who first affronted her smooth visage with a face like her own. The Emperor Julian never showed the luxuriancy of his genius to better advantage than in reviving the flowing beard. Look at Cardinal Bembo's picture — at Michael Angelo's — at Titian's — at Shakespeare's — at Fletcher's — at Spenser's — at Chaucer's — at Alfred's — at Plato's — I could name a great man for every tick of my watch. — Look at the Turks, a grave and otiose people. — Think of Haroun Al Raschid and Bed-ridden Hassan. — Think of Wortley Montagu, the worthy son of his mother, a man above the prejudice of his time. — Look at the Persian gentlemen, whom one is ashamed of meeting about the suburbs, their dress and appearance are so much finer than our own. — Lastly, think of the razor itself — how totally opposed to every sensation of bed — how cold, how edgy, how hard! how utterly different from anything like the warm and circling amplitude, which

> Sweetly recommends itself
> Unto our gentle senses.

Add to this, benumbed fingers, which may help you to cut yourself, a quivering body, a frozen towel, and a ewer full of ice; and he that says there is nothing to oppose in all this, only shows, at any rate, that he has no merit in opposing it.

Thomson the poet, who exclaims in his Seasons —

> Falsely luxurious! Will not man awake?

used to lie in bed till noon, because he said he had no motive in getting up. He could imagine the good of rising; but then he would also imagine the good of lying still; and his exclamation, it must be allowed, was made upon summer-time, not winter. We must proportion the argument to the individual character. A money-getter may be drawn out of his bed by three and four pence; but this will not suffice for a student. A proud man may say, "What shall I think of myself, if I don't get up?" but the more humble one will be content to waive this prodigious notion of himself, out of respect to his kindly bed. The mechanical man shall get up without any ado at all; and so shall the barometer. An ingenious lier in bed will find hard matter of discussion even on the score of health and longevity. He will ask us for our proofs and precedents of the ill effects of lying later in cold weather; and sophisticate much on the advantages of an even temperature of body; of the natural propensity (pretty universal) to have one's way; and of the animals that roll themselves up, and sleep all the winter. As to longevity, he will ask whether the longest life is of necessity the best; and whether Holborn is the handsomest street in London.

We only know of one confounding, not to say confounded argument, fit to overturn the huge luxury, the "enormous bliss"—of the vice in question. A lier in bed may be allowed to profess a disinterested indifference for his health or longevity; but while he is showing the reasonableness of consulting his own or one person's comfort, he must admit the proportionate claim of more than one; and the best way to deal with him is this, especially for a lady; for we earnestly recommend the use of that sex on such occasions, if not somewhat *over*-persuasive; since extremes have an awkward knack of meeting. First then, admit all the ingeniousness of what he says, telling him that the bar has been deprived of an excellent lawyer. Then look at him in the most good-natured manner in the world, with a mixture of assent and appeal in your countenance, and tell him that you are

waiting breakfast for him; that you never like to breakfast without him; that you really want it too; that the
servants want theirs; that you shall not know how to get
the house into order, unless he rises; and that you are
sure he would do things twenty times worse, even than
getting out of his warm bed, to put them all into good
humour and a state of comfort.   Then, after having said
this, throw in the comparatively indifferent matter, to
him, about his health; but tell him that it is no indifferent
matter to you; that the sight of his illness makes more
people suffer than one; but that if, nevertheless, he really
does feel so very sleepy and so very much refreshed by ——
Yet stay; we hardly know whether the frailty of a ——
Yes, yes; say that too, especially if you say it with sincerity; for if the weakness of human nature on the one
hand and the *vis inertiœ* on the other, should lead him
to take advantage of it once or twice, good-humour and
sincerity form an irresistible junction at last; and are
still better and warmer things than pillows and blankets.

Other little helps of appeal may be thrown in, as occasion
requires.   You may tell a lover, for instance, that lying in
bed makes people corpulent; a father, that you wish him
to complete the fine manly example he sets his children;
a lady, that she will injure her bloom or her shape, which
M. or W. admires so much; and a student or artist, that he
is always so glad to have done a good day's work, in his
best manner.

Reader.   And pray, Mr. Indicator, how do *you* behave
yourself in this respect?

Indic.   Oh, Madam, perfectly, of course; like all
advisers.

Reader.   Nay, I allow that your mode of argument does
not look quite so suspicious as the old way of sermonising
and severity, but I have my doubts, especially from that

laugh of yours.   If I should look in to-morrow morning —
    Indic.   Ah, Madam, the look in of a face like yours does
anything with me.   It shall fetch me up at nine, if you
please — *six*, I meant to say.

THE MAID–SERVANT

BY LEIGH HUNT

MUST be considered as young, or else she has married
the butcher, the butler, or *her cousin*, or has otherwise
settled into a character distinct from her original one, so
as to become what is properly called the domestic.   The
Maid-servant, in her apparel, is either slovenly and fine
by turns, and dirty always; or she is at all times snug
and neat, and dressed according to her station.   In the
latter case, her ordinary dress is black stockings, a stuff
gown, a cap, and a neck-handkerchief pinned cornerwise
behind.   If you want a pin, she just feels about her, and
has always one to give you.   On Sundays and holidays,
and perhaps of afternoons, she changes her black stockings
for white, puts on a gown of better texture and fine pattern,
sets her cap and her curls jauntily, and lays aside the neck-
handkerchief for a high-body, which, by the way, is not
half so pretty.   There is something very warm and latent
in the handkerchief — something easy, vital, and genial.
A woman in a high-bodied gown, made to fit her like a case,
is by no means more modest, and is much less tempting.
She looks like a figure at the head of a ship.   We could
almost see her chucked out of doors into a cart, with as
little remorse as a couple of sugar-loaves.   The tucker is
much better, as well as the handkerchief, and is to the
other what the young lady is to the servant.   The one
always reminds us of the Sparkler in Sir Richard Steele;
the other of Fanny in "Joseph Andrews."

But to return. The general furniture of her ordinary room, the kitchen, is not so much her own as her Master's and Mistress's, and need not be described: but in a drawer of the dresser or the table, in company with a duster and a pair of snuffers, may be found some of her property, such as a brass thimble, a pair of scissors, a thread-case, a piece of wax much wrinkled with the thread, an odd volume of "Pamela", and perhaps a sixpenny play, such as "George Barnwell", or Mrs. Behn's "Oroonoko." There is a piece of looking-glass in the window. The rest of her furniture is in the garret, where you may find a good looking-glass on the table, and in the window a Bible, a comb, and a piece of soap. Here stands also, under stout lock and key, the mighty mystery, — the box, — containing, among other things, her clothes, two or three song-books, consisting of nineteen for the penny; sundry Tragedies at a halfpenny the sheet; the "Whole Nature of Dreams Laid Open", together with the "Fortune-teller" and the "Account of the Ghost of Mrs. Veal; " the "Story of the Beautiful Zoa" "who was cast away on a desert island, showing how", etc.; some half-crowns in a purse, including pieces of country-money, with the good Countess of Coventry on one of them, riding naked on the horse; a silver penny wrapped up in cotton by itself; a crooked sixpence, given her before she came to town, and the giver of which has either forgotten or been forgotten by her, she is not sure which; — two little enamel boxes, with looking-glass in the lids, one of them a fairing, the other "a Trifle from Margate"; and lastly, various letters, square and ragged, and directed in all sorts of spellings, chiefly with little letters for capitals. One of them, written by a girl who went to a day-school, is directed "Miss."

In her manners, the Maid-servant sometimes imitates her young mistress; she puts her hair in papers, cultivates a shape, and occasionally contrives to be out of spirits. But her own character and condition overcome all sophistications of this sort : her shape, fortified by the mop and scrubbing-brush, will make its way ; and exercise keeps her healthy and cheerful. From the same cause her temper is good ; though she gets into little heats when a stranger is over-saucy, or when she is told not to go so heavily down stairs, or when some unthinking person goes up her wet stairs with dirty shoes, — or when she is called away often from dinner ; neither does she much like to be seen scrubbing the street-door steps of a morning ; and sometimes she catches herself saying, "Drat that butcher," but immediately adds, "God forgive me." The tradesmen indeed, with their compliments and arch looks, seldom give her cause to complain. The milkman bespeaks her good-humour for the day with "Come, pretty maids :" — then follow the butcher, the baker, the oilman, etc., all with their several smirks and little loiterings ; and when she goes to the shops herself, it is for her the grocer pulls down his string from its roller with more than the ordinary whirl, and tosses his parcel into a tie.

Thus pass the mornings between working, and singing, and giggling, and grumbling, and being flattered. If she takes any pleasure unconnected with her office before the afternoon, it is when she runs up the area-steps or to the door to hear and purchase a new song, or to see a troop of soldiers go by ; or when she happens to thrust her head out of a chamber window at the same time with a servant at the next house, when a dialogue infallibly ensues, stimulated by the imaginary obstacles between. If the Maid-servant is wise, the best part of her work is done by dinner-time ; and nothing else is necessary to give perfect zest to the meal. She tells us what she thinks of it, when she calls it "a bit o' dinner." There is the same sort of eloquence in her other phrase, "a cup o' tea;" but the old ones, and the washerwomen, beat her at that. After tea in great houses, she goes with the other servants to hot cockles, or What-are-my-thoughts-like, and tells Mr. John to "have done then"; or if there is a ball given that night, they throw open the doors, and make use of the music up stairs to dance by. In smaller houses, she receives the visits of her aforesaid cousin; and sits down alone, or with a fellow maid-servant, to work; talks of her young master or mistress and Mr. Ivins (Evans); or else she calls to mind her own friends in the country; where she thinks the cows and "all that" beautiful, now she is away. Meanwhile, if she is lazy, she snuffs the candle with her scissors; or if she has eaten more heartily than usual, she sighs double the usual number of times, and thinks that tender hearts were born to be unhappy.

Such being the Maid-servant's life in-doors, she scorns, when abroad, to be anything but a creature of sheer enjoyment. The Maid-servant, the sailor, and the school-boy, are the three beings that enjoy a holiday beyond all the rest of the world; — and all for the same reason, — because their inexperience, peculiarity of life, and habit of being with persons of circumstances or thoughts above them, give them all, in their way, a cast of the romantic. The most active of the money-getters is a vegetable compared with them. The Maid-servant when she first goes to Vauxhall, thinks she is in heaven. A theatre is all pleasure to her, whatever is going forward, whether the play or the music, or the waiting which makes others impatient, or the munching of apples and gingerbread, which she and her party commence almost as soon as they have seated themselves. She prefers tragedy to comedy, because it is grander, and less like what she meets with in general; and because she thinks it more in earnest also, especially in the love-scenes. Her favourite play is "Alexander the Great, or the Rival Queens." Another great delight is in going a shopping. She loves to look at the pictures in the windows, and the fine things labelled with those corpulent numerals of "only 7s." — "only 6s. 6d." She has also, unless born and bred in London, been to see my Lord Mayor, the fine people coming out of Court, and the "beasties" in the Tower; and at all events she has been to Astley's and the Circus, from which she comes away, equally smitten with the rider, and sore with laughing at the clown. But it is difficult to say what pleasure she enjoys most. One of the completest of all is the fair, where she walks through an endless round of noise, and toys, and gallant apprentices, and wonders. Here she is invited in by courteous and well-dressed people, as if she were a mistress. Here also is the conjuror's booth, where the operator himself, a most stately and genteel person all in white, calls her Ma'am; and says to John by her side, in spite of his laced hat, "Be good enough, sir, to hand the card to the lady."

Ah! may her "cousin" turn out as true as he says he is; or may she get home soon enough and smiling enough to be as happy again next time.

Washington Irving serves better than any other as link between the essayists of the old world and the new.   These short essays in his Sketch Book *are frankly in imitation of Addison though his own personality is so distinct.   Following still further the leadership of Addison and Steele, Irving, too, edited a literary periodical.*

THE ART OF BOOK-MAKING

BY WASHINGTON IRVING

I HAVE often wondered at the extreme fecundity of the press, and how it comes to pass that so many heads, on which Nature seems to have inflicted the curse of barrenness, yet teem with voluminous productions.   As a man travels on, however, in the journey of life, his objects of wonder daily diminish, and he is continually finding out some very simple cause for some great matter of marvel. Thus have I chanced, in my peregrinations about this great metropolis, to blunder upon a scene which unfolded to me some of the mysteries of the book-making craft, and at once put an end to my astonishment.

I was one summer's day loitering through the great saloons of the British Museum, with that listlessness with which one is apt to saunter about a room in warm weather ; sometimes lolling over the glass cases of minerals, sometimes studying the hieroglyphics on an Egyptian mummy, and sometimes trying, with nearly equal success, to comprehend the allegorical paintings on the lofty ceilings. While I was gazing about in this idle way, my attention was attracted to a distant door, at the end of a suite of apartments. It was closed, but every now and then it would open, and some strange-favored being, generally clothed in black, would steal forth, and glide through the rooms, without noticing any of the surrounding objects. There was an air of mystery about this that piqued my languid curiosity, and I determined to attempt the passage of that strait, and to explore the unknown regions that lay beyond. The door yielded to my hand, with all that facility with which the portals of enchanted castles yield to the adventurous knight-errant. I found myself in a spacious chamber, surrounded with great cases of venerable books. Above the cases, and just under the cornice, were arranged a great number of black-looking portraits of ancient authors. About the room were placed long tables, with stands for reading and writing, at which sat many pale, cadaverous personages, poring intently over dusty volumes, rummaging among mouldy manuscripts, and taking copious notes of their contents. The most hushed stillness reigned through this mysterious apartment, excepting that you might hear the racing of pens over sheets of paper, or, occasionally, the deep sigh of one of these sages, as he shifted his position to turn over the page of an old folio, — doubtless arising from that hollowness and flatulency incident to learned research.

Now and then some of these personages would write something on a small slip of paper, and ring a bell, whereupon a familiar would appear, take the paper in profound silence, glide out of the room, and return shortly, loaded with ponderous tomes, upon which the other would fall, tooth and nail, with famished voracity. I had no longer a doubt that I had happened upon a body of magi, deeply engaged in the study of occult sciences. The scene reminded me of an old Arabian tale, of a philosopher who was shut up in an enchanted library, in the bosom of a mountain, that opened only once a year; where he made the spirits of the place obey his commands, and bring him books of all kinds of dark knowledge, so that at the end of a year, when the magic portal once more swung open on its hinges, he issued forth so versed in forbidden lore as to be able to soar above the heads of the multitude, and to control the powers of nature.

My curiosity being now fully aroused, I whispered to one of the familiars, as he was about to leave the room, and begged an interpretation of the strange scene before me. A few words were sufficient for the purpose: I found that these mysterious personages, whom I had mistaken for magi, were principally authors, and were in the very act of manufacturing books. I was, in fact, in the reading-room of the great British Library, an immense collection of volumes of all ages and languages, many of which are now forgotten, and most of which are seldom read. To these sequestered pools of obsolete literature, therefore, do many modern authors repair, and draw buckets full of classic lore, or "pure English, undefiled," wherewith to swell their own scanty rills of thought.

Being now in possession of the secret, I sat down in a corner, and watched the process of this book manufactory. I noticed one lean, bilious-looking wight, who sought none but the most worm-eaten volumes, printed in black-letter. He was evidently constructing some work of profound erudition, that would be purchased by every man who wished to be thought learned, placed upon a conspicuous shelf of his library, or laid open upon his table — but never read. I observed him, now and then, draw a large fragment of biscuit out of his pocket, and gnaw; whether it was his dinner, or whether he was endeavoring to keep off that exhaustion of the stomach produced by much pondering over dry works, I leave harder students than myself to determine.

There was one dapper little gentleman in bright-colored clothes, with a chirping, gossiping expression of countenance, who had all the appearance of an author on good terms with his bookseller. After considering him attentively, I recognized in him a diligent getter-up of miscellaneous works, which bustled off well with the trade. I was curious to see how he manufactured his wares. He made more show and stir of business than any of the others; dipping into various books, fluttering over the leaves of manuscripts, taking a morsel out of one, a morsel out of another, "line upon line, precept upon precept, here a little and there a little." The contents of his book seemed to be as heterogeneous as those of the witches' cauldron in *Macbeth*. It was here a finger and there a thumb, toe of frog and blind-worm's sting, with his own gossip poured in like "baboon's blood", to make the medley "slab and good."

After all, thought I, may not this pilfering disposition be implanted in authors for wise purposes? May it not be the way in which Providence has taken care that the seeds of knowledge and wisdom shall be preserved from age to age, in spite of the inevitable decay of the works in which they were first produced? We see that Nature has wisely, though whimsically, provided for the conveyance of seeds from clime to clime, in the maws of certain birds; so that animals which in themselves are little better than carrion, and apparently the lawless plunderers of the orchard and the corn-field, are in fact Nature's carriers to disperse and perpetuate her blessings. In like manner, the beauties and fine thoughts of ancient and obsolete writers are caught up by these flights of predatory authors, and cast forth, again to flourish and bear fruit in a remote and

distant tract of time.   Many of their works, also, undergo
a kind of metempsychosis, and spring up under new forms.
What was formerly a ponderous history revives in the
shape of a romance, — an old legend changes into a modern
play, — and a sober philosophical treatise furnishes the
body for a whole series of bouncing and sparkling essays.
Thus it is in the clearing of our American woodlands;
where we burn down a forest of stately pines, a progeny of
dwarf oaks start up in their place; and we never see the
prostrate trunk of a tree, mouldering into soil, but it gives
birth to a whole tribe of fungi.

Let us not, then, lament over the decay and oblivion into
which ancient writers descend; they do but submit to the
great law of nature, which declares that all sublunary
shapes of matter shall be limited in their duration, but
which decrees also that their elements shall never perish.
Generation after generation, both in animal and vegetable
life, passes away, but the vital principle is transmitted to
posterity, and the species continue to flourish.   Thus also
do authors beget authors, and, having produced a numerous progeny, in a good old age they sleep with their fathers,
— that is to say, with the authors who preceded them, and
from whom they had stolen.

Whilst I was indulging in these rambling fancies I had
leaned my head against a pile of reverend folios.   Whether
it was owing to the soporific emanations from these works,
or to the profound quiet of the room, or to the lassitude
arising from much wandering, or to an unlucky habit of
napping at improper times and places with which I am
grievously afflicted, so it was that I fell into a doze.   Still,
however, my imagination continued busy, and indeed the
same scene remained before my mind's eye, only a little
changed in some of the details.   I dreamt that the chamber
was still decorated with the portraits of ancient authors,

but the number was increased. The long tables had disappeared, and in place of the sage magi I beheld a ragged, threadbare throng, such as may be seen plying about the great repository of cast-off clothes, Monmouth Street. Whenever they seized upon a book, by one of those incongruities common to dreams, methought it turned into a garment of foreign or antique fashion, with which they proceeded to equip themselves. I noticed, however, that no one pretended to clothe himself from any particular suit, but took a sleeve from one, a cape from another, a skirt from a third, thus decking himself out piece-meal, while some of his original rags would peep out from among his borrowed finery.

There was a portly, rosy, well-fed parson, whom I observed ogling several mouldy polemical writers through an eye-glass. He soon contrived to slip on the voluminous mantle of one of the old fathers, and, having purloined the gray beard of another, endeavored to look exceedingly wise; but the smirking commonplace of his countenance set at naught all the trappings of wisdom. One sickly looking gentleman was busied embroidering a very flimsy garment with gold thread drawn out of several old court dresses of the reign of Queen Elizabeth. Another had trimmed himself magnificently from an illuminated manuscript, had stuck a nosegay in his bosom, culled from "The Paradise of Dainty Devices," and, having put Sir Philip Sidney's hat on one side of his head, strutted off with an exquisite air of vulgar elegance. A third, who was but of puny dimensions, had bolstered himself out bravely with the spoils from several obscure tracts of philosophy, so that he had a very imposing front; but he was lamentably tattered in rear, and I perceived that he had patched his small-clothes with scraps of parchment from a Latin author.

There were some well-dressed gentlemen, it is true, who only helped themselves to a gem or so, which sparkled among their own ornaments without eclipsing them. Some, too, seemed to contemplate the costumes of the old writers, merely to imbibe their principles of taste, and to catch their air and spirit; but I grieve to say that too many were apt to array themselves, from top to toe, in the patchwork manner I have mentioned. I should not omit to speak of one genius, in drab breeches and gaiters, and an Arcadian hat, who had a violent propensity to the pastoral, but whose rural wanderings had been confined to the classic haunts of Primrose Hill and the solitudes of the Regent's Park. He had decked himself in wreaths and ribbons from all the old pastoral poets, and, hanging his head on one side, went about with a fantastical, lackadaisical air, "babbling about green fields." But the personage that most struck my attention was a pragmatical old gentleman, in clerical robes, with a remarkably large and square but bald head. He entered the room wheezing and puffing, elbowed his way through the throng with a look of sturdy self-confidence, and, having laid hands upon a thick Greek quarto, clapped it upon his head, and swept majestically away in a formidable frizzled wig.

In the height of this literary masquerade, a cry suddenly resounded from every side, of "Thieves! thieves!" I looked, and lo! the portraits about the walls became animated! The old authors thrust out first a head, then a shoulder, from the canvas, looked down curiously, for an instant, upon the motley throng, and then descended, with fury in their eyes, to claim their rifled property. The scene of scampering and hubbub that ensued baffles all description. The unhappy culprits endeavored in vain to escape with their plunder. On one side might be seen half a dozen old monks, stripping a modern professor; on another, there was sad devastation carried into the ranks of modern dramatic writers. Beaumont and Fletcher, side by side, raged round the field like Castor and Pollux, and sturdy Ben Jonson enacted more wonders than when a volunteer with the army in Flanders. As to the dapper little compiler of farragos, mentioned some time since, he had arrayed himself in as many patches and colors as Harlequin, and there was as fierce a contention of claimants about him as about the dead body of Patroclus. I was grieved to see many men, to whom I had been accustomed to look up with awe and reverence, fain to steal off with scarce a rag to cover their nakedness. Just then my eye was caught by the pragmatical old gentleman in the Greek grizzled wig who was scrambling away in sore affright with half a score of authors in full cry after him. They were close upon his haunches; in a twinkling off went his wig; at every turn some strip of raiment was peeled away; until in a few moments, from his domineering pomp he shrunk into a little pursy, "chopp'd bald shot", and made his exit with only a few tags and rags fluttering at his back.

There was something so ludicrous in the catastrophe of this learned Theban, that I burst into an immoderate fit of laughter, which broke the whole illusion. The tumult and the scuffle were at an end. The chamber resumed its usual appearance. The old authors shrunk back into their picture-frames, and hung in shadowy solemnity along the walls. In short, I found myself wide awake in my corner, with the whole assemblage of bookworms gazing at me with astonishment. Nothing of the dream had been real but my burst of laughter, a sound never before heard in that grave sanctuary, and so abhorrent to the ears of wisdom as to electrify the fraternity. The librarian now stepped up to me, and demanded whether I had a card of admission. At first I did not comprehend him, but I soon found that the library was a kind of literary "preserve," subject to game laws, and that no one must presume to hunt there without special license and permission. In a word, I stood convicted of being an arrant poacher, and was glad to make a precipitate retreat, lest I should have a whole pack of authors let loose upon me.

Thackeray and Dickens are names often mentioned together because of their place as English novelists. As essayists there is the wide contrast one would expect to find, because of differing temperaments and interests. Though little of each is here inserted, it is enough to illustrate diction and other marked characteristics.

TUNBRIDGE TOYS

By William Makepeace Thackeray

I wonder whether those little silver pencil-cases with a movable almanac at the butt-end are still favourite implements with boys, and whether pedlars still hawk them about the country? Are there pedlars and hawkers still, or are rustics and children grown too sharp to deal with them? Those pencil-cases, as far as my memory serves me, were not of much use. The screw, upon which the movable almanac turned, was constantly getting loose. The 1 of the table would work from its moorings, under Tuesday or Wednesday, as the case might be, and you would find, on examination, that Th. or W. was the $23\frac{1}{2}$ of the month (which was absurd on the face of the thing), and in a word your cherished pencil-case an utterly unreliable time-keeper. Nor was this a matter of wonder. Consider the position of a pencil-case in a boy's pocket. You had hardbake in it; marbles, kept in your purse when the money was all gone; your mother's purse knitted so fondly and supplied with a little bit of gold, long since — prodigal little son! — scattered amongst the swine — I mean amongst brandy-balls, open tarts, three-cornered puffs, and similar abominations. You had a top and string; a knife; a piece of cobbler's wax; two or three bullets; a "Little Warbler"; and I, for my part, remember, for a considerable period, a brass-barrelled pocket-pistol (which would fire beautifully, for with it I shot off a button from Butt Major's jacket); — with all these things, and ever so many more, clinking and rattling in your pockets, and your hands, of course, keeping them in perpetual movement, how could you expect your movable almanac not to be twisted out of its place now and again — your pencil-case to be bent — your liquorice water not to leak out of your bottle over the cobbler's wax, your bull's eye not to ram up the lock and barrel of your pistol, and so forth?

In the month of June, thirty-seven years ago, I bought one of those pencil-cases from a boy whom I shall call Hawker, and who was in my form. Is he dead? Is he a millionaire? Is he a bankrupt now? He was an immense screw at school, and I believe to this day that the value of the thing for which I owed and eventually paid three-and-sixpence, was in reality not one-and-nine.

I certainly enjoyed the case at first a good deal, and amused myself with twiddling round the movable calendar. But this pleasure wore off. The jewel, as I said, was not paid for, and Hawker, a large and violent boy, was exceedingly unpleasant as a creditor. His constant remark was, "When are you going to pay me that three-and-sixpence? What sneaks your relations must be! They come to see you. You go out to them on Saturdays and Sundays, and they never give you anything! Don't tell *me*, you little humbug!" and so forth. The truth is that my relations were respectable; but my parents were making a tour in Scotland; and my friends in London, whom I used to go and see, were most kind to me, certainly, but somehow never tipped me. That term, of May to August 1823, passed in agonies, then, in consequence of my debt to Hawker. What was the pleasure of a calendar pencil-case in comparison with the doubt and torture of mind occasioned by the sense of the debt, and the constant reproach in that fellow's scowling eyes and gloomy coarse reminders? How was I to pay off such a debt out of sixpence a week? ludicrous! Why did not some one come to see me, and tip me? Ah! my dear sir, if you have any little friends at school, go and see them, and do the natural thing by them. You won't miss the sovereign. You don't know what a blessing it will be to them. Don't fancy they are too old — try 'em. And they will remember you, and bless you in future days; and their gratitude shall accompany your dreary after life; and they shall meet you kindly when thanks for kindness are scant. Oh mercy! shall I ever forget that sovereign you gave me, Captain Bob? or the agonies of being in debt to Hawker? In that very term, a relation of mine was going to India. I actually was fetched from school in order to take leave of him. I am afraid I told Hawker of this circumstance. I own I speculated upon my friend's giving me a pound. A pound. Pooh! A relation going to India, and deeply affected at parting from his darling kinsman, might give five pounds to the dear fellow! . . . There was Hawker when I came back — of course there he was. As he looked in my scared face, he turned livid with rage. He muttered curses, terrible from the lips of so young a boy. My relation, about to cross the ocean to fill a lucrative appointment, asked me with much interest about my progress at school, heard me construe a passage of Eutroplus, the pleasing Latin work on which I was then engaged; gave me a God bless you, and sent me back to school;

upon my word of honour, without so much as a half-crown!
It is all very well, my dear sir, to say that boys contract
habits of expecting tips from their parents' friends, that
they become avaricious, and so forth. Avaricious!
fudge! Boys contract habits of tart and toffee eating,
which they do not carry into after life. On the contrary,
I wish I *did* like 'em. What raptures of pleasure one
could have now for five shillings, if one could but pick it off
the pastry-cook's tray! No. If you have any little
friends at school, out with your half-crowns, my friends,
and impart to those little ones the little fleeting joys of
their age.

Well, then. At the beginning of August 1823, Bartlemytide holidays came, and I was to go to my parents, who
were at Tunbridge Wells. My place in the coach was
taken by my tutor's servants — "Bolt-in-Tun", Fleet
Street, seven o'clock in the morning was the word. My
tutor, the Reverend Edward P——, to whom I hereby
present my best compliments, had a parting interview
with me: gave me my little account for my governor:
the remaining part of the coach-hire; five shillings for my
own expenses; and some five-and-twenty shillings on an
old account which had been over-paid, and was to be
restored to my family.

Away I ran and paid Hawker his three-and-six. Ouf!
what a weight it was off my mind! (He was a Norfolk
boy, and used to go home from Mrs. Nelson's "Bell Inn,"
Aldgate — but that is not to the point.) The next morning, of course, we were an hour before the time. I and
another boy shared a hackney-coach, two-and-six; porter
for putting luggage on coach, threepence. I had no more
money of my own left. Rasherwell, my companion, went
into the "Bolt-in-Tun" coffee-room, and had a good
breakfast. I could n't: because, though I had five-and-

twenty shillings of my parents' money, I had none of my own, you see.

I certainly intended to go without breakfast, and still remember how strongly I had that resolution in my mind. But there was that hour to wait. A beautiful August morning — I am very hungry. There is Rasherwell "tucking" away in the coffee-room. I pace the street, as sadly almost as if I had been coming to school, not going thence. I turn into a court by mere chance — I vow it was by mere chance — and there I see a coffee-shop with a placard in the window. "Coffee, Twopence, Round of buttered toast, Twopence." And here am I hungry, penniless, with five-and-twenty shillings of my parents' money in my pocket.

What would you have done? You see I had had my money, and spent it in that pencil-case affair. The five-and-twenty shillings were a trust — by me to be handed over.

But then would my parents wish their only child to be actually without breakfast? Having this money and being so hungry, so *very* hungry, might n't I take ever so little? Might n't I at home eat as much as I chose?

Well, I went into the coffee-shop, and spent four-pence. I remember the taste of the coffee and toast to this day — a peculiar, muddy, not-sweet-enough, most fragrant coffee — a rich, rancid, yet not-buttered-enough, delicious toast. The waiter had nothing. At any rate, fourpence, I know, was the sum I spent. And the hunger appeased, I got on the coach a guilty being.

At the last stage, — what is its name? I have forgotten in seven-and-thirty years, — there is an inn with a little green and trees before it; and by the trees there is an open carriage. It is our carriage. Yes, there are Prince and

Blucher, the horses; and my parents in the carriage.   Oh! how I had been counting the days until this one came! Oh! how happy had I been to see them yesterday!   But there was that fourpence.   All the journey down the toast had choked me, and the coffee poisoned me.

I was in such a state of remorse about the four pence, that I forgot the maternal joy and caresses, the tender paternal voice.   I pulled out the twenty-four shillings and eightpence with a trembling hand.

"Here's your money," I gasp out, "which Mr. P—— owes you, all but fourpence.   I owed three-and-sixpence to Hawker out of my money for a pencil-case, and I had none left, and I took fourpence of yours, and had some coffee at a shop."

I suppose I must have been choking whilst uttering this confession.

"My dear boy," says the governor, "why didn't you go and breakfast at the hotel?"

"He must be starved," says my mother.

I had confessed; I had been a prodigal; I had been taken back to my parents' arms again.   It was not a very great crime as yet, or a very long career of prodigality; but don't we know that a boy who takes a pin which is not his own, will take a thousand pounds when occasion serves, bring his parents' gray heads with sorrow to the grave, and carry his own to the gallows?   Witness the career of Dick Idle, upon whom our friend Mr. Sala has been discoursing.   Dick only began by playing pitch-and-toss on a tombstone: playing fair, for what we know: and even for that sin he was promptly caned by the beadle. The bamboo was ineffectual to cane that reprobate's bad courses out of him.   From pitch-and-toss he proceeded to manslaughter if necessary: to highway robbery; to Tyburn and the rope there.   Ah! Heaven be thanked, my parents' heads are still above the grass, and mine still out of the noose.

As I look up from my desk, I see Tunbridge Wells Common and the rocks, the strange familiar place which I remember forty years ago. Boys saunter over the green with stumps and cricket-bats. Other boys gallop by on the riding-master's hacks. I protest it is "Cramp, Riding Master," as it used to be in the reign of George IV., and that Centaur Cramp must be at least a hundred years old. Yonder comes a footman with a bundle of novels from the library. Are they as good as *our* novels? Oh! how delightful they were! Shades of Valancour, awful ghost of Manfroni, how I shudder at your appearance! Sweet image of Thaddeus of Warsaw, how often has this almost infantile hand tried to depict you in a Polish cap and richly embroidered tights! And as for Corinthian Tom in light blue pantaloons and hessians, and Jerry Hawthorn from the country, can all the fashion, can all the splendour of real life which these eyes have subsequently beheld, can all the wit I have heard or read in later times, compare with your fashion, with your brilliancy, with your delightful grace, and sparkling vivacious rattle?

Who knows? They *may* have kept those very books at the library still — at the well-remembered library on the Pantiles, where they sell that delightful, useful Tunbridge ware. I will go and see. I wend my way to the Pantiles, the queer little old-world Pantiles, where, a hundred years since, so much good company came to take its pleasure. Is it possible, that in the past century, gentlefolks of the first rank (as I read lately in a lecture on George II. in the *Cornhill Magazine*) assembled here and entertained each other with gaming, dancing, fiddling, and tea? There are fiddlers, harpers, and trumpeters performing at this moment in a weak little old balcony, but where is the fine company? Where are the earls, duchesses, bishops, and magnificent embroidered gamesters? A half-dozen of children and their nurses are listening to the musicians; an old lady or two in a poke bonnet passes; and for the rest, I see but an uninteresting population of native tradesmen. As for the library, its window is full of pictures of burly theologians, and their works, sermons, apologues, and so forth. Can I go in and ask the young ladies at the counter for "Manfroni, or the One-handed Monk", and "Life in London, or the Adventures of Corinthian Tom, Jeremiah Hawthorn, Esquire, and their friend Bob Logic"? — absurd. I turn away abashed from the casement — from the Pantiles — no longer Pantiles — but Parade. I stroll over the Common and survey the beautiful purple hills around, twinkling with a thousand bright villas, which have sprung up over this charming ground since first I saw it. What an admirable scene of peace and plenty! What a delicious air breathes over the heath, blows the cloud-shadows across it, and murmurs through the full-clad trees! Can the world show a land fairer, richer, more cheerful? I see a portion of it when I look up from the window at which I write. But fair scene, green woods, bright terraces gleaming in sunshine, and purple clouds swollen with summer rain — nay, the very pages over which my head bends — disappear from before my eyes. They are looking backwards, back into forty years off, into a dark room, into a little house hard by on the Common here, in the Bartlemytide holidays. The parents have gone to town for two days: the house is all his own, his own and a grim old maid-servant's, and a little boy is seated at night in the lonely drawing-room poring over "Manfroni, or the One-handed Monk", so frightened that he scarcely dares to turn round.

NIGHT WALKS (*Incomplete*)

By Charles Dickens

SOME years ago, a temporary inability to sleep, referable to a distressing impression, caused me to walk about the streets all night, for a series of several nights. The disorder might have taken a long time to conquer, if it had been faintly experimented on in bed; but, it was soon defeated by the brisk treatment of getting up directly after lying down, and going out, and coming home tired at sunrise.

In the course of those nights, I finished my education in a fair amateur experience of houselessness. My principal object being to get through the night, the pursuit of it brought me into sympathetic relations with people who have no other object every night in the year.

The month was March, and the weather damp, cloudy, and cold. The sun not rising before half-past five, the night perspective looked sufficiently long at half-past twelve: which was about my time for confronting it.

The restlessness of a great city, and the way in which it tumbles and tosses before it can get to sleep, formed one of the first entertainments offered to the contemplation of us houseless people. It lasted about two hours. We lost a great deal of companionship when the late public-houses turned their lamps out, and when the potmen thrust the last brawling drunkards into the street; but stray vehicles and stray people were left us, after that. If we were very lucky, a policeman's rattle sprang and a fray turned up; but, in general, surprisingly little of this diversion was provided. Except in the Haymarket, which is the worst kept part of London, and about Kent-street in the Borough, and along a portion of the line of the Old Kent-road, the peace was seldom violently broken. But, it was always the case that London, as if in imitation of individual citizens belonging to it, had expiring fits and starts of restlessness. After all seemed quiet, if one cab rattled by, half-a-dozen would surely follow; and Houselessness even observed that intoxicated people appeared to be magnetically attracted towards each other: so that we knew when we saw one drunken object staggering against the shutters of a shop, that another drunken object would stagger up before five minutes were out, to fraternise or fight with it. When we made a divergence from the regular species of drunkard, the thin-armed, puff-faced, leaden-lipped gin-drinker, and encountered a rarer specimen of a more decent appearance, fifty to one but that specimen was dressed in soiled mourning. As the street experience in the night, so the street experience in the day; the common folk who come unexpectedly into a little property, come unexpectedly into a deal of liquor.

At length these flickering sparks would die away, worn out — the last veritable sparks of waking life trailed from some late pieman or hot-potato man — and London would sink to rest. And then the yearning of the houseless mind would be for any sign of company, any lighted place, any movement, anything suggestive of any one being up — nay, even so much as awake, for the houseless eye looked out for lights in windows.

Walking the streets under the pattering rain, Houselessness would walk and walk and walk, seeing nothing but the interminable tangle of streets, save at a corner, here and there, two policemen in conversation, or the sergeant or inspector looking after his men. Now and then in the night — but rarely — Houselessness would become aware of a furtive head peering out of a doorway a few yards before him, and, coming up with the head, would find a man standing bolt upright to keep within the doorway's shadow, and evidently intent upon no particular service to society. Under a kind of fascination, and in a ghostly silence suitable to the time, Houselessness and this gentleman would eye one another from head to foot, and so, without exchange of speech, part, mutually suspicious. Drip, drip, drip, from ledge and coping, splash from pipes and water-spouts, and by-and-by the houseless shadow would fall upon the stones that pave the way to Waterloo-bridge; it being in the houseless mind to have a halfpenny worth of excuse for saying "Good night" to the toll-keeper, and catching a glimpse of his fire. A good fire and a good great-coat and a good woollen neck-shawl, were comfortable things to see in conjunction with the toll-keeper; also his brisk wakefulness was excellent company when he rattled the change of halfpence down upon that mental table of his, like a man who defied the night, with all its sorrowful thoughts, and didn't care for the coming of dawn. There was need of encouragement on the threshold of the bridge, for the bridge was dreary. The chopped-up murdered man, had not been lowered with a rope over the parapet when those nights were; he was alive, and slept then quietly enough most likely, and undisturbed by any dream of where he was to come. But the river had an awful look, the buildings on the banks were muffled in black shrouds, and the reflected lights seemed to originate deep in the water, as if the spectres of suicides were holding them to show where they went down. The wild moon and clouds were as restless as an evil conscience in a tumbled bed, and the very shadow of the immensity of London seemed to lie oppressively upon the river. . . .

When a church clock strikes, on houseless ears in the dead of the night, it may be at first mistaken for company and hailed as such. But, as the spreading circles of vibration, which you may perceive at such a time with great clearness, go opening out, for ever and ever afterwards widening perhaps (as the philosopher has suggested) in eternal space, the mistake is rectified and the sense of loneliness is profounder. Once — it was after leaving the Abbey and turning my face north — I came to the great steps of St. Martin's church as the clock was striking Three. Suddenly, a thing that in a moment more I should have trodden upon without seeing, rose up at my feet with a cry of loneliness and houselessness, struck out of it by the bell, the like of which I never heard. We then stood face to face looking at one another, frightened by one another. The creature was like a bettle-browed hair-lipped youth of twenty, and it had a loose bundle of rags on, which it held together with one of its hands. It shivered from head to foot, and its teeth chattered, and as it stared at me — persecutor, devil, ghost, whatever it thought me — it made with its whining mouth as if it were snapping at me, like a worried dog. Intending to give this ugly object money, I put out my hand to stay it — for it recoiled as it whined and snapped — and laid my hand upon its shoulder. Instantly, it twisted out of its garment, like the young man in the New Testament, and left me standing alone with its rags in my hands.

Covent-garden Market, when it was market morning, was wonderful company. The great waggons of cab-bages, with growers' men and boys lying asleep under them, and with sharp dogs from market-garden neigh-bourhoods looking after the whole, were as good as a party. But one of the worst night sights I know in London, is to be found in the children who prowl about this place; who sleep in the baskets, fight for the offal, dart at any object they think they can lay their thieving hands on, dive under the carts and barrows, dodge the constables, and are perpetually making a blunt pattering on the pavement of the Piazza with the rain of their naked feet. A painful and unnatural result comes of the comparison one is forced to institute between the growth of corruption as displayed in the so much improved and cared for fruits of the earth, and the growth of corruption as displayed in these all uncared for (except inasmuch as ever-hunted) savages.

There was early coffee to be got about Covent-garden Market, and there was more company — warm company, too, which was better. Toast of a very substantial quality, was likewise procurable: though the towzled-headed man who made it, in an inner chamber within the coffee-room, hadn't got his coat on yet, and was so heavy with sleep that in every interval of toast and coffee he went off anew behind the partition into complicated cross-roads of choke and snore, and lost his way directly. Into one of these establishments (among the earliest) near Bow-street, there came one morning as I sat over my houseless cup, pondering where to go next, a man in a high and long snuff-coloured coat, and shoes, and, to the best of my belief, nothing else but a hat, who took out of his hat a large cold meat pudding; a meat pudding so large that it was a very tight fit, and brought the lining of the hat out with it. This mysterious man was known by his pudding, for on his entering, the man of sleep brought him a pint of hot tea, a small loaf, and a large knife and fork and plate. Left to himself in his box, he stood the pudding on the bare table, and, instead of cutting it, stabbed it, over-hand, with the knife, like a mortal enemy; then took the knife out, wiped it on his sleeve, tore the pudding asunder with his fingers, and ate it all up. The remembrance of this man with the pudding remains with me as the remembrance of the most spectral person my house-

lessness encountered.   Twice only was I in that establishment, and twice I saw him stalk in (as I should say, just
out of bed, and presently going back to bed), take out his
pudding, stab his pudding, wipe the dagger, and eat his
pudding all up.   He was a man whose figure promised
cadaverousness, but who had an excessively red face,
though shaped like a horse's.   On the second occasion
of my seeing him, he said huskily to the man of sleep,
"Am I red to-night?"   "You are," he uncompromisingly
answered.   "My mother," said the spectre, "was a red-
faced woman that liked drink, and I looked at her hard
when she laid in her coffin, and I took the complexion."
Somehow, the pudding seemed an unwholesome pudding
after that, and I put myself in its way no more.

When there was no market, or when I wanted variety,
a railway terminus with the morning mails coming in, was
remunerative company.   But like most of the company to
be had in this world, it lasted only a very short time.   The
station lamps would burst out ablaze, the porters would
emerge from places of concealment, the cabs and trucks
would rattle to their places (the post-office carts were
already in theirs), and, finally, the bell would strike up, and
the train would come banging in.   But there were few
passengers and little luggage, and everything scuttled
away with the greatest expedition.   The locomotive post-
offices, with their great nets — as if they had been drag-
ging the country for bodies — would fly open as to their
doors, and would disgorge a smell of lamp, an exhausted
clerk, a guard in a red coat, and their bags of letters; the
engine would blow and heave and perspire, like an engine
wiping its forehead and saying what a run it had had;
and within ten minutes the lamps were out, and I was
houseless and alone again.

But now, there were driven cattle on the high road

near, wanting (as cattle always do) to turn into the midst of stone walls, and squeeze themselves through six inches' width of iron railing, and getting their heads down (also as cattle always do) for tossing-purchase at quite imaginary dogs, and giving themselves and every devoted creature associated with them a most extraordinary amount of unnecessary trouble. Now, too, the conscious gas began to grow pale with the knowledge that daylight was coming, and straggling work-people were already in the streets, and, as waking life had become extinguished with the last pieman's sparks, so it began to be rekindled with the fires of the first street-corner breakfast-sellers. And so by faster and faster degrees, until the last degrees were very fast, the day came, and I was tired and could sleep. And it is not, as I used to think, going home at such times, the least wonderful thing in London, that in the real desert region of the night, the houseless wanderer is alone there. I knew well enough where to find Vice and Misfortune of all kinds, if I had chosen ; but they were put out of sight, and my houselessness had many miles upon miles of streets in which it could, and did, have its own solitary way.

*Emerson, Thoreau — there is no reason for grouping
these names in this book except that they are American
essayists of the past, contemporaries, whose writings still live,
and whose influence upon letters here and in the Old World
has been considerable. Holmes is added to the group, though
the genial humor of his prose sets him apart from those other
two while proving his closer kinship to Cowley and Lamb.*

GIFTS

By Ralph Waldo Emerson

Gifts of one who loved me, —
'T was high time they came;
When he ceased to love me,
Time they stopped for shame.

IT is said that the world is in a state of bankruptcy, that
the world owes the world more than the world can pay,
and ought to go into chancery, and be sold.   I do not think
this general insolvency, which involves in some sort all the
population, to be the reason of the difficulty experienced at
Christmas and New Year, and other times, in bestowing
gifts; since it is always so pleasant to be generous, though
very vexatious to pay debts.   But the impediment lies in
the choosing.   If, at any time, it comes into my head, that
a present is due from me to somebody, I am puzzled what
to give, until the opportunity is gone.   Flowers and fruits
are always fit presents; flowers, because they are a proud
assertion that a ray of beauty outvalues all the utilities of
the world.   These gay natures contrast with the some-

what stern countenance of ordinary nature: they are like
music heard out of a workhouse. Nature does not cocker
us: we are children, not pets: she is not fond: everything is dealt to us without fear or favor, after severe
universal laws. Yet these delicate flowers look like the
frolic and interference of love and beauty. Men use to tell
us that we love flattery, even though we are not deceived
by it, because it shows that we are of importance enough
to be courted. Something like that pleasure, the flowers
give us: what am I to whom these sweet hints are addressed? Fruits are acceptable gifts, because they are the
flowers of commodities, and admit of fantastic values being
attached to them. If a man should send to me to come a
hundred miles to visit him, and should set before me a
basket of fine summer-fruit, I should think there was some
proportion between the labor and the reward.

For common gifts, necessity makes pertinences and
beauty every day, and one is glad when an imperative
leaves him no option, since if the man at the door have no
shoes, you have not to consider whether you could procure him a paint-box. And as it is always pleasing to see a
man eat bread, or drink water, in the house or out of doors,
so it is always a great satisfaction to supply these first
wants. Necessity does everything well. In our condition of universal dependence, it seems heroic to let the
petitioner be the judge of his necessity, and to give all that
is asked, though at great inconvenience. If it be a fantastic desire, it is better to leave to others the office of
punishing him. I can think of many parts I should prefer
playing to that of the Furies. Next to things of necessity,
the rule for a gift, which one of my friends prescribed, is,
that we might convey to some person that which properly
belonged to his character, and was easily associated with
him in thought. But our tokens of compliment and love

are for the most part barbarous.   Rings and other jewels
are not gifts, but apologies for gifts.   The only gift is a
portion of thyself.   Thou must bleed for me.   Therefore
the poet brings his poem; the shepherd, his lamb; the
farmer, corn; the miner, a gem; the sailor, coral and shells;
the painter, his picture; the girl, a handkerchief of her own
sewing.   This is right and pleasing, for it restores society in
so far to the primary basis, when a man's wealth is an index
of his merit.   But it is a cold, lifeless business when you
go to the shops to buy me something, which does not
represent your life and talent, but a goldsmith's.   This
is fit for kings, and rich men who represent kings, and a
false state of property, to make presents of gold and silver
stuffs, as a kind of symbolical sin-offering, or payment
of blackmail.

The law of benefits is a difficult channel, which requires
careful sailing, or rude boats.   It is not the office of a man
to receive gifts.   How dare you give them?   We wish
to be self-sustained.   We do not quite forgive a giver.
The hand that feeds us is in some danger of being bitten.
We can receive anything from love, for that is a way of
receiving it from ourselves; but not from any one who
assumes to bestow.   We sometimes hate the meat which
we eat, because there seems something of degrading
dependence in living by it.

"Brother, if Jove to thee a present make,
Take heed that from his hands thou nothing take."

We ask the whole.   Nothing less will content us.   We
arraign society, if it do not give us besides earth, and fire,
and water, opportunity, love, reverence, and objects of
veneration.

He is a good man, who can receive a gift well.   We are
either glad or sorry at a gift, and both emotions are unbe-

coming. Some violence, I think, is done, some degradation
borne, when I rejoice or grieve at a gift. I am sorry when
my independence is invaded, or when a gift comes from
such as do not know my spirit, and so the act is not sup-
ported; and if the gift pleases me overmuch, then I should
be ashamed that the donor should read my heart, and see
that I love his commodity, and not him. The gift, to be
true, must be the flowing of the giver unto me, cor-
respondent to my flowing unto him. When the waters are
at level, then my goods pass to him, and his to me. All his
are mine, all mine his. I say to him, How can you give me
this pot of oil, or this flagon of wine, when all your oil and
wine is mine, which belief of mine this gift seems to deny?
Hence the fitness of beautiful, not useful things for gifts.
This giving is flat usurpation, and therefore when the beneficiary is ungrateful, as all beneficiaries hate all Timons,
not at all considering the value of the gift, but looking
back to the greater store it was taken from, I rather
sympathize with the beneficiary, than with the anger of
my lord, Timon. For, the expectation of gratitude is
mean, and is continually punished by the total insensibility
of the obliged person. It is a great happiness to get off
without injury and heart-burning, from one who has had
the ill luck to be served by you. It is a very onerous business, this of being served and the debtor naturally
wishes to give you a slap. A golden text for these gentlemen is that which I so admire in the Buddhist, who never
thanks, and who says, "Do not flatter your benefactors."

The reason of these discords I conceive to be, that there
is no commensurability between a man and any gift. You
cannot give anything to a magnanimous person. After
you have served him, he at once puts you in debt by his
magnanimity. The service a man renders his friend is
trivial and selfish, compared with the service he knows his

friend has stood in readiness to yield him, alike before he had begun to serve his friend, and now also.   Compared with that good will I bear my friend, the benefit it is in my power to render him seems small.   Besides, our action on each other, good as well as evil, is so incidental and at random, that we can seldom hear the acknowledgments of any person who would thank us for a benefit, without some shame and humiliation.   We can rarely strike a direct stroke, but must be content with an oblique one;   we seldom have the satisfaction of yielding a direct benefit, which is directly received.   But rectitude scatters favors on every side without knowing it, and receives with wonder the thanks of all people.

I fear to breathe any treason against the majesty of love, which is the genius and god of gifts, and to whom we must not affect to prescribe.   Let him give kingdoms or flower-leaves indifferently.   There are persons, from whom we always expect fairy-tokens; let us not cease to expect them.   This is prerogative, and not to be limited by our municipal rules.   For the rest, I like to see that we cannot be bought and sold.   The best of hospitality and of generosity is also not in the will, but in fate.   I find that I am not much to you; you do not need me; you do not feel me; then am I thrust out of doors, though you proffer me house and lands.   No services are of any value, but only likeness.   When I have attempted to join myself to others by services, it proved an intellectual trick, — no more. They eat your service like apples, and leave you out.   But love them, and they feel you, and delight in you all the time.

WHERE I LIVED, AND WHAT
I LIVED FOR (*Incomplete*)

HENRY DAVID THOREAU

WHEN first I took up my abode in the woods, that is, began to spend my nights as well as days there, which, by accident, was on Independence Day, or the Fourth of July, 1845, my house was not finished for winter, but was merely a defence against the rain, without plastering or chimney, the walls being of rough, weather-stained boards, with wide chinks, which made it cool at night. The upright white hewn studs and freshly planed door and window casings gave it a clean and airy look, especially in the morning, when its timbers were saturated with dew, so that I fancied that by noon some sweet gum would exude from them. To my imagination it retained throughout the day more or less of this auroral character, reminding me of a certain house on a mountain which I had visited a year before. This was an airy and unplastered cabin, fit to entertain a travelling god, and where a goddess might trail her garments. The winds which passed over my dwelling were such as sweep over the ridges of mountains, bearing the broken strains, or celestial parts only of terrestrial music. The morning wind forever blows, the poem of creation is uninterrupted; but few are the ears that hear it. Olympus is but the outside of the earth everywhere. . . .

I went to the woods because I wished to live deliberately, to front only the essential facts of life, and see if I could not learn what it had to teach, and not, when I came to die, discover that I had not lived. I did not wish to live what was not life, living is so dear; nor did I wish to practise resignation, unless it was quite necessary. I wanted to live deep and suck out all the marrow of life, to live so sturdily and

Spartan-like as to put to rout all that was not life, to cut a broad swath and shave close, to drive life into a corner, and reduce it to its lowest terms, and, if it proved to be mean, why then to get the whole and genuine meanness of it, and publish its meanness to the world; or if it were sublime, to know it by experience, and be able to give a true account of it in my next excursion. For most men, it appears to me, are in a strange uncertainty about it, whether it is of the devil or of God, and have *somewhat hastily* concluded that it is the chief end of man here to "glorify God and enjoy him forever."

Still we live meanly, like ants; though the fable tells us that we were long ago changed into men; like pygmies we fight with cranes; it is error upon error, and clout upon clout, and our best virtue has for its occasion a superfluous and evitable wretchedness. Our life is frittered away by detail. An honest man has hardly need to count more than his ten fingers, or in extreme cases he may add his ten toes, and lump the rest. Simplicity, simplicity, simplicity! I say, let your affairs be as two or three, and not a hundred or a thousand; instead of a million count half a dozen, and keep your accounts on your thumb-nail. In the midst of this chopping sea of civilized life, such are the clouds and storms and quicksands and thousand-and-one items to be allowed for, that a man has to live, if he would not founder and go to the bottom and not make his port at all, by dead reckoning, and he must be a great calculator indeed who succeeds. Simplify, simplify. Instead of three meals a day, if it be necessary eat but one; instead of a hundred dishes, five; and reduce other things in proportion. Our life is like a German Confederacy, made up of petty states, with its boundary forever fluctuating, so that even a German cannot tell you how it is bounded at any moment. The nation itself, with all its so-called internal improvements, which, by the way are all external and superficial, is just such an unwieldy and overgrown establishment, cluttered with furniture and tripped up by its own traps, ruined by luxury and heedless expense, by want of calculation and a worthy aim, as the million households in the land; and the only cure for it, as for them, is in a rigid economy, a stern and more than Spartan simplicity of life and elevation of purpose. It lives too fast. Men think that it is essential that the *Nation* have commerce, and export ice, and talk through a telegraph, and ride thirty miles an hour, without a doubt, whether *they* do or not; but whether we should live like baboons or like men, is a little uncertain. If we do not get out sleepers, and forge rails, and devote days and nights to the work, but go to tinkering upon our *lives* to improve *them*, who will build railroads? And if railroads are not built, how shall we get to heaven in season? But if we stay at home and mind our business, who will want railroads? We do not ride on the railroad; it rides upon us. Did you ever think what those sleepers are that underlie the railroad? Each one is a man, an Irishman, or a Yankee man. The rails are laid on them, and they are covered with sand, and the cars run smoothly over them. They are sound sleepers, I assure you. And every few years a new lot is laid down and run over; so that, if some have the pleasure of riding on a rail, others have the misfortune to be ridden upon. And when they run over a man that is walking in his sleep, a supernumerary sleeper in the wrong position, and wake him up, they suddenly stop the cars, and make a hue and cry about it, as if this were an exception. I am glad to know that it takes a gang of men for every five miles to keep the sleepers down and level in their beds as it is, for this is a sign that they may sometime get up again.

Why should we live with such hurry and waste of life?

We are determined to be starved before we are hungry. Men say that a stitch in time saves nine, and so they take a thousand stitches to-day to save nine to-morrow. As for *work*, we haven't any of any consequence. We have the Saint Vitus' dance, and cannot possibly keep our heads still. If I should only give a few pulls at the parish bell-rope, as for a fire, that is, without setting the bell, there is hardly a man on his farm in the outskirts of Concord, notwithstanding that press of engagements which was his excuse so many times this morning, nor a boy, nor a woman, I might almost say, but would forsake all and follow that sound, not mainly to save property from the flames, but, if we will confess the truth, much more to see it burn, since burn it must, and we, be it known, did not set it on fire, — or to see it put out, and have a hand in it, if that is done as handsomely; yes, even if it were the parish church itself. Hardly a man takes a half hour's nap after dinner, but when he wakes he holds up his head and asks, "What's the news?" as if the rest of mankind had stood his sentinels. Some give directions to be waked every half-hour, doubtless for no other purpose; and then, to pay for it, they tell what they have dreamed. After a night's sleep the news is as indispensable as the breakfast. "Pray tell me anything new that has happened to a man anywhere on this globe," — and he reads it over his coffee and rolls, that a man has had his eyes gouged out this morning on the Wachito River; never dreaming the while that he lives in the dark unfathomed mammoth cave of this world, and has but the rudiment of an eye himself.

For my part, I could easily do without the post-office. I think that there are very few important communications made through it. To speak critically, I never received more than one or two letters in my life — I wrote this some years ago — that were worth the postage. The penny-

post is, commonly, an institution through which you
seriously offer a man that penny for his thoughts which is
so often safely offered in jest.   And I am sure that I never
read any memorable news in a newspaper.   If we read of
one man robbed, or murdered, or killed by accident, or
one house burned, or one vessel wrecked, or one steam-
boat blown up, or one cow run over on the Western
Railroad, or one mad dog killed, or one lot of grasshoppers
in the winter, — we never need read of another.   One is
enough.   If you are acquainted with the principle, what
do you care for a myriad instances and applications?   To
a philosopher all *news*, as it is called, is gossip, and they who
edit and read it are old women over their tea.   Yet not a
few are greedy after this gossip.   There was such a rush, as
I hear, the other day at one of the offices to learn the
foreign news by the last arrival, that several large squares
of plate glass belonging to the establishment were broken
by the pressure, — news which I seriously think a ready wit
might write a twelvemonth, or twelve years, beforehand
with sufficient accuracy.   As for Spain, for instance, if
you know how to throw in Don Carlos and the Infanta,
and Don Pedro and Seville and Granada, from time to
time in the right proportions, — they may have changed
the names a little since I saw the papers, — and serve up a
bull-fight when other entertainments fail, it will be true to
the letter, and give us as good an idea of the exact state or
ruin of things in Spain as the most succinct and lucid
reports under this head in the newspapers : and as for
England, almost the last significant scrap of news from that
quarter was the revolution of 1649; and if you have
learned the history of her crops for an average year, you
never need attend to that thing again, unless your speculations are of a merely pecuniary character.   If one may
judge who rarely looks into the newspapers, nothing new

does ever happen in foreign parts, a French revolution not excepted.

What news! how much more important to know what that is which was never old! "Kieou-he-yu (great dignitary of the state of Wei) sent a man to Khoung-tseu to know his news. Khoung-tseu caused the messenger to be seated near him, and questioned him in these terms: What is your master doing? The messenger answered with respect: My master desires to diminish the number of his faults, but he cannot come to the end of them. The messenger being gone, the philosopher remarked: What a worthy messenger! What a worthy messenger!" The preacher, instead of vexing the ears of drowsy farmers on their day of rest at the end of the week, — for Sunday is the fit conclusion of an ill-spent week, and not the fresh and brave beginning of a new one, — with this one other draggle-tail of a sermon, should shout with thundering voice, "Pause! Avast! Why so seeming fast, but deadly slow?"

Shams and delusions are esteemed for soundest truths, while reality is fabulous. If men would steadily observe realities only, and not allow themselves to be deluded, life, to compare it with such things as we know, would be like a fairy tale and the Arabian Nights' Entertainments. If we respected only what is inevitable and has a right to be, music and poetry would resound along the streets. When we are unhurried and wise, we perceive that only great and worthy things have any permanent and absolute existence, that petty fears and petty pleasures are but the shadow of the reality. This is always exhilarating and sublime. By closing the eyes and slumbering, and consenting to be deceived by shows, men establish and confirm their daily life of routine and habit everywhere, which still is built on purely illusory foundations. Children, who play life, discern its true law and relations more clearly than men, who fail to live it worthily, but who think that they are wiser by experience, that is, by failure. I have read in a Hindoo book, that "there was a king's son, who, being expelled in infancy from his native city, was brought up by a forester, and, growing up to maturity in that state, imagined himself to belong to the barbarous race with which he lived. One of his father's ministers having discovered him, revealed to him what he was, and the misconception of his character was removed, and he knew himself to be a prince. So soul," continues the Hindoo philosopher, "from the circumstances in which it is placed, mistakes its own character, until the truth is revealed to it by some holy teacher, and then it knows itself to be *Brahme*." I perceive that we inhabitants of New England live this mean life that we do because our vision does not penetrate the surface of things. We think that that *is* which *appears* to be. If a man should walk through this town and see only the reality, where, think you, would the "Mill-dam" go to? If he should give us an account of the realities he beheld there, we should not recognize the place in his description. Look at a meeting-house, or a court-house, or a jail, or a shop, or a dwelling-house, and say what that thing really is before a true gaze, and they would all go to pieces in your account of them. Men esteem truth remote, in the outskirts of the system, behind the farthest star, before Adam and after the last man. In eternity there is indeed something true and sublime. But all these times and places and occasions are now and here. God himself culminates in the present moment, and will never be more divine in the lapse of all the ages. And we are enabled to apprehend at all what is sublime and noble only by the perpetual instilling and drenching of the reality that surrounds us. The universe constantly and obediently answers to our conceptions;

whether we travel fast or slow, the track is laid for us.   Let
us spend our lives in conceiving then.   The poet or the
artist never yet had so fair and noble a design but some of
his posterity at least could accomplish it.

   Let us spend one day as deliberately as Nature, and not
be thrown off the track by every nutshell and mosquito's
wing that falls on the rails.   Let us rise early and fast, or
break fast, gently and without perturbation; let company
come and let company go, let the bells ring and the children
cry, — determined to make a day of it.   Why should we
knock under and go with the stream?   Let us not be upset
and overwhelmed in that terrible rapid and whirlpool called
a dinner, situated in the meridian shallows.   Weather this
danger and you are safe, for the rest of the way is down
hill.   With unrelaxed nerves, with morning vigor, sail by
it, looking another way, tied to the mast like Ulysses.
If the engine whistles, let it whistle till it is hoarse for its
pains.   If the bell rings, why should we run?   We will
consider what kind of music they are like.   Let us settle
ourselves, and work and wedge our feet downward through
the mud and slush of opinion, and prejudice, and tradition,
and delusion, and appearance, that alluvion which covers
the globe, through Paris and London, through New York
and Boston and Concord, through Church and State,
through poetry and philosophy and religion, till we come
to a hard bottom and rocks in place, which we can call
reality and say, This is, and no mistake; and then begin,
having a *point d'appui*, below freshet and frost and fire, a
place where you might found a wall or a state, or set a
lamp-post safely, or perhaps a gauge, not a Nilometer,
but a Realometer, that future ages might know how deep
a freshet of shams and appearances had gathered from
time to time.   If you stand right fronting and face to face
to a fact, you will see the sun glimmer on both its surfaces,

as if it were a cimeter, and feel its sweet edge dividing you through the heart and marrow, and so you will happily conclude your mortal career. Be it life or death, we crave only reality. If we are really dying, let us hear the rattle in our throats and feel cold in the extremities; if we are alive, let us go about our business.

Time is but the stream I go a-fishing in. I drink at it; but while I drink I see the sandy bottom and detect how shallow it is. Its thin current slides away, but eternity remains. I would drink deeper; fish in the sky, whose bottom is pebbly with stars. I cannot count one. I know not the first letter of the alphabet. I have always been regretting that I was not as wise as the day I was born. The intellect is a cleaver; it discerns and rifts its way into the secret of things. I do not wish to be any more busy with my hands than is necessary. My head is hands and feet. I feel all my best faculties concentrated in it. My instinct tells me that my head is an organ for burrowing, as some creatures use their snout and fore paws, and with it I would mine and burrow my way through these hills. I think that the richest vein is somewhere hereabouts; so by the divining-rod and thin rising vapors I judge; and here I will begin to mine.

THE AUTOCRAT OF THE BREAKFAST
TABLE (an Extract)

By Oliver Wendell Holmes

I would have a woman true as Death. At the first real lie which works from the heart outward, she should be tenderly chloroformed into a better world, where she can have an angel for a governess, and feed on strange fruits which will make her all over again, even to her bones and marrow. — Whether gifted with the accident of beauty

or not, she should have been molded in the rose-red clay
of Love before the breath of life made a moving mortal
of her.   Love capacity is a congenital endowment; and
I think after a while one gets to know the warm-hued
natures it belongs to from the pretty pipe-clay counterfeits
of them. — Proud she may be, in the sense of respecting
herself; but pride in the sense of contemning others less
gifted than herself deserves the two lowest circles of a
vulgar woman's Inferno where the punishments are
smallpox and bankruptcy. — She who nips off the end of a
brittle courtesy, as one breaks the tip of an icicle, to bestow
upon those whom she ought cordially and kindly to
recognize, proclaims the fact that she comes not merely
of low blood, but of bad blood.   Consciousness of unques-
tioned position makes people gracious in proper measure to
all; but if a woman put on airs with her real equals, she has
something about herself or her family she is ashamed of, or
ought to be.   Middle and more than middle aged people,
who know family histories, generally see through it.
An official of standing was rude to me once.   "Oh, that is
the maternal grandfather," said a wise old friend to me:
"he was a boor." — Better too few words from the woman
we love than too many; while she is silent, Nature is working for her; while she talks she is working for herself. —
Love is sparingly soluble in the words of men, therefore
they speak much of it; but one syllable of woman's
speech can dissolve more of it than a man's heart can hold.
— Whether I say any or all of these things to the schoolmistress, or not, — whether I stole them out of Lord
Bacon, — whether I cribbed them from Balsac, — whether
I dipped them from the ocean of Tupperian wisdom, — or
whether I have just found them in my head, laid there by
that solemn fowl Experience (who, according to my
observation, cackles oftener than she drops real live eggs),

— I cannot say.   Wise men have said more foolish things
— and foolish men, I don't doubt, have said as wise things.
Anyhow, the schoolmistress and I had pleasant walks and
long talks, all of which I do not feel bound to report.

— You are a stranger to me, Ma'am.   I don't doubt
you would like to know all I said to the schoolmistress.   I
shan't do it; — I had rather get the publishers to return
the money you have invested in these pages.   Besides,
I have forgotten a good deal of it.   I shall tell only what I
like of what I remember.

.   .   .   .

I don't know anything sweeter than this leaking in of
Nature through all the cracks in the walls and floors of
cities.   You heap up a million tons of hewn rocks on a
square mile or two of earth which was green once.   The
trees look down from the hillsides and ask each other, as
they stand on tiptoe, "What are these people about?"
And the small herbs at their feet look up and whisper back,
"We will go and see."   So the small herbs pack themselves
up in the least possible bundles, and wait until the wind
steals to them at night and whispers, "Come with me."
Then they go softly with it into the great city, — one to a
cleft in the pavement, one to a spout on the roof, one to a
seam in the marbles over a rich gentleman's bones, and
one to the grave without a stone where nothing but a man
is buried, — and there they grow, looking down on the
generations of men from moldy roofs, looking up from
between the less-trodden pavements, looking out through
iron cemetery railings.   Listen to them, when there is
only a light breath stirring, and you will hear them saying
to each other, "Wait awhile!"   The words run along the
telegraph of those narrow green lines that border the
roads leading from the city, until they reach the slope of
the hills, and the trees repeat in low murmurs to each other,

"Wait awhile!"   By-and-by the flow of life in the streets
ebbs, and the old leafy inhabitants — the smaller tribes
always in front — saunter in, one by one, very careless
seemingly, but very tenacious, until they swarm so that
the great stones gape from each other with the crowding of
their roots, and the feldspar begins to be picked out of the
granite to find them food.   At last the trees take up their
solemn line of march, and never rest until they have
encamped in the market-place.   Wait long enough and
you will find an old doting oak hugging a huge worn block
in its yellow underground arms; that was the corner-
stone of the State House.   Oh, so patient she is, this
imperturbable Nature!

Carlyle and Ruskin are here together, not because of the personal friendship that existed between them, but because students interested in the essay as a vehicle for criticism should become well acquainted with both. Yet Carlyle's writings in general do not reveal the man himself but only his subject-matter. It is in "Sartor Resartus" that he shows the influence of the true essayists of his day and in an unaccustomed playfulness takes on the personality of a German professor. Ruskin's critical essays are actually platform talks, addressed directly to the audience for which they are planned.

SYMBOLS

FROM *Sartor Resartus*

BY THOMAS CARLYLE

PROBABLY it will elucidate the drift of these foregoing obscure utterances, if we here insert somewhat of our Professor's speculations on *Symbols*. To state his whole doctrine, indeed, were beyond our compass : nowhere is he more mysterious, impalpable, than in this of "Fantasy being the organ of the God-like"; and how "Man thereby, though based, to all seeming, on the small Visible, does nevertheless extend down into the infinite deeps of the Invisible, of which Invisible, indeed, his Life is properly the bodying forth." Let us, omitting these high transcendental aspects of the matter, study to glean (whether from the Paper-bags or the Printed Volume) what little seems logical and practical, and cunningly arrange it into such degree of coherence as it will assume. By way of proem, take the following not injudicious remarks :

"The benignant efficacies of Concealment," cries our Professor, "who shall speak or sing? SILENCE and SECRECY ! Altars might still be raised to them (were this an altar-building time) for universal worship. Silence is the element in which great things fashion themselves together; that at length they may emerge, full-formed and majestic, into the daylight of Life, which they are thenceforth to rule. Not William the Silent only, but all the considerable men I have known, and the most undiplomatic and unstrategic of these, forbore to babble of what they were creating and projecting. Nay, in thy own mean perplexities, do thou thyself but *hold thy tongue for one day:* on the morrow, how much clearer are thy purposes and duties; what wreck and rubbish have those mute workmen within thee swept away, when intrusive noises were shut out ! Speech is too often not, as the Frenchman defined it, the art of concealing Thought; but of quite stifling and suspending Thought, so that there is none to conceal. Speech too is great, but not the greatest. As the Swiss Inscription says : *Sprechen ist silbern, Schweigen ist golden* (Speech is silvern, Silence is golden); or as I might rather express it : Speech is of Time, Silence is of Eternity.

"Bees will not work except in darkness; Thought will not work except in Silence : neither will Virtue work except in Secrecy. Let not thy left hand know what thy right hand doeth ! Neither shalt thou prate even to thy own heart of 'those secrets known to all.' Is not Shame (*Scham*) the soil of all Virtue, of all good manners and good morals ? Like other plants, Virtue will not grow unless its root be hidden, buried from the eye of the sun. Let the sun shine on it, nay do but look at it privily thyself, the root withers, and no flower will glad thee. O my Friends, when we view the fair clustering flowers that over-wreathe, for example, the Marriage-bower, and encircle man's life with the fragrance and hues of Heaven, what hand will not smite the foul plunderer that grubs them up by the roots, and with grinning, grunting satisfaction, shows us the dung they flourish in! Men speak much of the Printing-Press with its Newspapers: *du Himmel!* what are these to Clothes and the Tailor's Goose?"

"Of kin to the so incalculable influences of Concealment, and connected with still greater things, is the wondrous agency of *Symbols*. In a Symbol there is concealment and yet revelation: here therefore, by Silence and by Speech acting together, comes a double significance. And if both the Speech be itself high, and the Silence fit and noble, how expressive will their union be! Thus in many a painted Device, or simple Seal-emblem, the commonest Truth stands out to us proclaimed with quite new emphasis.

"For it is here that Fantasy with her mystic wonderland plays into the small prose domain of Sense, and becomes incorporated therewith. In the Symbol proper, what we can call a Symbol, there is ever, more or less distinctly and directly, some embodiment and revelation of the Infinite; the Infinite is made to blend itself with the Finite, to stand visible, and as it were, attainable there. By Symbols, accordingly, is man guided and commanded, made happy, made wretched. He everywhere finds himself encompassed with Symbols, recognized as such or not recognized: the Universe is but one vast Symbol of God; nay if thou wilt have it, what is man himself but a Symbol of God; is not all that he does symbolical; a revelation to Sense of the mystic god-given force that is in him; a 'Gospel of Freedom,' which he, the 'Messias of Nature,' preaches, as he can, by act and word? Not a Hut he builds but is the visible embodiment of a Thought; but bears visible record of invisible things; but is, in the transcendental sense, symbolical as well as real."

"Man," says the Professor elsewhere, in quite antipodal contrast with these high-soaring delineations, which we have here cut-short on the verge of the inane, "Man is by birth somewhat of an owl. Perhaps, too, of all the owleries that ever possessed him, the most owlish, if we consider it, is that of your actually existing Motive-Millwrights. Fantastic tricks enough man has played, in his times; has fancied himself to be most things, down even to an animated heap of Glass: but to fancy himself a dead Iron-Balance for weighing Pains and Pleasures on, was reserved for this his latter era. There stands he, his Universe one huge Manger, filled with hay and thistles to be weighed against each other; and looks long-eared enough. Alas, poor devil! specters are appointed to haunt him: one age he is hag-ridden, bewitched; the next, priest-ridden, befooled; in all ages, bedevilled. And now the Genius of Mechanism smothers him worse than any Nightmare did; till the Soul is nigh choked out of him, and only a kind of Digestive, Mechanic life remains. In Earth and in Heaven he can see nothing but Mechanism; has fear for nothing else, hope in nothing else: the world would indeed grind him to pieces; but cannot he fathom the Doctrine of Motives, and cunningly compute these, and mechanize them to grind the other way?

"Were he not, as has been said, purblinded by enchantment, you had but to bid him open his eyes and look. In which country, in which time, was it hitherto that man's history, or the history of any man, went-on by calculated or calculable 'Motives'? What make ye of your Christianities, and Chivalries, and Reformations, and Marseilles Hymns, and Reigns of Terror? Nay, has not perhaps the

Motive-grinder himself been *in Love?*   Did he never stand
so much as a contested Election?   Leave him to Time, and
the medicating virtue of Nature."

"Yes, Friends," elsewhere observes the Professor, "not
our Logical, Mensurative faculty, but our Imaginative one
is King over us; I might say, Priest and Prophet to lead us
heavenward; or Magician and Wizard to lead us hellward.
Nay, even for the basest Sensualist, what is Sense but the
implement of Fantasy; the vessel it drinks out of?   Ever
in the dullest existence there is a sheen either of Inspiration
or of Madness (thou partly hast it in thy choice, which of
the two), that gleams-in from the circumambient Eternity,
and colors with its own hues our little islet of Time.   The
Understanding is indeed thy window, too clear thou
canst not make it; but Fantasy is thy eye, with its color-
giving retina, healthy or diseased.   Have not I myself
known five-hundred living soldiers sabered into crows'-
meat for a piece of glazed cotton, which they called their
Flag; which, had you sold it at any market-cross, would
not have brought above three groschen?   Did not the
whole Hungarian Nation rise, like some tumultuous
moon-stirred Atlantic, when Kaiser Joseph pocketed their
Iron Crown; an implement, as was sagaciously observed,
in size and commercial value little differing from a horse-
shoe?   It is in and through *Symbols* that man, consciously
or unconsciously, lives, works, and has his being: those
ages, moreover, are accounted the noblest which can the
best recognize symbolical worth, and prize it the highest.
For is not a Symbol ever, to him who has eyes for it, some
dimmer or clearer revelation of the Godlike?

"Of Symbols, however, I remark farther, that they have
both an extrinsic and intrinsic value oftenest the former
only.   What, for instance, was in that clouted Shoe, which
the Peasants bore aloft with them as ensign in their

Bauernkrieg (Peasants' War) ?   Or in the Wallet-and-staff
round which the Netherland *Gueux*, glorying in that nick-
name of Beggars, heroically rallied and prevailed, though
against King Philip himself ?   Intrinsic significance these
had none : only extrinsic ; as the accidental Standards of
multitudes more or less sacredly uniting together ; in which
union itself, as above noted, there is ever something
mystical and borrowing of the Godlike.   Under a like
category, too, stand, or stood, the stupidest heraldic
Coats-of-arms ; military Banners everywhere ; and generally all national or other sectarian Costumes and Customs : they have no intrinsic, necessary divineness, or even
worth ; but have acquired an extrinsic one.   Nevertheless
through all these there glimmers something of a Divine
Idea ; as through military Banners themselves, the Divine
Idea of Duty, of heroic Daring ; in some instances of
Freedom, of Right.   Nay the highest ensign that men ever
met and embraced under, the Cross itself, had no meaning
save an accidental extrinsic one.

"Another matter it is, however, when your Symbol has
intrinsic meaning, and is of itself *fit* that men should unite
round it.   Let but the Godlike manifest itself to Sense ;
let but Eternity look, more or less visibly, through the
Time-Figure (*Zeitbild*) !   Then it is fit that men unite
there ; and worship together before such Symbol ; and
so from day to day, and from age to age, superadd to it
new divineness.

"Of this latter sort are all true Works of Art : in them
(if thou know a Work of Art from a Daub of Artifice) wilt
thou discern Eternity looking through Time ; the Godlike
rendered visible.   Here too may an extrinsic value gradually superadd itself : thus certain *Iliads*, and the like, have,
in three-thousand years, attained quite new significance.
But nobler'than all in this kind are the Lives of heroic god-

inspired Men; for what other Work of Art is so divine?
In Death too, in the Death of the Just, as the last perfection of a Work of Art, may we not discern symbolic
meaning? In that divinely transfigured Sleep, as of
Victory, resting over the beloved face which now knows
thee no more, read (if thou canst for tears) the confluence
of Time with Eternity, and some gleam of the latter peering
through.

OF KINGS' TREASURIES

FROM *Sesame and Lilies*

BY JOHN RUSKIN

MY first duty this evening is to ask your pardon for the
ambiguity of title under which the subject of my lecture has
been announced : for indeed I am not going to talk of kings,
known as regnant, nor of treasuries, understood to contain
wealth ; but of quite another order of royalty, and another
material of riches, than those usually acknowledged. I
had even intended to ask your attention for a little while
on trust, and (as sometimes one contrives, in taking a
friend to see a favorite piece of scenery) to hide what I
wanted most to show, with such imperfect cunning as I
might, until we unexpectedly reached the best point of view
by winding paths. But — and as also I have heard it said,
by men practised in public address, that hearers are never
so much fatigued as by the endeavor to follow a speaker
who gives them no clue to his purpose — I will take the
slight mask off at once, and tell you plainly that I want to
speak to you about the treasures hidden in books; and
about the way we find them, and the way we lose them.
A grave subject, you will say; and a wide one! Yes; so
wide that I shall make no effort to touch the compass of it.
I will try only to bring before you a few simple thoughts

about reading, which press themselves upon me every day
more deeply, as I watch the course of the public mind with
respect to our daily enlarging means of education; and
the answeringly wider spreading on the levels, of the
irrigation of literature.

It happens that I have practically some connection
with schools for different classes of youth; and I receive
many letters from parents respecting the education of their
children.   In the mass of these letters I am always struck
by the precedence which the idea of a "position in life"
takes above all other thoughts in the parents' — more
especially in the mothers' — minds.   "The education
befitting such and such a *station in life*" — this is the
phrase, this the object, always.   They never seek, as far
as I can make out, an education good in itself; even the
conception of abstract rightness in training rarely seems
reached by the writers.   But, an education "which shall
keep a good coat on my son's back; — which shall enable
him to ring with confidence the visitors' bell at double-
belled doors; which shall result ultimately in the establishment of a double-belled door to his own house; — in a
word, which shall lead to advancement in life; — *this* we
pray for on bent knees — and this is *all* we pray for."   It
never seems to occur to the parents that there may be an
education which, in itself, *is* advancement in Life; — that
any other than that may perhaps be advancement in
Death; and that this essential education might be more
easily got, or given, than they fancy, if they set about it in
the right way; while it is for no price, and by no favor, to
be got, if they set about it in the wrong.

Indeed, among the ideas most prevalent and effective
in the mind of this busiest of countries, I suppose the first
— at least that which is confessed with the greatest
frankness, and put forward as the fittest stimulus to youth-

ful exertion — is this of "Advancement in life."   May I
ask you to consider with me, what this idea practically
includes, and what it should include?

Practically, then, at present, "advancement in life"
means, becoming conspicuous in life; obtaining a position
which shall be acknowledged by others to be respectable or
honorable.   We do not understand by this advancement,
in general, the mere making of money, but the being known
to have made it; not the accomplishment of any great
aim, but the being seen to have accomplished it.   In a
word, we mean the gratification of our thirst for applause.
That thirst, if the last infirmity of noble minds, is also the
first infirmity of weak ones; and on the whole, the strongest impulsive influence of average humanity: the greatest
efforts of the race have always been traceable to the love of
praise, as its greatest catastrophes to the love of pleasure.

I am not about to attack or defend this impulse.   I
want you only to feel how it lies at the root of effort; especially of all modern effort.   It is the gratification of vanity
which is, with us, the stimulus of toil and balm of repose;
so closely does it touch the very springs of life that the
wounding of our vanity is always spoken of (and truly) as
in its measure *mortal;* we call it "mortification", using the
same expression which we should apply to a gangrenous
and incurable bodily hurt.   And although few of us may be
physicians enough to recognize the various effects of this
passion upon health and energy, I believe most honest men
know, and would at once acknowledge, its leading power
with them as a motive.   The seaman does not commonly
desire to be made captain only because he knows he can
manage the ship better than any other sailor on board.
He wants to be made captain that he may be *called*
captain.   The clergyman does not usually want to be made
a bishop only because he believes that no other hand can,

as firmly as his, direct the diocese through its difficulties.
He wants to be made bishop primarily that he may be
called "My Lord."   And a prince does not usually desire
to enlarge, or a subject to gain, a kingdom, because he
believes that no one else can as well serve the State, upon
its throne; but, briefly, because he wishes to be addressed
as "Your Majesty," by as many lips as may be brought to
such utterance.

This, then, being the main idea of "advancement in
life", the force of it applies, for all of us, according to our
station, particularly to that secondary result of such
advancement which we call "getting into good society."
We want to get into good society not that we may have it,
but that we may be seen in it; and our notion of its
goodness depends primarily on its conspicuousness.

Will you pardon me if I pause for a moment to put what
I fear you may think an impertinent question?   I never
can go on with an address unless I feel, or know, that my
audience are either with me or against me: I do not much
care which, in beginning; but I must know where they are;
and I would fain find out, at this instant, whether you think
I am putting the motives of popular action too low.   I am
resolved, to-night, to state them low enough to be admitted
as probable; for whenever, in my writings on Political
Economy, I assume that a little honesty, or generosity —
or what used to be called "virtue" — may be calculated
upon as a human motive of action, people always answer
me, saying, "You must not calculate on that: that is not
in human nature: you must not assume anything to be
common to men but acquisitiveness and jealousy; no
other feeling ever has influence on them, except acci-
dentally, and in matters out of the way of business."   I
begin, accordingly, to-night low in the scale of motives;
but I must know if you think me right in doing so.   There

fore, let me ask those who admit the love of praise to be usually the strongest motive in men's minds in seeking advancement, and the honest desire of doing any kind of duty to be an entirely secondary one, to hold up their hands. (*About a dozen hands held up — the audience, partly, not being sure the lecturer is serious, and, partly, shy of expressing opinion.*) I am quite serious — I really do want to know what you think; however, I can judge by putting the reverse question. Will those who think that duty is generally the first, and love of praise the second, motive, hold up their hands? (*One hand reported to have been held up, behind the lecturer.*) Very good: I see you are with me, and that you think I have not begun too near the ground. Now, without teasing you by putting farther question, I venture to assume that you will admit duty as at least a secondary or tertiary motive. You think that the desire of doing something useful, or obtaining some real good, is indeed an existent collateral idea, though a secondary one, in most men's desire of advancement. You will grant that moderately honest men desire place and office, at least in some measure, for the sake of beneficent power; and would wish to associate rather with sensible and well-informed persons than with fools and ignorant persons, whether they are seen in the company of the sensible ones or not. And finally, without being troubled by repetition of any common truisms about the preciousness of friends, and the influence of companions, you will admit, doubtless, that according to the sincerity of our desire that our friends may be true, and our companions wise, — and in proportion to the earnestness and discretion with which we choose both, — will be the general chances of our happiness and usefulness.

But granting that we had both the will and the sense to choose our friends well, how few of us have the power!

or, at least, how limited, for most, is the sphere of choice!
Nearly all our associations are determined by chance, or
necessity; and restricted within a narrow circle. We
cannot know whom we would; and those whom we know,
we cannot have at our side when we most need them.
All the higher circles of human intelligence are, to those
beneath, only momentarily and partially open. We
may, by good fortune, obtain a glimpse of a great poet,
and hear the sound of his voice; or put a question to a
man of science, and be answered good humoredly. We
may intrude ten minutes' talk on a cabinet minister,
answered probably with words worse than silence, being
deceptive; or snatch, once or twice in our lives, the
privilege of throwing a bouquet in the path of a princess,
or arresting the kind glance of a queen. And yet these
momentary chances we covet; and spend our years, and
passions, and powers in pursuit of little more than these;
while, meantime, there is a society, continually open to us,
of people who will talk to us as long as we like, whatever
our rank or occupation; — talk to us in the best words they
can choose, and of the things nearest their hearts. And
this society, because it is so numerous and so gentle, and
can be kept waiting round us all day long, — kings and
statesmen lingering patiently, not to grant audience, but
to gain it! — in those plainly furnished and narrow ante-
rooms, our bookcase shelves, — we make no account of
that company, — perhaps never listen to a word they
would say, all day long!

You may tell me, perhaps, or think within yourselves,
that the apathy with which we regard this company of the
noble, who are praying us to listen to them; and the passion with which we pursue the company, probably of the
ignoble, who despise us, or who have nothing to teach us,
are grounded in this, — that we can see the faces of the

living men, and it is themselves, and not their sayings, with which we desire to become familiar. But it is not so. Suppose you never were to see their faces : — suppose you could be put behind a screen in the statesman's cabinet, or the prince's chamber, would you not be glad to listen to their words, though you were forbidden to advance beyond the screen? And when the screen is only a little less, folded in two instead of four, and you can be hidden behind the cover of the two boards that bind a book, and listen all day long, not to the casual talk, but to the studied, determined, chosen addresses of the wisest of men; — this station of audience, and honorable privy council, you despise !

But perhaps you will say that it is because the living people talk of things that are passing, and are of immediate interest to you, that you desire to hear them. Nay; that cannot be so, for the living people will themselves tell you about passing matters, much better in their writings than in their careless talk. But I admit that this motive does influence you, so far as you prefer those rapid and ephemeral writings to slow and enduring writings — books, properly so called. For all books are divisible into two classes : the books of the hour, and the books of all time. Mark this distinction — it is not one of quality only. It is not merely the bad book that does not last, and the good one that does. It is a distinction of species. There are good books for the hour, and good ones for all time; bad books for the hour, and bad ones for all time. I must define the two kinds before I go farther.

The good book of the hour, then, — I do not speak of the bad ones, — is simply the useful or pleasant talk of some person whom you cannot otherwise converse with, printed for you. Very useful often, telling you what you need to know; very pleasant often, as a sensible friend's

present talk would be.   These bright accounts of travels;
good-humored and witty discussions of questions; lively or
pathetic story-telling in the form of novel; firm fact-
telling, by the real agents concerned in the events of passing
history; — all these books of the hour, multiplying among
us as education becomes more general, are a peculiar
possession of the present age: we ought to be entirely
thankful for them, and entirely ashamed of ourselves if
we make no good use of them.   But we make the worst
possible use if we allow them to usurp the place of true
books: for, strictly speaking, they are not books at all,
but merely letters or newspapers in good print.   Our
friend's letter may be delightful, or necessary, to-day:
whether worth keeping or not, is to be considered.   The
newspaper may be entirely proper at breakfast-time, but
assuredly it is not reading for all day.   So, though bound
up in a volume, the long letter which gives you so pleasant
an account of the inns, and roads, and weather last year
at such a place, or which tells you that amusing story, or
gives you the real circumstances of such and such events,
however valuable for occasional reference, may not be, in
the real sense of the word, a "book" at all, nor in the real
sense, to be "read."   A book is essentially not a talked
thing, but a written thing; and written not with a view of
mere communication, but of permanence.   The book of
talk is printed only because its author cannot speak to
thousands of people at once; if he could, he would — the
volume is mere *multiplication* of his voice.   You cannot
talk to your friend in India; if you could, you would; you
write instead: that is mere *conveyance* of voice.   But a
book is written, not to multiply the voice merely, not to
carry it merely, but to perpetuate it.   The author has
something to say which he perceives to be true and useful,
or helpfully beautiful.   So far as he knows, no one has yet

said it; so far as he knows, no one else can say it. He is
bound to say it, clearly and melodiously if he may; clearly,
at all events. In the sum of his life he finds this to be the
thing, or group of things, manifest to him; — this, the
piece of true knowledge, or sight, which his share of sunshine and earth has permitted him to seize. He would
fain set it down forever; engrave it on rock, if he could;
saying, "This is the best of me; for the rest, I ate, and
drank, and slept, loved and hated, like another; my life
was as the vapor, and is not; but this I saw and knew:
this if anything of mine, is worth your memory." That
is his "writing"; it is, in his small human way, and with
whatever degree of true inspiration is in him, his inscription, or scripture. That is a "Book."

Perhaps you think no books were ever so written?

But, again, I ask you, do you at all believe in honesty, or
at all in kindness? or do you think there is never any honesty or benevolence in wise people? None of us, I hope,
are so unhappy as to think that. Well, whatever bit of a
wise man's work is honestly and benevolently done, that
bit is his book, or his piece of art. It is mixed always with
evil fragments — ill-done, redundant, affected work. But
if you read rightly, you will easily discover the true bits,
and those *are* the book.

Now, books of this kind have been written in all ages
by their greatest men, — by great readers, great statesmen,
and great thinkers. These are all at your choice; and Life
is short. You have heard as much before; — yet, have
you measured and mapped out this short life and its
possibilities? Do you know, if you read this, that you
cannot read that — that what you lose to-day you cannot
gain to-morrow? Will you go and gossip with your house-
maid, or your stable-boy, when you may talk with queens
and kings; or flatter yourselves that it is with any worthy

consciousness of your own claims to respect, that you jostle with the hungry and common crowd for *entrée* here, and audience there, when all the while this eternal court is open to you, with its society, wide as the world, multitudinous as its days, the chosen, and the mighty, of every place and time? Into that you may enter always; in that you may take fellowship and rank according to your wish; from that, once entered into it, you can never be an outcast but by your own fault; by your aristocracy of companionship there, your own inherent aristocracy will be assuredly tested, and the motives with which you strive to take high place in the society of the living, measured, as to all the truth and sincerity that are in them, by the place you desire to take in this company of the Dead.

"The place you desire", and the place *you fit yourself for*, I must also say; because, observe, this court of the past differs from all living aristocracy in this : — it is open to labor and to merit, but to nothing else. No wealth will bribe, no name overawe, no artifice deceive, the guardian of those Elysian gates. In the deep sense, no vile or vulgar person ever enters there. At the portières of that silent Faubourg St. Germain, there is but brief question : "Do you deserve to enter? Pass. Do you ask to be the companion of nobles? Make yourself noble, and you shall be. Do you long for the conversation of the wise? Learn to understand it, and you shall hear it. But on other terms? — no. If you will not rise to us, we cannot stoop to you. The living lord may assume courtesy, the living philosopher explain his thought to you with considerate pain; but here we neither feign nor interpret; you must rise to the level of our thoughts if you would be gladdened by them, and share our feelings if you would recognize our presence."

This, then, is what you have to do, and I admit that it is much. You must, in a word, love these people, if you are to be among them.   No ambition is of any use.   They scorn your ambition.   You must love them, and show your love in these two following ways.

I. First, by a true desire to be taught by them, and to enter into their thoughts.   To enter into theirs, observe; not to find your own expressed by them.   If the person who wrote the book is not wiser than you, you need not read it; if he be, he will think differently from you in many respects.

Very ready we are to say of a book, "How good this is — that's exactly what I think!"   But the right feeling is, "How strange that is !   I never thought of that before, and yet I see it is true; or if I do not now, I hope I shall, some day."   But whether thus submissively or not, at least be sure that you go to the author to get at *his* meaning, not to find yours.   Judge it afterwards if you think yourself qualified to do so; but ascertain it first.   And be sure also, if the author is worth anything, that you will not get at his meaning all at once; — nay, that at his whole meaning you will not for a long time arrive in any wise.   Not that he does not say what he means, and in strong words too; but he cannot say it all; and what is more strange, *will* not, but in a hidden way and in parable, in order that he may be sure you want it.   I cannot quite see the reason of this, nor analyze that cruel reticence in the breasts of wise men which makes them always hide their deeper thought.   They do not give it you by way of help, but of reward; and will make themselves sure that you deserve it before they allow you to reach it.   But it is the same with the physical type of wisdom, gold.   There seems, to you and me, no reason why the electric forces of the earth should not carry whatever there is of gold within it at once to the mountain tops, so that kings and people might know that all the gold they could get was there; and without any trouble of digging, or anxiety, or chance, or waste of time, cut it away, and coin as much as they needed. But Nature does not manage it so. She puts it in little fissures in the earth, nobody knows where; you may dig long and find none; you must dig painfully to find any.

And it it just the same with men's best wisdom. When you come to a good book, you must ask yourself, "Am I inclined to work as an Australian miner would? Are my pickaxes and shovels in good order, and am I in good trim myself, my sleeves well up to the elbow, and my breath good, and my temper?" And, keeping the figure a little longer, even at cost of tiresomeness, for it is a thoroughly useful one, the metal you are in search of being the author's mind or meaning, his words are as the rock which you have to crush and smelt in order to get at it. And your pickaxes are your own care, wit, and learning; your smelting furnace is your own thoughtful soul. Do not hope to get at any good author's meaning without those tools and that fire; often you will need sharpest, finest chiselling, and patientest fusing, before you can gather one grain of the metal.

And, therefore, first of all, I tell you earnestly and authoritatively (I *know* I am right in this), you must get into the habit of looking intensely at words, and assuring yourself of their meaning, syllable by syllable — nay, letter by letter. For though it is only by reason of the opposition of letters in the function of signs, to sounds in the function of signs, that the study of books is called "literature", and that a man versed in it is called, by the consent of nations, a man of letters instead of a man of books, or of words, you may yet connect with that accidental nomenclature this real fact, — that you might read all the books in the British Museum (if you could live long enough), and remain an utterly "illiterate", uneducated person; but that if you read ten pages of a good book, letter by letter, — that is to say, with real accuracy, — you are forevermore in some measure an educated person. The entire difference between education and non-education (as regards the merely intellectual part of it) consists in this accuracy. A well-educated gentleman may not know many languages, — may not be able to speak any but his own, — may have read very few books. But whatever language he knows, he knows precisely; whatever word he pronounces, he pronounces rightly; above all, he is learned in the *peerage* of words; knows the words of true descent and ancient blood, at a glance, from words of modern canaille; remembers all their ancestry, their intermarriages, distant relationships, and the extent to which they were admitted, and offices they held, among the national noblesse of words at any time, and in any country. But an uneducated person may know, by memory, many languages, and talk them all, and yet truly know not a word of any, — not a word even of his own. An ordinarily clever and sensible seaman will be able to make his way ashore at most ports; yet he has only to speak a sentence of any language to be known for an illiterate person; so also the accent, or turn of expression of a single sentence, will at once mark a scholar. And this is so strongly felt, so conclusively admitted, by educated persons, that a false accent or a mistaken syllable is enough, in the parliament of any civilized nation, to assign to a man a certain degree of inferior standing forever.

And this is right; but it is a pity that the accuracy insisted on is not greater, and required to a serious purpose. It is right that a false Latin quantity should excite a smile in the House of Commons; but it is wrong that a false English *meaning* should *not* excite a frown there. Let the accent of words be watched, and closely; let their meaning be watched more closely still, and fewer will do the work.

A few words, well chosen and distinguished, will do work that a thousand cannot, when every one is acting equivocally, in the function of another. Yes; and words, if they are not watched, will do deadly work sometimes. There are masked words droning and skulking about us in Europe just now — (there never were so many, owing to the spread of a shallow, blotching, blundering, infectious "information", or rather deformation, everywhere, and to the teaching of catechisms and phrases at schools instead of human meanings) — there are masked words abroad, I say, which nobody understands, but which everybody uses, and most people will also fight for, live for, or even die for, fancying they mean this or that, or the other, of things dear to them: for such words wear chameleon cloaks — "ground-lion" cloaks, of the color of the ground of any man's fancy: on that ground they lie in wait, and rend him with a spring from it. There never were creatures of prey so mischievous, never diplomatists so cunning, never poisoners so deadly, as these masked words; they are the unjust stewards of all men's ideas: whatever fancy or favorite instinct a man most cherishes, he gives to his favorite masked word to take care of for him; the word at last comes to have an infinite power over him, — you cannot get at him but by its ministry.

And in languages so mongrel in breed as the English, there is a fatal power of equivocation put into men's hands, almost whether they will or no, in being able to use Greek or Latin words for an idea when they want it to be awful; and Saxon or otherwise common words when they want it to be vulgar. What a singular and salutary effect, for instance, would be produced on the minds of people who are in the habit of taking the Form of the "Word" they live by, for the Power of which that Word tells them, if we always either retained, or refused, the Greek form

"biblos", or "biblion", as the right expression for "book"
— instead of employing it only in the one instance in which
we wish to give dignity to the idea, and translating it into
English everywhere else.   How wholesome it would be for
many simple persons if, in such places (for instance) as
Acts xix. 19, we retained the Greek expression, instead of
translating it, and they had to read — "Many of them also
which used curious arts, brought their bibles together, and
burnt them before all men; and they counted the price of
them, and found it fifty thousand pieces of silver"!   Or if,
on the other hand, we translated where we retain it, and
always spoke of "the Holy Book", instead of "Holy
Bible", it might come into more heads than it does at
present, that the Word of God, by which the heavens were,
of old, and by which they are now kept in store, cannot be
made a present of to anybody in morocco binding, nor
sown on any wayside by help either of steam plough or
steam press; but is nevertheless being offered to us daily,
and by us with contumely refused; and sown in us daily,
and by us, as instantly as may be, choked.

So, again, consider what effect has been produced on the
English vulgar mind by the use of the sonorous Latin
form "damno", in translating the Greek κατακρίνω, when
people charitably wish to make it forcible; and the sub-
stitution of the temperate "condemn" for it, when they
choose to keep it gentle; and what notable sermons have
been preached by illiterate clergymen on — "He that
believeth not shall be damned"; though they would
shrink with horror from translating Heb. xi. 7, "The
saving of his house, by which he damned the world," or
John viii. 10–11, "Woman, hath no man damned thee?
She saith, No man, Lord.   Jesus answered her, Neither do
I damn thee: go, and sin no more."   And divisions in the
mind of Europe, which have cost seas of blood, and in the

defence of which the noblest souls of men have been cast
away in frantic desolation, countless as forest leaves, —
though, in the heart of them, founded on deeper causes, —
have nevertheless been rendered practically possible,
mainly, by the European adoption of the Greek word for a
public meeting, "ecclesia", to give peculiar respectability
to such meetings, when held for religious purposes; and
other collateral equivocations, such as the vulgar English
one of using the word "priest" as a contraction for
"presbyter."

Now, in order to deal with words rightly, this is the
habit you must form.   Nearly every word in your language
has been first a word of some other language — of Saxon,
German, French, Latin, or Greek (not to speak of Eastern
and primitive dialects).   And many words have been all
these; — that is to say, have been Greek first, Latin next,
French or German next, and English last: undergoing a
certain change of sense and use on the lips of each nation;
but retaining a deep vital meaning, which all good scholars
feel in employing them, even at this day.   If you do not
know the Greek alphabet, learn it; young or old — girl or
boy — whoever you may be, if you think of reading seriously (which, of course, implies that you have some leisure
at command), learn your Greek alphabet; then get good
dictionaries of all these languages, and whenever you are in
doubt about a word, hunt it down patiently.   Read Max
Müller's lectures thoroughly, to begin with; and, after
that, never let a word escape you that looks suspicious.   It
is severe work; but you will find it, even at first, interesting, and at last, endlessly amusing.   And the general
gain to your character, in power and precision, will be quite
incalculable.

As in the case of Lamb, to select one essay from the many by Robert Louis Stevenson is a troublesome task. Here is the spirit of Montaigne, inherited and strengthened; here is the gentleness and humor of Lamb, and a fanciful quality that can be traced to no one back of the writer himself. The one selection is here included by permission of Charles Scribner's Sons, the American publishers of all of Stevenson's works.

A COLLEGE MAGAZINE

By ROBERT LOUIS STEVENSON

I

ALL through my boyhood and youth, I was known and pointed out for the pattern of an idler; and yet I was always busy on my own private end, which was to learn to write. I kept always two books in my pocket, one to read, one to write in. As I walked, my mind was busy fitting what I saw with appropriate words; when I sat by the roadside, I would either read, or a pencil and a penny version-book would be in my hand, to note down the features of the scene or commemorate some halting stanzas. Thus I lived with words. And what I thus wrote was for no ulterior use, it was written consciously for practice. It was not so much that I wished to be an author (though I wished that too) as that I had vowed that I would learn to write. That was a proficiency that tempted me; and I practised to acquire it, as men learn to whittle, in a wager with myself. Description was the principal field of my exercise; for to any one with senses there is always something worth describing, and town and country are but one continuous subject. But I worked in other ways also; often accompanied my walks with dramatic dialogues, in which I played many parts; and often exercised myself in writing down conversations from memory.

This was all excellent, no doubt; so were the diaries I sometimes tried to keep, but always and very speedily discarded, finding them a school of posturing and melancholy self-deception. And yet this was not the most efficient part of my training. Good though it was, it only taught me (so far as I have learned them at all) the lower and less intellectual elements of the art, the choice of the essential note and the right word: things that to a happier constitution had perhaps come by nature. And regarded as training, it had one grave defect; for it set me no standard of achievement. So that there was perhaps more profit, as there was certainly more effort, in my secret labors at home. Whenever I read a book or a passage that particularly pleased me, in which a thing was said or an effect rendered with propriety, in which there was either some conspicuous force or some happy distinction in the style, I must sit down at once and set myself to ape that quality. I was unsuccessful, and I knew it; and tried again, and was again unsuccessful and always unsuccessful; but at least in these vain bouts, I got some practice in rhythm, in harmony, in construction, and in the co-ordination of parts. I have thus played the sedulous ape to Hazlitt, to Lamb, to Wordsworth, to Sir Thomas Browne, to Defoe, to Hawthorne, to Montaigne, to Baudelaire, and to Obermann. I remember one of these monkey tricks, which was called *The Vanity of Morals;* it was to have had a second part, *The Vanity of Knowledge;* and as I had neither morality nor scholarship, the names were apt; but the second part was never attempted, and the first part was written (which is my reason for recalling it, ghostlike, from its ashes) no less than three times: first in the manner of Hazlitt, second in the manner of Ruskin, who had cast on me a passing spell, and third, in a laborious pasticcio of Sir Thomas Browne. So with my other works: *Cain*, an epic, was (save the mark!) an imitation of *Sordello; Robin Hood*, a tale in verse, took an eclectic middle course among the fields of Keats, Chaucer, and Morris; in *Monmouth*, a tragedy, I reclined on the bosom of Mr. Swinburne; in my innumerable gouty-footed lyrics, I followed many masters; in the first draft of *The King's Pardon*, a tragedy, I was on the trail of no lesser man than John Webster; in the second draft of the same piece, with staggering versatility, I had shifted my allegiance to Congreve, and of course conceived my fable in a less serious vein — for it was not Congreve's verse, it was his exquisite prose, that I admired and sought to copy. Even at the age of thirteen I had tried to do justice to the inhabitants of the famous city of Peebles in the style of the *Book of Snobs*. So I might go on forever, through all my abortive novels, and down to my later plays, of which I think more tenderly, for they were not only conceived at first under the bracing influence of old Dumas, but have met with resurrections: one, strangely bettered by another hand, came on the stage itself and was played by bodily actors; the other, originally known as *Semiramis: A Tragedy*, I have observed on book-stalls under the *alias* of *Prince Otto*. But enough has been said to show by what arts of impersonation, and in what purely ventriloquial efforts I first saw my words on paper.

That, like it or not, is the way to learn to write; whether I have profited or not, that is the way. It was so Keats learned, and there was never a finer temperament for literature than Keats's; it was so, if we could trace it out, that all men have learned; and that is why a revival of letters is always accompanied or heralded by a cast back to earlier and fresher models.   Perhaps I hear some one cry out: But this is not the way to be original!   It is not; nor is there any way but to be born so.   Nor yet, if you are born original, is there anything in this training that shall clip the wings of your originality.   There can be none more original than Montaigne, neither could any be more unlike Cicero; yet no craftsman can fail to see how much the one must have tried in his time to imitate the other. Burns is the very type of a prime force in letters; he was of all men the most imitative.   Shakespeare himself, the imperial, proceeds directly from a school.   It is only from a school that we can expect to have good writers; it is almost invariably from a school that great writers, these lawless exceptions, issue.   Nor is there anything here that should astonish the considerate.   Before he can tell what cadences he truly prefers, the student should have tried all that are possible; before he can choose and preserve a fitting key of words, he should long have practised the literary scales; and it is only after years of such gymnastic that he can sit down at last, legions of words swarming to his call, dozens of turns of phrase simultaneously bidding for his choice, and he himself knowing what he wants to do and (within the narrow limit of a man's ability) able to do it.

And it is the great point of these imitations that there still shines beyond the student's reach his inimitable model. Let him try as he please, he is still sure of failure; and it is a very old and a very true saying that failure is the only high road to success.   I must have had some disposition to learn; for I clear-sightedly condemned my own perform- ances.   I liked doing them indeed; but when they were done, I could see they were rubbish.   In consequence, I very rarely showed them even to my friends; and such friends as I chose to be my confidants I must have chosen well, for they had the friendliness to be quite plain with me. "Padding," said one. Another wrote: "I cannot understand why you do lyrics so badly." No more could I! Thrice I put myself in the way of a more authoritative rebuff, by sending a paper to a magazine. These were returned; and I was not surprised nor even pained. If they had not been looked at, as (like all amateurs) I suspected was the case, there was no good in repeating the experiment; if they had been looked at — well, then I had not yet learned to write, and I must keep on learning and living. Lastly, I had a piece of good fortune, which is the occasion of this paper, and by which I was able to see my literature in print, and to measure experimentally how far I stood from the favor of the public.

II

THE Speculative Society is a body of some antiquity, and has counted among its members Scott, Brougham, Jeffery, Horner, Benjamin Constant, Robert Emmet, and many a legal and local celebrity besides. By an accident, variously explained, it has its rooms in the very buildings of the University of Edinburgh: a hall, Turkey-carpeted, hung with pictures, looking, when lighted up at night with fire and candle, like some goodly dining-room; a passage-like library, walled with books in their wire cages; and a corridor with a fireplace, benches, a table, many prints of famous members, and a mural tablet to the virtues of a former secretary. Here a member can warm himself and loaf and read; here, in defiance of Senatus-consults, he can smoke. The Senatus looks askance at these privileges; looks even with a somewhat vinegar aspect on the whole society; which argues a lack of proportion in the learned mind, for the world, we may be sure, will prize far higher this haunt of dead lions than all the living dogs of the professorate.

I sat one December morning in the library of the Speculative; a very humble-minded youth, though it was a virtue I never had much credit for; yet proud of my privileges as a member of the Spec.; proud of the pipe I was smoking in the teeth of the Senatus; and in particular, proud of being in the next room to three very distinguished students, who were then conversing beside the corridor fire. One of these has now his name on the back of several volumes, and his voice, I learn, is influential in the law courts. Of the death of the second, you have just been reading what I had to say. And the third also has escaped out of that battle of life in which he fought so hard, it may be so unwisely. They were all three, as I have said, notable students; but this was the most conspicuous. Wealthy, handsome, ambitious, adventurous, diplomatic, a reader of Balzac, and of all men that I have known, the most like to one of Balzac's characters, he led a life, and was attended by an ill fortune, that could be properly set forth only in the *Comédie Humaine*. He had then his eye on Parliament; and soon after the time of which I write, he made a showy speech at a political dinner, was cried up to heaven next day in the *Courant*, and the day after was dashed lower than earth with a charge of plagiarism in the *Scotsman*. Report would have it (I dare say, very wrongly) that he was betrayed by one in whom he particularly trusted, and that the author of the charge had learned its truth from his own lips. Thus, at least, he was up one day on a pinnacle, admired and envied by all; and the next, though still but a boy, he was publicly disgraced. The blow would have broken a less finely tempered spirit;

and even him I suppose it rendered reckless; for he took flight to London, and there, in a fast club, disposed of the bulk of his considerable patrimony in the space of one winter. For years thereafter he lived I know not how; always well dressed, always in good hotels and good society, always with empty pockets. The charm of his manner may have stood him in good stead; but though my own manners are very agreeable, I have never found in them a source of livelihood; and to explain the miracle of his continued existence, I must fall back upon the theory of the philosopher, that in his case, as in all of the same kind, "there was a suffering relative in the background." From this genteel eclipse he reappeared upon the scene, and presently sought me out in the character of a generous editor. It is in this part that I best remember him; tall, slender, with a not ungraceful stoop; looking quite like a refined gentleman, and quite like an urbane adventurer; smiling with an engaging ambiguity; cocking at you one peaked eyebrow with a great appearance of finesse; speaking low and sweet and thick, with a touch of burr; telling strange tales with singular deliberation and, to a patient listener, excellent effect. After all these ups and downs, he seemed still, like the rich student that he was of yore, to breathe of money; seemed still perfectly sure of himself and certain of his end. Yet he was then upon the brink of his last overthrow. He had set himself to found the strangest thing in our society : one of those periodical sheets from which men suppose themselves to learn opinions; in which young gentlemen from the universities are encouraged, at so much a line, to garble facts, insult foreign nations, and calumniate private individuals; and which are now the source of glory, so that if a man's name be often enough printed there, he becomes a kind of demigod; and people will pardon him when he talks back and forth, as they do for Mr. Gladstone; and crowd him to suffocation on railway platforms, as they did the other day to General Boulanger; and buy his literary works, as I hope you have just done for me. Our fathers, when they were upon some great enterprise, would sacrifice a life; building, it may be, a favorite slave into the foundations of their palace. It was with his own life that my companion disarmed the envy of the gods. He fought his paper single-handed; trusting no one, for he was something of a cynic; up early and down late, for he was nothing of a sluggard; daily ear-wigging influential men, for he was a master of ingratiation. In that slender and silken fellow there must have been a rare vein of courage, that he should thus have died at his employment; and doubtless ambition spoke loudly in his ear, and doubtless love also, for it seems there was a marriage in his view had he succeeded. But he died, and his paper died after him; and of all this grace, and tact, and courage, it must seem to our blind eyes as if there had come literally nothing.

These three students sat, as I was saying, in the corridor, under the mural tablet that records the virtues of Macbean, the former secretary. We would often smile at that ineloquent memorial, and thought it a poor thing to come into the world at all and leave no more behind one than Macbean. And yet of these three, two are gone and have left less; and this book, perhaps, when it is old and foxy, and some one picks it up in a corner of a book-shop, and glances through it, smiling at the old, graceless turns of speech, and perhaps for the love of *Alma Mater* (which may be still extant and flourishing) buys it, not without haggling, for some pence — this book may alone preserve a memory of James Walter Ferrier and Robert Glasgow Brown.

Their thoughts ran very differently on that December

morning; they were all on fire with ambition; and when
they had called me in to them, and made me a sharer in
their design, I too became drunken with pride and hope.
We were to found a University magazine. A pair of little,
active brothers — Livingstone by name, great skippers on
the foot, great rubbers of the hands, who kept a book-
shop over against the University building — had been
debauched to play the part of publishers. We four were
to be conjunct editors and, what was the main point of the
concern, to print our own works; while, by every rule of
arithmetic — that flatterer of credulity — the adventure
must succeed and bring great profit. Well, well: it was a
bright vision. I went home that morning walking upon air.
To have been chosen by these three distinguished students
was to me the most unspeakable advance; it was my first
draught of consideration; it reconciled me to myself and to
my fellowmen; and as I steered round the railings at the
Tron, I could not withhold my lips from smiling publicly.
Yet, in the bottom of my heart, I knew that magazine
would be a grim fiasco; I knew it would not be worth
reading; I knew, even if it were, that nobody would read
it; and I kept wondering how I should be able, upon my
compact income of twelve pounds per annum, payable
monthly, to meet my share in the expense. It was a
comfortable thought to me that I had a father.

The magazine appeared, in a yellow cover which was the
best part of it, for at least it was unassuming; it ran four
months in undisturbed obscurity, and died without a gasp.
The first number was edited by all four of us with prodigious bustle; the second fell principally into the hands
of Ferrier and me; the third I edited alone; and it has
long been a solemn question who it was that edited the
fourth. It would perhaps be still more difficult to say who
read it. Poor yellow sheet, that looked so hopefully in the

Livingstones' window! Poor, harmless paper, that might have gone to print a *Shakespeare* on, and was instead so clumsily defaced with nonsense! And, shall I say, Poor Editors? I cannot pity myself, to whom it was all pure gain. It was no news to me, but only the wholesome confirmation of my judgment, when the magazine struggled into half-birth, and instantly sickened and subsided into night. I had sent a copy to the lady with whom my heart was at that time somewhat engaged, and who did all that in her lay to break it; and she, with some tact, passed over the gift and my cherished contributions in silence. I will not say that I was pleased at this; but I will tell her now, if by any chance she takes up the work of her former servant, that I thought the better of her taste. I cleared the decks after this lost engagement; had the necessary interview with my father, which passed off not amiss; paid over my share of the expense to the two little, active brothers, who rubbed their hands as much, but methought skipped rather less than formerly, having perhaps, these two also, embarked upon the enterprise with some graceful illusions; and then, reviewing the whole episode, I told myself that the time was not yet ripe, nor the man ready; and to work I went again with my penny version-books, having fallen back in one day from the printed author to the manuscript student.

Three essays by living English essayists follow. "The Whole Duty of Woman", by Sir Edmund Gosse, reprinted here by permission from his book entitled "The Realm", suggests a pleasant fashion of essaying; for he has taken a book that represents a social standard of another period, and built what might otherwise have been a mere book review into a comparison of certain manners of today and yesterday. "On Lying in Bed" is reprinted here from "Tremendous Trifles", by Gilbert K. Chesterton, by arrangement with his publishers, Dodd, Mead & Co. There is an embarrassment of riches in Chesterton's works, and through them all one finds certain literary mannerisms peculiarly his own which give vividness and personality to his ideas. "A Relic" by Max Beerbohm, artist and essayist — humorist with brush and pen, — is reprinted from his book "And Even Now" by permission of E. P. Dutton & Co.

THE WHOLE DUTY OF WOMAN

By Edmund Gosse

It is universally conceded that our great-grandmothers were women of the most precise life and austere manners. The girls nowadays display a shocking freedom; but they were partly led into it by the relative laxity of their mothers, who, in their turn, gave great anxiety to a still earlier generation. To hear all the "Ahs" and the "Well, I nevers" of the middle-aged, one would fancy that propriety of conduct was a thing of the past, and that never had there been a "gaggle of girls" (the phrase belongs to Dame Juliana Berners) so wanton and rebellious as the race of 1895.   Still, there must be a fallacy somewhere.   If each generation is decidedly wilder, more independent, more revolting, and more insolent than the one before, how exceedingly good people must have been four or five generations ago !   Outside the pages of the people so sweetly advertised as "sexual female fictionists", the girls of to-day do not strike one as extremely bad.   Some of them are quite nice ; the average is not very low.   How lofty, then, must have been the standard one hundred years ago, to make room for such a steady decline ever since !   Poor J. K. S. wrote : —

> "If all the harm that's been done by men
>   Were doubled and doubled and doubled again,
>   And melted and fused into vapour, and then
>   Were squared and raised to the power of ten,
>   There wouldn't be nearly enough, not near,
>   To keep a small girl for a tenth of a year."

This is the view of a cynic.   To the ordinary observer, the "revolting daughters", of whom we hear so much, do not revolt nearly enough to differentiate them duly from their virtuous great-grandmothers.

We fear that there was still a good deal of human nature in girls a hundred, or even two hundred, years ago. That eloquent and animated writer, the author of *The Whole Duty of Man*, published in the reign of Charles II, a volume which, if he had had the courage of his opinions, he would have named *The Whole Duty of Woman*.   Under the tamer title of *The Ladies' Calling* it achieved a great success.   In the frontispiece to this work a doleful dame, seated on what seems to be a bare altar in an open landscape, is raising one hand to grasp a crown dangled out of her reach in the clouds, and in the other, with an air of great affectation is lifting her skirt between finger and thumb. A purse, a coronet, a fan, a mirror, rings, dice, coins, and other useful articles lie strewn at her naked feet; she spurns them, and lifts her streaming eyes to heaven. This is the sort of picture which does its best to prevent the reader from opening the book; but *The Ladies' Calling*, nevertheless, is well worth reading. It excites in us a curious wish to know more exactly what manner of women it was addressed to. How did the great-grandmothers of our great-grandmothers behave? When we come to think of it, how little we know about them!

The customary source of information is the play-book of the time. There, indeed, we come across some choice indications of ancient women's behaviour. Nor did the women spare one another. The woman dramatists out-did the men in attacking the manners of their sex, and what is perhaps the most cynical comedy in all literature was written by a woman. It will be some time before the Corinnas of *The Yellow Book* contrive to surpass *The Town Fop* in outrageous frankness. Our ideas of the fashions of the seventeenth century are, however, taken too exclusively, if they are taken from these plays alone. We conceive every fine lady to be like Lady Brute, in *The Provok'd Wife*, who wakes about two o'clock in the after-noon, is "trailed" to her great chair for tea, leaves her bedroom only to descend to dinner, spends the night with a box and dice, and does not go to bed until the dawn. Comedy has always forced the note, and is a very unsafe (though picturesque) guide to historic manners. Perhaps we obtain a juster notion from the gallant pamphlets of the age, such as *The Lover's Watch* and *The Lady's Look-ing-Glass;* yet these were purely intended for people who we should nowadays call "smart", readers who hung about the outskirts of the Court.

For materials, then, out of which to construct a portrait

of the ordinary woman of the world in the reign of Charles
II, we are glad to come back to our anonymous divine.
His is the best-kept secret in English literature. In spite
of the immense success of *The Whole Duty of Man*, no
one has done more than conjecture, more or less vaguely,
who he may have been. He wrote at least five works
besides his most famous treatise, and in preparing each of
these for the press he took more pains than Junius did a
century later to conceal his identity. The publisher
of *The Ladies' Calling*, for example, assures us that he
knows no more than we do.   The MS. came to him from
an unknown source and in a strange handwriting, "as
from the Clouds dropt into my hands."   The anonymous
author made no attempt to see proofs of it, nor claimed
his foundling in any way whatever. In his *English Prose
Selections*, the recent third volume of which covers the
ground we are dealing with, Mr. Craik, although finding
room for such wretched writers as Bishop Cumberland and
William Sherlock, makes no mention of the author of *The
Whole Duty*. That is a curious oversight. There was no
divine of the age who wielded a more graceful pen.   Only
the exigencies of our space restrain us from quoting the
noble praise of the Woman-Confessor in the preface to
The Ladies' Calling. It begins "Queens and Empresses
knew then no title so glorious"; and the reader who is
curious in such matters will refer to it for himself.

The women of this time troubled our author by their
loudness of speech.   There seems some reason to believe
that with the Restoration, and in opposition to the affected
whispering of the Puritans, a truculent and noisy manner
became the fashion among Englishwomen. This was,
perhaps, the "barbarous dissonance" that Milton depre-
cated; it is, at all events, so distasteful to the writer of
The Ladies' Calling that he gives it an early prominence

in his exhortation. "A woman's tongue," he says, "should be like the imaginary music of the spheres, sweet and charming, but not to be heard at distance." *Modesty*, indeed, he inculcates as the first ornament of womanhood, and he intimates that there was much neglect of it in his day. We might fancy it to be Mrs. Lynn Linton speaking when, with uplifted hands, he cries, "Would God that they would take, in exchange for that virile Boldness, which is now too common among many even of the best Rank," such a solidity and firmness of mind as will permit them to succeed in — keeping a secret! Odd to hear a grave and polite divine urging the ladies of his congregation not to "adorn" their conversation with oaths and imprecations, of which he says, with not less truth than gallantry, that "out of a woman's mouth there is on this side Hell no noise that can be more amazingly odious." The revolting daughters of to-day do not curse and swear; at all events, they do not swear in print, where only we have met the shrews. On the other hand, they smoke, a contingency which does not seem to have occurred to the author of *The Ladies' Calling*, who nowhere warns the sisterhood against tobacco. The gravity of his indictment of excess in wine, not less than the evidence of such observers as Pepys, proves to us that drunkenness was by no means rare even among women of quality.

There never, we suppose, from the beginning of the world was a man-preacher who did not warn the women of his congregation against the vanity of fair raiment. The author of *The Ladies' Calling* is no exception; but he does his spiriting in a gentlemanlike way. The ladies came to listen to him bedizened with jewels, with all the objects which lie strewn at the feet of his penitent in the frontispiece. He does not scream to them to rend them off. He only remonstrates at their costliness. In that

perfectly charming record of a child's mind, the Memoir
of Marjorie Fleming, the delicious little wiseacre records
the fact that her father and mother have given a guinea
for a pineapple, remarking that that money would have
sustained a poor family during the entire winter. We are
reminded of that when our divine tells his auditors that
"any one of the baubles, the loosest appendage of the
dress, a fan, a busk, perhaps a black patch, bears a price
that would warm the empty bowels of a poor starving
wretch." This was long before the days of very elaborate
and expensive patches, which were still so new in Pepys's
days that he remarked on those of Mr. Penn's pretty sister
when he saw her in the new coach, "patched and very
fine." Our preacher is no ranter, nor does he shut the
door of mercy on entertainments; all he deprecates is their
excess. His penitents are not forbidden to spend an afternoon at the theatre, or an evening in dancing or at cards;
but they are desired to remember that, delightful as these
occupations are, devotion is more delightful still.

The attitude of the author to gaming is curious. "I
question not the lawfulness of this recreation," he says
distinctly; but he desires his ladies not to make cards the
business of their life, and especially not to play on Sundays. It appears that some great ladies, in the emptiness
of their heads and hearts, took advantage of the high
pews then always found in churches to play ombre or
quadrille under the very nose of the preacher. This conduct must have been rare; the legends of the age prove
that it was not unknown. The game might be concealed
from every one if it was desisted from at the moment of
the sermon, and in many cases the clergyman was a pitiful,
obsequious wretch who knew better than to find fault with
the gentlefolks "up at the house." It was not often that
a convenient flash of lightning came in the middle of

service to kill the impious gamester in his pew, as happened, to the immense scandal and solemnization of everybody, at Withycombe, in Devonshire.

On the whole, it is amusing to find that the same faults and the same dangers which occupy our satirists to-day were pronounced imminent for women two hundred years ago. The ladies of Charles II's reign were a little coarser, a little primmer, a good deal more ignorant than those of our age. Their manners were on great occasions much better, and on small occasions much worse, than those of their descendants of 1895; but the same human nature prevailed. The author of *The Ladies' Calling* considered that the greatest danger of his congregation lay in the fact that "the female Sex is eminent for its pungency in the sensible passion of love"; and, although we take other modes of saying it, that is true now.

ON LYING IN BED

From *Tremendous Trifles* by Gilbert K. Chesterton

Lying in bed would be an altogether perfect and supreme experience if only one had a coloured pencil long enough to draw on the ceiling. This, however, is not generally a part of the domestic apparatus on the premises. I think myself that the thing might be managed with several pails of Aspinall and a broom. Only if one worked in a really sweeping and masterly way, and laid on the colour in great washes, it might drip down again on one's face in floods of rich and mingled colour like some strange fairy rain; and that would have its disadvantages. I am afraid it would be necessary to stick to black and white in this form of artistic composition. To that purpose, indeed, the white ceiling would be of the greatest possible use; in fact it is the only use I think of a white ceiling being put to.

But for the beautiful experiment of lying in bed I might never have discovered it. For years I have been looking for some blank spaces in a modern house to draw on. Paper is much too small for any really allegorical design; as Cyrano de Bergerac says: "Il me faut des geants." But when I tried to find these fine clear spaces in the modern rooms such as we all live in I was continually disappointed. I found an endless pattern and complication of small objects hung like a curtain of fine links between me and my desire. I examined the walls; I found them to my surprise to be already covered with wall-paper, and I found the wall-paper to be covered with very uninteresting images, all bearing a ridiculous resemblance to each other. I could not understand why one arbitrary symbol (a symbol apparently entirely devoid of any religious or philosophical significance) should thus be sprinkled all over my nice walls like a sort of small-pox. The Bible must be referring to wall-papers, I think, when it says, "Use not vain repetitions, as the Gentiles do." I found the Turkey carpet a mass of unmeaning colours, rather like the Turkish Empire, or like the sweetmeat called Turkish Delight. I do not exactly know what Turkish Delight really is; but I suppose it is Macedonian Massacres. Everywhere that I went forlornly, with my pencil or my paint brush, I found that others had unaccountably been before me, spoiling the walls, the curtains, and the furniture with their childish and barbaric designs.

.   .   .   .

Nowhere did I find a really clear space for sketching until this occasion when I prolonged beyond the proper limit the process of lying on my back in bed. Then the light of that white heaven broke upon my vision, that breadth of mere white which is indeed almost the definition of Paradise, since it means purity and also means freedom. But alas! like all heavens, now that it is seen it is found to be unattainable; it looks more austere and more distant than the blue sky outside the window. For my proposal to paint on it with the bristly end of a broom has been discouraged — never mind by whom; by a person debarred from all political rights — and even my minor proposal to put the other end of the broom into the kitchen fire and turn it into charcoal has not been conceded. Yet I am certain that it was from persons in my position that all the original inspiration came for covering the ceilings of palaces and cathedrals with a riot of fallen angels or victorious gods. I am sure that it was only because Michael Angelo was engaged in the ancient and honourable occupation of lying in bed that he ever realised how the roof of the Sistine Chapel might be made into an awful imitation of a divine drama that could be enacted in the heavens.

The tone now commonly taken towards the practice of lying in bed is hypocritical and unhealthy. Of all the marks of modernity that seem to mean a kind of decadence, there is none more menacing and dangerous than the exaltation of very small and secondary matters of conduct at the expense of very great and primary ones, at the expense of eternal public and tragic human morality. If there is one thing worse than the modern weakening of major morals it is the modern strengthening of minor morals. Thus it is considered more withering to accuse a man of bad taste than of bad ethics. Cleanliness is not next to godliness nowadays, for cleanliness is made an essential and godliness is regarded as an offence. A playwright can attack the institution of marriage so long as he does not misrepresent the manners of society, and I have met Ibsenite pessimists who thought it wrong to take beer but right to take prussic acid.   Especially this is so in matters of hygiene; notably such matters as lying in bed.   Instead of being regarded, as it ought to be, as a matter of personal convenience and adjustment, it has come to be regarded by many as if it were a part of essential morals to get up early in the morning.   It is upon the whole a part of practical wisdom; but there is nothing good about it or bad about its opposite.

.   .   .   .

Misers get up early in the morning; and burglars, I am informed, get up the night before.   It is the great peril of our society that all its mechanism may grow more fixed while its spirit grows more fickle.   A man's minor actions and arrangements ought to be free, flexible, creative; the things that should be unchangeable are his principles, his ideals.   But with us the reverse is true; our views change constantly; but our lunch does not change.   Now, I should like men to have strong and rooted conceptions, but as for their lunch, let them have it sometimes in the garden, sometimes in bed, sometimes on the roof, sometimes in the top of a tree.   Let them argue from the same first principles, but let them do it in bed, or a boat, or a balloon.   This alarming growth of good habits really means a too great emphasis on those virtues which mere custom can misuse, it means too little emphasis on those virtues which custom can never quite ensure, sudden and splendid virtues of inspired pity or of inspired candour.   If ever that abrupt appeal is made to us we may fail.   A man can get used to getting up at 5 o'clock in the morning.   A man cannot very well get used to being burnt for his opinions; the first experiment is commonly fatal.   Let us pay a little more attention to these possibilities of the heroic and the unexpected.   I daresay that when I get out of this bed I shall do some deed of an almost terrible virtue.

For those who study the great art of lying in bed there is one emphatic caution to be added. Even for those who can do their work in bed (like journalists), still more for those whose work cannot be done in bed (as, for example, the professional harpooner of whales), it is obvious that the indulgence must be very occasional. But that is not the caution I mean. The caution is this: if you do lie in bed, be sure you do it without any reason or justification at all. I do not speak, of course, of the seriously sick. But if a healthy man lies in bed, let him do it without a rag of excuse; then he will get up a healthy man. If he does it for some secondary hygienic reason, if he has some scientific explanation, he may get up a hypochondriac.

A RELIC

By Max Beerbohm

YESTERDAY I found in a cupboard an old, small, battered portmanteau which, by the initials on it, I recognised as my own property. The lock appeared to have been forced. I dimly remembered having forced it myself, with a poker, in my hot youth, after some journey in which I had lost the key; and this act of violence was probably the reason why the trunk had so long ago ceased to travel. I unstrapped it, not without dust; it exhaled the faint scent of its long closure; it contained a tweed suit of Late Victorian pattern, some bills, some letters, a collar-stud, and — something which, after I had wondered for a moment or two what on earth it was, caused me suddenly to murmur, 'Down below, the sea rustled to and fro over the shingle.'

Strange that these words had, year after long year,

been existing in some obscure cell at the back of my brain !
— forgotten but all the while existing, like the trunk in
that cupboard. What released them, what threw open
the cell door, was nothing but the fragment of a fan ; just
the butt-end of an inexpensive fan. The sticks are of
white bone, clipped together with a semicircular ring that
is not silver. They are neatly oval at the base, but variously jagged at the other end. The longest of them
measures perhaps two inches. Ring and all, they have
no market value ; for a farthing is the least coin in our
currency. And yet, though I had so long forgotten them,
for me they are not worthless. They touch a chord. . . .
Lest this confession raise false hopes in the reader, I add
that I did not know their owner.

I did once see her, and in Normandy, and by moonlight,
and her name was Angélique. She was graceful, she was
even beautiful. I was but nineteen years old. Yet even
so I cannot say that she impressed me favourably. I was
seated at a table of a café on the terrace of a casino. I sat
facing the sea, with my back to the casino. I sat listening
to the quiet sea, which I had crossed that morning. The
hour was late, there were few people about. I heard the
swing-door behind me flap open, and was aware of a sharp
snapping and crackling sound as a lady in white passed
quickly by me. I stared at her erect thin back and her
agitated elbows. A short fat man passed in pursuit of
her — an elderly man in a black alpaca jacket that billowed.
I saw that she had left a trail of little white things on the
asphalt. I watched the efforts of the agonised short fat
man to overtake her as she swept wraithlike away to the
distant end of the terrace. What was the matter ? What
had made her so spectacularly angry with him ? The
three or four waiters of the café were exchanging cynical
smiles and shrugs, as waiters will. I tried to feel cynical,

but was thrilled with excitement, with wonder and curiosity. The woman out yonder had doubled on her tracks. She had not slackened her furious speed, but the man waddlingly contrived to keep pace with her now. With every moment they became more distinct, and the prospect that they would presently pass by me, back into the casino, gave me that physical tension which one feels on a wayside platform at the imminent passing of an express. In the rushingly enlarged vision I had of them, the wrath on the woman's face was even more saliently the main thing than I had supposed it would be. That very hard Parisian face must have been as white as the powder that coated it. 'Écoute, Angélique,' gasped the perspiring bourgeois, 'écoute, je te supplie —' The swing-door received them and was left swinging to and fro. I wanted to follow, but had not paid for my bock. I beckoned my waiter. On his way to me he stooped down and picked up something which, with a smile and a shrug, he laid on my table: 'Il semble que Mademoiselle ne s'en servira plus.' This is the thing I now write of, and at sight of it I understood why there had been that snapping and crackling, and what the white fragments on the ground were.

I hurried through the rooms, hoping to see a continuation of that drama — a scene of appeasement, perhaps, or of fury still implacable. But the two oddly-assorted players were not performing there. My waiter had told me he had not seen either of them before. I suppose they had arrived that day. But I was not destined to see either of them again. They went away, I suppose, next morning; jointly or singly; singly, I imagine.

They made, however, a prolonged stay in my young memory, and would have done so even had I not had that tangible memento of them. Who were they, those two of whom that one strange glimpse had befallen me? What,

I wondered, was the previous history of each? What, in particular, had all that tragic pother been about? Mlle. Angélique I guessed to be thirty years old, her friend perhaps fifty-five. Each of their faces was as clear to me as in the moment of actual vision — the man's fat shiny bewildered face; the taut white face of the woman, the hard red line of her mouth, the eyes that were not flashing, but positively dull, with rage. I presumed that the fan had been a present from him, and a recent present — bought perhaps that very day, after their arrival in the town. But what, *what* had he done that she should break it between her hands, scattering the splinters as who should sow dragon's teeth? I could not believe he had done anything much amiss. I imagined her grievance a trivial one. But this did not make the case less engrossing. Again and again I would take the fan-stump from my pocket, examining it on the palm of my hand, or between finger and thumb, hoping to read the mystery it had been mixed up in, so that I might reveal that mystery to the world. To the world, yes; nothing less than that. I was determined to make a story of what I had seen — a *conte* in the manner of great Guy de Maupassant. Now and again, in the course of the past year or so, it had occurred to me that I might be a writer. But I had not felt the impulse to sit down and write something. I did feel that impulse now. It would indeed have been an irresistible impulse if I had known just what to write.

I felt I might know at any moment, and had but to give my mind to it. Maupassant was an impeccable artist, but I think the secret of the hold he had on the young men of my day was not so much that we discerned his cunning as that we delighted in the simplicity which his cunning achieved. I had read a great number of his short stories, but none that had made me feel as though I, if I were a writer, mightn't have written it myself. Maupassant had an European reputation. It was pleasing, it was soothing and gratifying, to feel that one could at any time win an equal fame if one chose to set pen to paper. And now, suddenly, the spring had been touched in me, the time was come. I was grateful for the fluke by which I had witnessed on the terrace that evocative scene. I looked forward to reading the MS. of 'The Fan' — to-morrow, at latest. I was not wildly ambitious. I was not inordinately vain. I knew I couldn't ever, with the best will in the world, write like Mr. George Meredith. Those wondrous works of his, seething with wit, with poetry and philosophy and what not, never had beguiled me with the sense that I might do something similar. I had full consciousness of not being a philosopher, of not being a poet, and of not being a wit. Well, Maupassant was none of these things. He was just an observer like me. Of course he was a good deal older than I, and had observed a good deal more. But it seemed to me that he was not my superior in knowledge of life. I knew all about life through *him*.

Dimly, the initial paragraph of my tale floated in my mind. I — not exactly I myself, but rather that impersonal *je* familiar to me through Maupassant — was to be sitting at that table, with a bock before me, just as I *had* sat. Four or five short sentences would give the whole scene. One of these I had quite definitely composed. You have already heard it. 'Down below, the sea rustled to and fro over the shingle.'

These words, which pleased me much, were to do double duty. They were to recur. They were to be, by a fine stroke, the very last words of my tale, their tranquility striking a sharp ironic contrast with the stress of what had just been narrated. I had, you see, advanced further in the form of my tale than in the substance. But even the form was as yet vague. What, exactly, was to happen after Mlle. Angélique and M. Joumand (as I provisionally called him) had rushed back past me into the casino? It was clear that I must hear the whole inner history from the lips of one or the other of them. Which? Should M. Joumand stagger out on to the terrace, sit down heavily at the table next to mine, bury his head in his hands, and presently, in broken words, blurt out to me all that might be of interest? . . .

'"And I tell you I gave up everything for her — everything." He stared at me with his old hopeless eyes. "She is more than the fiend I have described to you. Yet I swear to you, monsieur, that if I had anything left to give, it should be hers."

'Down below, the sea rustled to and fro over the shingle.'

Or should the lady herself be my informant? For a while, I rather leaned to this alternative. It was more exciting, it seemed to make the writer more signally a man of the world. On the other hand, it was less simple to manage. Wronged persons might be ever so communicative, but I surmised that persons in the wrong were reticent. Mlle. Angélique, therefore, would have to be modified by me in appearance and behaviour, toned down, touched up; and poor M. Joumand must look like a man of whom one could believe anything. . . .

'She ceased speaking. She gazed down at the fragments of her fan, and then, as though finding in them an image of her own life, whispered, "To think what I once was, monsieur! — what, but for him, I might be, even now!" She buried her face in her hands, then stared out into the night. Suddenly she uttered a short, harsh laugh.

'Down below, the sea rustled to and fro over the shingle.'

I decided that I must choose the first of these two ways.

It was the less chivalrous as well as the less lurid way, but
clearly it was the more artistic as well as the easier.   The
'chose vue,' the 'tranche de la vie' — this was the thing
to aim at.   Honesty was the best policy.   I must be
nothing if not merciless.   Maupassant was nothing if not
merciless.   He would not have spared Mlle. Angélique.
Besides, why should I libel M. Joumand?   Poor — no,
not *poor* M. Joumand!   I warned myself against pitying
him.   One touch of 'sentimentality,' and I should be lost.
M. Joumand was ridiculous.   I must keep him so.   But —
what was his position in life?   Was he a lawyer perhaps?
— or the proprietor of a shop in the Rue de Rivoli?   I
toyed with the possibility that he kept a fan shop — that
˙he business had once been a prosperous one, but had gone
down, down, because of his infatuation for this woman to
whom he was always giving fans — which she *always*
smashed. . . .   '"Ah monsieur, cruel and ungrateful to
me though she is, I swear to you that if I had anything
left to give, it should be hers; but," he stared at me with
his old hopeless eyes, "the fan she broke tonight was the
last — the last, monsieur — of my stock."   Down below,'
— but I pulled myself together, and asked pardon of my
Muse.

   It may be that I had offended her by my fooling.   Or
it may be that she had a sisterly desire to shield Mlle.
Angélique from my mordant art.   Or it may be that she
was bent on saving M. de Maupassant from a dangerous
rivalry.   Anyway, she withheld from me the inspiration
I had so confidently solicited.   I *could not* think what had
led up to that scene on the terrace.   I tried hard and
soberly.   I turned the 'chose vue' over and over in my
mind, day by day, and the fan-stump over and over in
my hand.   But the 'chose à figurer' — what, oh what,
was that?   Nightly I revisited the café, and sat there with

an open mind — a mind wide-open to catch the idea that
should drop into it like a ripe golden plum. The plum
did not ripen. The mind remained wide-open for a week
or more, but nothing except that phrase about the sea
rustled to and fro in it. A full quarter of a century has
gone by. M. Joumand's death, so far too fat was he all
those years ago, may be presumed. A temper so violent
as Mlle. Angélique's must surely have brought its owner
to the grave, long since. But here, all unchanged, the
stump of her fan is; and once more I turn it over and over
in my hand, not learning its secret — no, nor even trying
to, now. The chord this relic strikes in me is not one of
curiosity as to that old quarrel, but (if you will forgive me)
one of tenderness for my first effort to write, and for my
first hopes of excellence.

This essay, published originally in the Atlantic Monthly *and* Atlantic Classics, *was the germ from which grew Mr. Schauffler's musical romance, "Fiddler's Luck", published by Houghton Mifflin and Company in 1920, and reprinted here by permission of the author. Just as there are many instances of a short story expanding later into a novel, so this is only one of many instances of an essay which has first served to suggest a writer's philosophy or vagrant fancy, and has later been expanded into a book.*

FIDDLERS ERRANT

By Robert Haven Schauffler

I

MUSICAL adventures largely depend on your instrument. Go traveling with a bassoon or clarionet packed in your trunk, and romance will pass you by. But far otherwise will events shape themselves if you set forth with a fiddle.

The moment I turned my back upon the humdrum flute and embraced the 'cello, that instrument of romance, things began happening thick and fast in a hitherto uneventful life. I found that to sally forth with your 'cello couchant under your arm, like a lance of the days of chivalry, was to invite adventure. You tempted Providence to make things interesting for you, up to the moment when you returned home and stood your fat, melodious friend in the corner on his one leg — like the stork, that other purveyor of joyful surprises.

One reason why the 'cellist is particularly liable to meet with musical adventures is because the nature of his talent is so plainly visible. The parcel under his arm labels him FIDDLER in larger scare-caps than Mr. Hearst ever invented for headlines. It is seen of all men. There is no concealment possible. For it would, indeed, be less practicable to hide your 'cello under a bushel than to hide a bushel under your 'cello.

The non-reducible obesity of this instrument is apt to bring you adventures of all sorts: wrathful sometimes, when urchins recognize it as a heaven-sent target for snowballs; or when adults audibly quote Dean Swift's asinine remark, 'He was a fiddler and therefore a rogue.' Absurd, sometimes, as when the ticket-chopper in the subway bars your path under the misapprehension that you are carrying a double-bass; and when the small boys at the exit offer you a *Saturday Evening Post* in return for 'a tune on that there banjo.' But more often the episodes are pleasant, as when your bulky trademark enables some kindred spirit to recognize you as his predestined companion on impromptu adventures in music.

I was at first almost painfully aware of my 'cello's conspicuousness because I had abandoned for it an instrument so retiring by nature that you might carry it till death in your side pocket, yet never have it contribute an unusual episode to your career. But from the moment when I discovered the exaggerated old fiddle in the attic, slumbering in its black coffin, and wondered what it was all about, and brought it resurrection and life, — events began. I have never known exactly what was the magic inherent in the dull, guttural, discouraged protests of the strings which I experimentally plucked that day. But their songs-without-words-or-music seemed to me pregnant with promises of beauty and romance far beyond the ken of the forthright flute. So then and there I decided to embark upon the delicate and dangerous enterprise of learning another instrument.

It was indeed delicate and dangerous because it had to be prosecuted as secretly as sketching hostile fortifications. Father must not suspect. I feared that if he heard the demonic groans of a G string in pain, or the ghoulish whimperings of a manhandled A, he would mount to the attic, throw back his head, look down upon me through those lower crescents of his spectacles which always made him look a trifle unsympathetic, and pronounce that baleful formula: 'My son, come into my study!' For I knew he labored under the delusion that I already 'blew in' too much time on the flute, away from the companionship of All Gaul, *enteuthen exelaunei*, and Q. E. D. As for any additional instrument, I feared that he would reduce it to a pulp at sight, and me too.

My first secret step was to secure a long strip of paper to be pasted on the finger-board under the strings. It was all pockmarked with black dots and letters, so that if the music told you to play the note G, all you had to do was to contort your neck properly and remove your left hand from the path of vision, then gaze cross-eyed and upside down at the finger-board until you discovered the particular dot labeled G. The next move was to clap your fingertip upon that dot and straighten out your neck and eyes and apply the bow. Then out would come a triumphant G, — that is, provided your fingers had not already rubbed G's characteristically undershot lip so much as to erase away the letter's individuality. In that case, to be sure, all your striving for G might result only in C after all.

It was fascinating work, though. And every afternoon as the hour of four, and father's 'constitutional', ap-

proached, I would 'get set' like a sprinter on my mark
in the upper hall. The moment the front door closed
definitely behind my parent I would dash for the attic and
commence my cervical and ocular contortions. It was
dangerous, too. For it was so hard to stop betimes that
one evening father made my blood run cold by inquiring,
'What were you moaning about upstairs before dinner?'
I fear that I attributed these sounds to travail in Latin
scholarship, and an alleged sympathy for the struggles
of the dying Gaul.

The paper finger-board was so efficacious that in a week
I felt ready to taste the first fruits of toil. So I insinuated
a pair of musical friends into the house one afternoon, to
try an easy trio. They were a brother and sister who
played violin and piano. Things went so brilliantly that
we resolved on a public performance within a few days, at
the South High School. Alas, if I had only taken the
supposed rapidity of my progress with a grain of attic salt!
But my only solicitude was over the problem how to
smuggle the too conspicuous instrument to school, on
the morning of the concert, without the knowledge of a
vigilant father. We decided at last that any such attempt
would be suicidal rashness. So I borrowed another
boy's father's 'cello, and, in default of the printed strip,
I penciled under the strings notes of the whereabouts of
G, C, and so forth, making G shoot out the lip with
extra decision.

Our public performance was a *succès fou*, — that is,
it was a *succès* up to a certain point, and *fou* beyond it,
when one disaster followed another. My fingers played
so hard as to rub out G's lower lip. They quite obliterated
A, turned E into F, and B into a fair imitation of D.
These involuntary revisions led me to introduce the very
boldest modern harmonies into one of the most naïvely

traditional strains of Cornelius Gurlitt. Now, in the practice of the art of music one never with impunity pours new harmonic wine into old bottles. The thing is simply not done.

Perhaps, though, we might have muddled through somehow, had not my violinist friend, during a rest, poked me cruelly in the ribs with his bow and remarked in a coarse stage whisper, 'Look who's there!'

I looked, and gave a gasp. It might have passed for an excellent rehearsal of my last gasp. In the very front row sat — father! He appeared sardonic and businesslike. The fatal formula seemed already to be trembling upon his lips. The remnants of B, C, D, and so forth suddenly blurred before my crossed eyes. With the most dismal report our old bottle of chamber music blew up, and I fled from the scene.

'My son, come into my study.'

In an ague I had waited half the evening for those hated words; and with laggard step and miserable forebodings I followed across the hall. But the day was destined to end in still another surprise. When father finally faced me in that awful sanctum, he was actually smiling in the jolliest manner, and I divined that the rod was going to be spared.

'What's all this?' he inquired. 'Thought you'd surprise your old dad, eh? Come, tell me about it.'

So I told him about it; and he was so sympathetic that I found courage for the great request.

'Pa,' I stammered, 'sometimes I think p'raps I don't hold the bow just right. It scratches so. Please might I take just four lessons from a regular teacher so I could learn all about how to play the 'cello?'

Father choked a little. But he looked jollier than ever as he replied, 'Yes, my son, on condition that you promise to lay the flute entirely aside until you have learned *all* about how to play the 'cello.'

I promised.

I have faithfully kept that promise.

II

FIDDLERS errant are apt to rush in and occupy the centre of the stage where angels in good and regular practice fear even to tune up. One of the errant's pet vagaries is to volunteer his services in orchestras too good for him. Not long after discovering that I would need more than four lessons to learn quite all there was to know about the 'cello, — in fact, just nine months after discovering the coffin in the attic, — I 'rushed in.' Hearing that *The Messiah* was to be given at Christmas, I approached the conductor and magniloquently informed him that I was a 'cellist and that, seeing he was he, I would contribute my services without money and without price to the coming performance.

With a rather dubious air my terms were accepted. That same evening at rehearsal I found that the entire bass section of the orchestra consisted of three 'cellos. These were presided over by an inaudible, and therefore negligible, little girl, a hoary sage who always arrived very late and left very early, and myself. I shall never forget my sensations when the sage, at a crucial point, suddenly packed up and left me, an undeveloped musical Atlas, to bear the entire weight of the orchestra on one pair of puny shoulders. Under these conditions it was a memorable ordeal to read at sight 'The Trumpet Shall Sound.' The trumpet sounded, indeed. That was more than the 'cello did in certain passages! As for the dead being raised, however, that happened according to programme.

After this high-tension episode, I pulled myself together,

only to fall into a cruel and unusual pit which the treacherous Händel dug for 'cellists by writing one single passage in that unfamiliar alto clef which looks so much like the usual tenor clef that before the least suspicion of impending disaster dawns, you are down in the pit, hopelessly floundering.

I emerged from this rehearsal barely alive; but I had really enjoyed myself so much more than I had suffered, or made others suffer, that my initial impulse to rush at sight into strange orchestras now became stereotyped into a habit. Since then what delightful evenings I have spent in the old Café Martin and in the old Café Boulevard where my 'cellist friends in the orchestras were ever ready to resign their instruments into my hands for a course or two, and the leader always let me pick out the music!

But one afternoon in upper Broadway I met with the sort of adventure that figures in the fondest dreams of fiddlers errant. I had strolled into the nearest hotel to use the telephone. As I passed through the restaurant, my attention was caught by a vaguely familiar strain from the musicians' gallery. Surely this was unusual spiritual provender to offer a crowd of typical New York diners! More and more absorbed in trying to recognize the music, I sank into an armchair in the lobby, the telephone quite forgotten. The instruments were working themselves up to some magnificent climax, and working me up at the same time. It began to sound more and more like the greatest of all music, — the musician's very holiest of holies. Surely I must be dreaming! My fingers crooked themselves for a pinch. But just then the unseen instruments swung back into the opening theme of the Brahms piano quartette in A major. Merciful heavens! A Brahms quartette in Broadway? Pan in Wall Street?

Silence.   With three jumps I was up in the little gallery, wringing the hands of those performers and calling down blessings upon their quixotism as musical missionaries. 'Missionaries?' echoed the leader in amusement.   'Ah, no.   We could never hope to convert those down there.' He waved a scornful hand at the consumers of lobster below.   'Now and then we play Brahms just in order that we may save our own souls.'   The 'cellist rose, saluted, and extended his bow in my direction, like some proud commander surrendering his sword.   'Will it please you,' he inquired, 'to play the next movement?'   It pleased me.

III

FIDDLERS errant find that traveling with a 'cello is almost as good — and almost as bad — as traveling with a child.   It helps you, for example, in cultivating friendly relations with fellow passengers.   Suppose there is a broken wheel, or the engineer is waiting for Number 26 to pass, or you are stalled for three days in a blizzard, — what more jolly than to undress your 'cello and play each of those present the tune he would most like to hear, and lead the congregational singing of 'Dixie', 'Tipperary', 'Drink to me only', and 'Home, Sweet Home'?   A fiddle may even make tenable one of those railway junctions which Stevenson cursed as the nadir of intrinsic uninterestingness, and which Mr. Clayton Hamilton praised with such *brio*.   But this is only the bright side.   In some ways traveling with a 'cello is as uncomfortable as traveling, not only with a baby, but with a donkey.   Unless indeed you have an instrument with a convenient hinged door in the back so that you may pack it full of pyjamas, collars, brushes, MSS, and so forth, thus dispensing with a bag; or unless you can calk up its *f* holes and use the instrument as a canoe on occasion, a 'cello is about as inconvenient a traveling companion as the corpse in R. L. S.'s tale, which would insist on getting into the wrong box.

Some idea of the awkwardness of taking the 'cello along in a sleeping car may be gathered from its nicknames. It is called the 'bull-fiddle.' It is called the 'dog-house.' But, unlike either bulls or kennels, it cannot safely be forwarded by freight or express. The formula for Pullman travel with a 'cello is as follows: First ascertain whether the conductor will let you aboard with the instrument. If not, try the next train. When successful, fee the porter heavily at sight, thus softening his heart so that he will assign the only spare upper berth to your baby. And warn him in impressive tones that the instrument is priceless, and on no account to touch it. You need not fear thieves. Sooner than steal a 'cello, the light-fingered would button his coat over a baby white elephant and let it tusk his vitals.

I have cause to remember my first and only holiday trip with the Princeton Glee, Mandolin, and Banjo Clubs. My function being to play solos and to assist the Mandolin Club, I demanded for the 'cello an upper berth in the special car. But I was overwhelmed with howls of derision and assurances that I was a very fresh soph indeed. The first night, my instrument reposed in some mysterious recess under a leaky cooler, where all too much water flowed under its bridge before the dawn. The second night it was compressed into a strait and narrow closet with brushes and brooms, whence it emerged with a hollow chest, a stoop, a consumptive quality of voice, and the malady known as *compressio pontis*. Thereafter it occupied the same upper with me. Twice I overlaid it, with well-nigh fatal consequences.

Short-distance travel with a 'cello is not much more agreeable. In trolleys you have to hold it more deli-

cately than any babe, and be ready to give a straight-
arm to any one who lurches in your direction, and to raise
it from the floor every time you jolt over crosstracks or
run over pedestrians, for fear of jarring the delicate adjustment of the sound-post. As for a holiday crush down
town, the best way to negotiate it with a 'cello is to fix the
sharp end-pin in place, and then, holding the instrument
at charge like a bayonet, impale those who seem most likely
to break its ribs.

After my full share of such experiences, I learned
that if you are a fiddler errant it is better to leave your
instrument at home and live on the country, as it were,
trusting to the fact that you can beg, borrow, or rent some
kind of fiddle and of chamber music almost anywhere, if
you know how to go about it.

IV

ONLY don't try it in Sicily !

For several months I had buried the fiddler in the errant
pure and simple, when, one sunset, across a gorge in
Monte Venere, my first strain of Sicilian music floated,
to reawaken in me all the primeval instincts of the musical
adventurer. The melody came from the reed pipe of a
goat-herd as he drove his flock down into Taormina. Such
a pipe was perhaps to Theocritus what the fiddles of Strad-
ivarius are to us. It was pleasant to imagine that this
goat-herd's music might possibly be the same that used to
inspire the tenderest of Sicilian poets twenty-three hundred
years ago.

Piercingly sweet, indescribably pathetic, the melody
recalled the Largo in Dvořák's New World Symphony.
Yet, there on the mountain-side, with Ætna rosy on the
right, and the purple Mediterranean shimmering far
below, the voice of the reed sounded more divine than any

English horn or Boehm flute I had ever heard singing in
the depths of a modern orchestra.   And I began to doubt
whether music was so completely a product of the last
three centuries as it purported to be.

But that evening, when the goat-herd, ensnared by
American gold, turned himself into a modern chamber
musician in our hotel room, I regained poise.   Removed
from its properly romantic setting, like seaweed from the
sea, the pastoral stop of Theocritus became unmistakably
a penny whistle, with an intonation of the whistle's conventional purity.   Our captured Comatas seemed to
realize that the environment was against him and that
things were going 'contrairy'; for he refused to venture
on any of the soft Lydian airs of Monte Venere, and confined himself strictly to tarantellas, native dances, which
he played with a magnificent feeling for rhythm (if not
for in-tuneness) while, with a pencil, I caught — or
muffed — them on the fly.   One was to this effect : —

Da Capo, al Fine

While this was going on, a chance hotel acquaintance dropped into the room and revealed himself as a
professor by explaining that the tarantella was named
for its birthplace, the old Greek city of Taranto over
yonder in the heel of the Italian boot; that dancing it was
once considered the only cure for the maddening bite of
the spider known as the *Lycosa Tarantula;* and that some
of the melodies our goat-herd was playing might possibly
be ancient Greek tunes, handed down traditionally in
Taranto, and later dispersed over Calabria and Sicily.

This all sounded rather academic.   But his next words
sent the little professor soaring in our estimation.   He
disclosed himself as a fiddler errant by wistfully remarking
that all this made him long for two things: his violin, and
a chance to play trios.   Right heartily did we introduce
ourselves as pianist and 'cellist errant at his service.   And
he and I decided to visit Catania next day to scout for
fiddles and music.   We thought we would look for the
music first.

Next day, accordingly, we invaded the largest music
store in Catania.   Did they have trios for violin, violon-
cello, and piano? 'Certainly!' We were shown a
derangement of *La Somnambula* for violin and piano,
and another for 'cello and piano.   If we omitted one of
the piano parts, we were assured, a very beautiful trio
would result, as surely as one from four makes three.

Finding us hard to please, the storekeeper referred us

to the conductor of the Opera, who offered to rent us all the standard works of chamber music. The 'trios' he offered us turned out to be elementary pieces labeled 'For Piano and Violin or 'Cello.' But nothing we could say was able to persuade our conductor that 'or' did not mean 'and.' To this day I feel sure that he is ready to defend his interpretation of this word against all comers.

We turned three more music stores upside down and had already abandoned the hunt in despair when we discovered a fourth in a narrow side street. There were only five minutes in which to catch the train; but in thirty seconds we had unearthed a genuine piece of chamber music. Hallelujah! it was the finale of the first Beethoven trio!

Suddenly the oil of joy curdled to mourning. The thing was an arrangement for piano solo! We left hurriedly when the proprietor began assuring us that the original effect would be secured if the piano was doubled in the treble by the violin and in the bass by the 'cello.

This piano solo was the nearest approach to chamber music that a thorough search and research revealed in the island of Trinacria. But afterwards, recollecting the misadventure in tranquillity, we concluded that it was as absurd to look for chamber music in Sicily as to look for 'Die Wacht am Rhein' among the idylls of Theocritus.

V

SCENE: a city composed of one department store and three houses, on the forbidding shores of Newfoundland.

TIME: one of those times when a fellow needs a friend, — when he's in a stern, strange land on pleasure bent — and has to have a check cashed. I don't know why it is that one always runs out of ready money in Newfoundland.

Perhaps because salmon flies are such fleeting creatures of a day that you must send many postal orders to St. Johns for more.   Perhaps because the customs officials at Port au Basques make you deposit so much duty on your fishing tackle.   At any rate, there I was penniless, with the burly storekeeper scowling in a savage manner at my check and not knowing at all whether to take a chance on it. Finally he thought he would n't, but conceded that I might spend a night under his roof, as there was really nowhere else to go.

At this pass something made me think of music.   Perhaps it was the parlor piano which, when new, back in the stone age, had probably been in tune.   I inquired whether there were any other instruments.   The wreckage of a violin was produced.   With two pieces of string and a table fork I set up the prostrate sound-post.   I glued together the bridge and put it in position.   The technique of the angler proved helpful in splicing together some strange-looking strings.   The A was eked out with a piece of salmon leader, while an old mandolin yielded a wire E.

When all was at last ready, a fresh difficulty occurred to me.   The violin was an instrument which I had never learned to play!   But necessity is the mother of pretension.   I thought of that check.   And placing the small fiddle between my knees, I pretended that it was a 'cello.

So the daughter of the house seated herself at the relic of the stone age, and we had a concert.   Newfoundland appeared not to be over-finicky in the matter of pitch and tone-quality.   And how it did enjoy music!   As the audience was of Scotch-English-Irish descent, we rendered equal parts of 'Comin' Through the Rye', 'God Save the King', and 'Kathleen Mavourneen.'   Then the proprietor requested the Sextette from *Lucia*.   While it was forthcoming he toyed furtively with his bandana.   When

it ceased he encored it with all his might.   Then he slipped
out storewards and presently returned with the fattest,
blackest, most formidable-looking cigar I ever saw, which
he gravely proffered me.

'We like,' he remarked in his quaint idiom, 'to hear
music at scattered times.' He was trying to affect
indifference.   But his gruff voice shook, and I knew then
that music hath charms to cash the savage check.

VI

THIS essay has rambled on an unconscionable while.
The shades of editorial night are already descending;
and still I have not yet described one of those unexpected
and perfect orgies of chamber music, — one of those little
earthly paradises full of

> Soul-satisfying strains — alas! too few, —

which true fiddlers errant hope to find in each new place
they visit, but which usually keep well in advance of them,
like the foot of the rainbow.

One such adventure came to me not long ago in a
California city, while I was gathering material for a book
of travel.   On my first evening there I was taken to dine
with a well-known writer in his beautiful home, which he
had built with his own two hands in the Spanish misssion
style during fourteen years of joyous labor.   This gentleman had no idea that I was to be thrust upon him.   But
his hospitality went so far as to insist, before the evening
was over, that I must stay a week.   He would not take no
for an answer.   And for my part I had no desire to say no,
because he was a delightful person, his home with its leaf-
filled patio was most alluring, and I had discovered
promising possibilities for fiddlers errant in the splendid
music-room and the collection of phonograph records of

Indian music which mine host had himself made in Arizona and New Mexico. Then too there were rumors of skillful musical vagabonds in the vicinity.

Such an environment fairly cried aloud for impromptu fiddling. So, armed with a note to the best violinist in that part of California, I set forth next morning on the trail of the ideal orgy. At the address given I was told that my man had moved and his address was not known. That was a setback, indeed! But determined fiddlers errant usually land on their feet. On the way back I chanced to hear some masterly strains of Bach-on-the-violin issuing from a brown bungalow. And ringing at a venture I was confronted by the very man I sought.

Blocking the doorway, he read the note, looking as bored as professionals usually do when asked to play with amateurs. But just as he began to tell me how busy he was and how impossible, and so forth, he happened to glance again at the envelope, and a very slight gleam came into his eye.

'You're not by any chance the fellow who wrote that thing about fiddlers in the *Atlantic*, are you?' he inquired. At my nod he very flatteringly unblocked the doorway and dragged me inside, pumping my hand up and down in a painful manner, shouting for his wife, and making various kind representations, all at the same time. And his talk gradually simmered down into an argument that of course the only thing to do was to fiddle together that very night.

I asked who had the best 'cello in town. He told me the man's name, but looked dubious. 'The trouble is, he loves that big Amati as if it were twins. I doubt if he could bring himself to lend it to any one. Anyway, let's try.'

He scribbled a card to his 'cellist friend and promised, if I were successful, to bring along a good pianist and play trios in the evening. So I set forth on the trail of the Amati. Its owner had just finished his noonday stint in a hotel orchestra and looked somewhat tired and cross. He glanced at the card and then assumed a most conservative expression and tried to fob off on me a cheap 'cello belonging to one of his pupils, which sounded very much as a three-cent cigar tastes. At this point I gave him the secret thumb-position grip and whispered into his ear one of those magic pass words of the craft which in a trice convinced him that I was in a position to dandle a 'cello with as tender solicitude as any man alive. On my promising, moreover, to taxicab it both ways with the sacred burden, he passed the Amati over, and the orgy of fiddlers errant was assured.

And that night how those beautiful Spanish walls did resound to Beethoven and Dvořák and Brahms, most originally interspersed with the voice of the Mexican serv-ant's guitar, with strange, lovely songs of the aboriginal West and South, — and with the bottled sunshine of Californian hill-slopes; while El Alcalde Maiore, the lone gnarled tree-giant that filled the patio, looked in through the open windows and contributed, by way of accompani-ment, leafy arpeggios *sotto voce*. And sometimes, during rests, I remembered to be thankful that I had once snapped my fingers at the howling wolf, and at fat pot-boilers, while I scribbled for the *Atlantic* that little essay on fiddlers which had gained me this priceless evening.

Here are several contemporary American essayists, writing on bookish themes, selected from among the many who find pleasure in the essayist's art. "Literary Borrowing" from Imaginary Obligations, *by the late Frank Moore Colby, is reprinted by permission of Dodd Mead & Co., his publishers, and Mrs. Colby. Kindly humor and biting satire both may be found throughout his essays, and a shrewd discernment of values.* "Comfortable Books", *reprinted from* The Jonathan Papers *by Elisabeth Woodbridge Morris, by permission of Mrs. Morris and her publishers, Houghton Mifflin Co., is another comment upon a single book built into an essay about books in general.* "Confession in Prose", *by Walter Prichard Eaton, reprinted here by permission of the author, discusses certain tendencies in dramatic as well as general prose writing, illustrating them by specific cases. Christopher Morley should stand in a group by himself, were it not that his essays are associated in readers' minds with book reviewing. This little bit from his pen is more illustrative of that whimsicality which made possible such a book as* Where the Blue Begins, *and is reprinted from* The Romany Stain *by permission of Doubleday Page & Company.*

LITERARY BURROWING

From *Imaginary Obligations*

BY FRANK MOORE COLBY

THE *Iliad* is a great symbolical poem, according to a certain critic, because Homer makes a group of old men, on seeing Helen pass by, remark: "After all, she was worth it," or words to that effect. This according to our commentator, proves that the *Iliad* contains a great moral idea; in other words, is symbolical. Now, Homer was the most utterly unsymbolical person (if he was a person) that ever enjoyed good health. He never had anything of that kind the matter with him, and his poems are as free from it as they are from germs. The way our sophisticated modern critic will read complex innuendoes into what is elemental is enough to wear one's patience to the bone. Must poor old Homer father a lot of esoteric things? Is the *Iliad* to have four or five layers of meaning, one below the other, like a pile of sandwiches? This digging up of unsuspected meanings goes too far. It spoils a poem to be all the time spading it or boring through its imagery with a steam drill. These critics spend too much of their time underground, and they look pale and unwholesome when they come up. And it often happens that what they bring up is something they have dropped themselves. There are commentators who have been digging all their lives and come up with their own pocket handkerchief. They expect you to be glad about it. They think a poet, like a dog, no sooner happens on a good thing than he wants to bury it.

A few years ago an inmate of one of our state asylums was taken out for a walk in a pleasant park. As soon as his keeper's back was turned he jumped down a manhole and ran along a sewer main. When dug up at great expense he complained of the interference, saying he was "keeping store" down there. So of a symbolist when you let him into a poem. One would think Homer might have escaped this. The meaning of the *Iliad* is so accessible it seems foolish to try and enter it through a gopher hole. But if we must we must. — Helen is divine beauty, Menelaus is the soul; Paris the heart of humanity; Nestor the onlooking, judging thought; Thersites the ego, and Achilles the personification of world energy. And whenever one of them does anything it means six or eight other things, and they never can take a step without leaving a footnote. Then it will amount to something to say you understand Homer. It will rank you among the seven deepest thinkers in the world, and even in regard to the other six you may reasonably entertain suspicions.

That is really the ambitious motive at the root of this kind of criticism. Below every great poem there is a little subterranean aristocracy where rank is measured by its distance from the surface. Each is aiming at the point furthest down. A few years ago a Shakespearian critic showed that when Falstaff was made to babble of green fields he was really quoting from one of the psalms. This proved that he had received a religious education, and was probably a choir boy in his youth. The man who hit upon this illuminating thought was for weeks a marvel among critics. Since then they have no doubt found Falstaff to be nine different kinds of an allegory; so rapidly does the work advance. Why need every honest poet be suspected of leading a quadruple life? Sometimes the second or third meaning is less interesting than the first, and the only really difficult thing about a poem is the critic's explanation of it. But active minds must find employment, and if you cannot burrow how can you be deep? And if you are not deep you are that wretched vulgar thing, a casual reader, and will be snubbed to the end of your days by these haughty troglodytes. So when one of them comes along, never let him see you feeding on the surface of a poem. Dive to the bottom like a loon. You can bring up queer things from the deepest part. Then he will feel degraded and superficial and blush awkwardly like a casual reader.

COMFORTABLE BOOKS

From *The Jonathan Papers*

By Elisabeth Woodbridge Morris

Jonathan methodically tucked his bookmark into "The Virginians", and, closing the fat green volume, began to knock the ashes out of his pipe against the bricked sides of the fireplace.

"'The Virginians' is a very comfortable sort of book," he remarked.

"Is it?" I said. "I wonder why."

He ruminated. "Well, chiefly, I suppose, because it's so good and long. You get to know all the people, you get used to their ways, and when they turn up again, after a lot of chapters, you don't have to find out who they are — you just feel comfortably acquainted."

I sighed. I had just finished a magazine story — condensed, vivid, crushing a whole life-tragedy into seven pages and a half. In that space I had been made acquainted with sixteen different characters, seven principal ones and the rest subordinate, but all clearly drawn. I had found it interesting, stimulating; as a tour de force it was noteworthy even among the crowd of short-stories — all condensed, all vivid, all interesting — that had appeared that month. But — comfortable? No. And I felt envious of Jonathan. He had been reading "The Virginians" all winter. His bookmark was at page 597, and there were 803 pages in all, so he had a great deal of comfort left.

Perhaps comfort is not quite all that one should expect from one's reading. Certainly it is the last thing one gets from the perusal of our current literature, and any one who reads nothing else is missing something which, whether he realizes it or not, he ought for his soul's sake to have —

something which Jonathan roughly indicated when he called it "comfort." The ordinary reader devours short-stories by the dozen, by the score — short short-stories, long short-stories, even short-stories laboriously expanded to a volume, but still short-stories. He glances, less frequently, at verses, chiefly quatrains, at columns of jokes, at popularized bits of history and science, at bits of anecdotal biography, and nowhere in all this medley does he come in contact with what is large and leisurely. Current literature is like a garden I once saw. Its proud owner led me through a maze of smooth-trodden paths, and pointed out a vast number of horticultural achievements. There were sixty-seven varieties of dahlias, there were more than a hundred kinds of roses, there were untold wonders which at last my weary brain refused to record. Finally I escaped, exhausted, and sought refuge on a hillside I knew, from which I could look across the billowing green of a great rye-field, and there, given up to the beauty of its manifold simplicity, I invited my soul.

It is even so with our reading. When I go into one of our public reading-rooms, and survey the serried ranks of magazines and the long shelves full of "Recent fiction, not to be taken out for more than five days", — nay, even when I look at the library tables of some of my friends, — my brain grows sick and I long for my rye-field.

Happily, there is always a rye-field at hand to be had for the seeking. Jonathan finds refuge from business in his pipe and "The Virginians." I have no pipe, but I sit under the curling rings of Jonathan's, and I, too, have my comfortable books, my literary rye-fields. Last summer it was Malory's "Morte d'Arthur", whose book I found indeed a comfortable one — most comfortable. I read much besides, many short-stories of surpassing cleverness and some of real excellence, but as I look back upon my summer's literary experience, all else gives place to the long pageant of Malory's story, gorgeous or tender or gay, seen like a fair vision against the dim background of an old New England apple orchard. Surely, though the literature of our library tables may sometimes weary me, it shall never enslave me.

But they must be read, these "comfortable" books, in the proper fashion, not hastily, nor cursorily, nor with any desire to "get on" in them. They must lie at our hand to be taken up in moments of leisure, the slowly shifting bookmark recording our half-reluctant progress. (I remember with what dismay I found myself arrived at the fourth and last volume of Malory.) Thus read, thus slowly woven among the intricacies and distractions of our life, these precious books will link its quiet moments together and lend to it a certain quality of largeness, of deliberation, of continuity.

For it is surely a mistake to assume, as people so often do, that in a life full of distractions one should read only such things as can be finished at a single sitting and that a short one. It is a great misfortune to read only books that "must be returned within five days." For my part, I should like to see in our public libraries, to offset the shelves of such books, other shelves, labeled "Books that may and should be kept out six months." I would have there Thackeray and George Eliot and Wordsworth and Spenser, Malory and Homer and Cervantes and Shakespeare and Montaigne — oh, they should be shelves to rejoice the soul of the harassed reader!

No, if one can read but little, let him by all means read something big. I know a woman occupied with the demands of a peculiarly exigent social position. Finding her one day reading "The Tempest", I remarked on her enterprise. "Not a bit!" she protested. "I am not reading it to be enterprising, I am reading it to get rested. I find Shakespeare so peaceful, compared with the magazines." I have another friend who is taking entire charge of her children, besides doing a good deal of her own housework and gardening. I discovered her one day sitting under a tree, reading Matthew Arnold's poems, while the children played near by. I ventured to comment on what seemed to me the incongruity of her choice of a book. "But don't you see," she replied quickly. "That is just why! I am so busy from minute to minute doing lots of little practical, temporary things, that I simply have to keep in touch with something different — something large and quiet. If I did n't, I should die!"

I suppose in the old days, in a less "literary" age, all such busy folk found this necessary rest and refreshment in a single book — the Bible. Doubtless many still do so, but not so many; and this, quite irrespective of religious considerations, seems to me a great pity. The literary quality of the Scriptures has, to be sure, been partly vitiated by the lamentable habit of reading them in isolated "texts", instead of as magnificent wholes; yet, even so, I feel sure that this constant intercourse with the Book did for our predecessors in far larger measure what some of these other books of which I have been speaking do for us — it furnished that contact with greatness which we all crave.

It may be accident, though I hardly think so, that to find such books we must turn to the past. Doubtless others will arise in the future — possibly some are even now being brought to birth, though this I find hard to believe. For ours is the age of the short-story — a wonderful product, perhaps the finest flower of fiction, and one which has not yet achieved all its victories or realized all its possibilities. All the fiction of the future will show the influence of this highly specialized form. In sheer craftsmanship, novel-writing has progressed far; in technique, in dextrous manipulation of their material, the novices of to-day are ahead of the masters of yesterday. This often happens in an art, and it is especially true just now in the art of fiction. Yes, there are great things preparing for us in the future, there are excellent things being done momently about us. But while we wait for the great ones, the excellent ones sometimes create in us a sense of surfeit. We cannot hurry the future, and if meanwhile we crave repose, leisure, quiet, steadiness, the sense of magnitude, we must go to the past. There, and not in the yearly output of our own publishers, we shall find our "comfortable" books.

A CONFESSION IN PROSE

By Walter Prichard Eaton

Unlike M. Jourdain, who had been speaking prose all his life without knowing it, I have been writing it nearly all of mine, quite consciously, and earning my living thereby since I was twenty-one years old. I am now thirty-four. I have been a professional writer of prose, then, for thirteen years — or shall I say a writer of professional prose? Much of this writing has been done for various American magazines; still more has been done to fill the ravenous columns of American newspapers; some, even, has been immured between covers. I have tried never to write sloppily, though I have of necessity often written hastily. I can honestly say, too, that I have tried at times to write beautifully, by which I mean rhythmically, with a conscious adjustment of sound and melody to the sense, with the charm of word-chiming further to heighten heightened thought. But I can also as honestly say that in this latter effort I have never been encouraged by a newspaper editor, and I have been not infrequently discouraged by magazine editors. Not all magazines compel you to chop up your prose into a maximum paragraph length of ten lines, as does a certain one of large circulation. Not all newspapers compel you to be 'smart', as did one for which I worked compel us all. But the impression among editors is prevalent, none the less, that a conversational downrightness and sentence and paragraph brevity are the be-all and end-all of prose style, or at least of so much of prose style as can be grasped by the populace who read their publications; and that beautiful writing must be 'fine writing', and therefore never too much to be avoided. So I started out from the classroom of Professor Lewis E. Gates, one of the keenest and most inspiring analysts of prose beauties this country has produced, to be a professional writer of prose, and dreamed, as youth will, of wrapping my singing robes about me and ravishing the world. I was soon enough told to doff my singing robes for the overalls of journalism, and I have become a writer of professional prose instead.

These remarks have been inspired by a long and wistful evening just spent in perusing Professor Saintsbury's new book, called *The History of English Prose Rhythm*. I shall hold no brief for the good professor's method of scansion. It matters little to me, indeed, how he chooses to scan prose. What does matter to me is that he has chosen to scan it at all, that he has brought forward the finest examples in the stately procession of English literature, and demonstrated with all the weight of his learning, his authority, his fine enthusiasm, that this prose is no less consciously wrought to pleasing numbers than is verse.

We who studied under Professor Gates knew much of this
before, if not in so detailed and would-be methodical a
fashion. Charles Lamb knew it when he wrote, 'Even
ourself, in these our humbler lucubrations, tune our
best measured cadences (prose has her cadences) not unfrequently to the charm of the drowsier watchman,
"blessing the doors"; or the wild sweep of winds at
midnight.' Sir Thomas Browne was not exactly unaware
of it as he prepared his *Urn Burial* for the printer; nor
the authors of the King James Version of the Bible when
they translated — or if you prefer, paraphrased — the
rhapsodic chapters of Isaiah. But it is pleasant, and not
unimportant, to be once more reminded, in a generation
when written speech has sunk to the conversational level
of the man in the street, that 'prose has her cadences';
and to me, at least, it is melancholy, also. For I would
strive to write such prose, in my stumbling fashion, were
I permitted.

Writing about a fine art, as I am so often called upon to
do, I would endeavor with what might lay in me to write
about it finely. Suppose that art chances to be the drama.
Why, when some compact, weighty, and worthily performed example comes to our stage, should I be expected
to toss off a description of it in a style less compact and
weighty and worthily conducted? On the rare occasions
when a new play chances to be poetic, am I not justified
in writing of it in poetic prose? How else, indeed, can I
truly render back to my readers the subtler aspects of its
charm? But for such writing there is little room in our
hurrying and 'conversational' press, though now and then
a despised dramatic editor is found who understands.
Even the drama itself strives to be 'conversational' at all
costs, under the banner of 'realism', and profanity
flourishes on our stage in what we must infer to be a

most life-like manner, while we have almost forgotten
that the spoken word can be melodious or imaginative.
Criticism cries at its heels, and helps with flippant jest
and broken syntax and cacophonous combinations of
our poorest vernacular, in the general debasement.
Do not tell me that men do not exist who could write
differently of the stage, as men exist who can, and do,
write differently for it.   Every worthy dramatist can be
paralleled by at least one worthy critic, and more probably by three or four, since the true creative instinct in
drama is perhaps the rarest of human attributes, save
only charity.   But the editors appear to have determined
that the public does not want such critics — and perhaps
the editors are right.   At least, the public does not often
get them.

   We are speaking now of prose, not of opinions, and we
may safely introduce the name of a living critic, William
Winter.   For nearly half a century Mr. Winter has
written prose about the theatre, and although that
prose was produced for a morning newspaper it was
carefully and consistently balanced and welded, and,
when the subject demanded it, rose, according to its
creator's ideas of beauty, into the heightened eloquence
of sentence rhythm and syllabic harmony.   Leisure
may improve, but haste cannot prevent the rhythm of
prose, provided the instinct for it resides in the writer,
and the opportunity exists for practice and expression.
Two examples of Mr. Winter's use of rhythm come to
my memory, and I quote only phrases, not whole sentences, merely because I am sure of no more.   Writing
one morning of a new and very 'modern' play, presented
the previous evening by a well-known actress, he said:
'Sarah Bernhardt at least made her sexual monsters
interesting, wielding the lethal hatpin or the deadly hatchet

with Gallic grace and sweet celerity.' Again, in reviewing Pinero's *Iris*, he took up two of Henry Arthur Jones's phrases, recently made current in a lecture, and played with them, ending with mellifluous scorn, 'Such are "the great realities of modern life", flowers of disease and blight that fringe the charnel house of the "serious drama."'

These are certainly examples of rhythmic, or cadenced prose, and they are examples taken from journalistic reviews. They admirably express the writer's point of view toward his subject matter, but they also reveal his care for the manner of expression, they satisfy the ear; and therefore to one at all sensitive to literature they are doubly satisfying. The arrow of irony is ever more delightful when it sings on its flight. The trick, then, can be done. Mr. Winter, too often perhaps for modern ears, performed it by recourse to the Johnsonian balance of period and almost uniform, swelling roll. But that is neither here nor there. The point is that he performed it — and that it is no longer performed by the new generation, either in newspaper columns, or, we will add at once, anywhere else. Rhythmic prose, prose cadenced to charm the ear and by its melodies and harmonies properly adjusted to heighten, as with an under-song, the emotional appeal of the ideas expressed, is no longer written. It appears to be no longer wanted. We are fallen upon harsh and colloquial times.

No one with any ear at all would deny Emerson a style, even if his rhythms are often broken into the cross-chop of Carlyle. No one would deny Irving a style, or Poe, — certainly Poe at his best, — or, indeed, to hark far back, Cotton Mather in many passages of the *Magnalia*, where to a quaint iambic simplicity he added a Biblical fervor which redeems and melodizes the monotony.

Mather suggests Milton, Irving suggests Addison, Emerson suggests Carlyle, Poe, shall we say, is often the too conscious workman typified by De Quincey. But thereafter, in this country, we descend rapidly into second-hand imitations, into rhythm become, in truth, mere 'fine writing', until its death within recent memory. Yet we do not find even to-day the true cadenced prose either uninteresting or out of date. Emerson is as modern as the morning paper. Newman's description of the ideal site for a university, in the clear air of Attica beside the blue Ægean, charms us still with its perfect blend of sound and sense, its clear intellectual idea borne on a cadenced undersong, as of distant surf upon the shore; and the exquisite epilogue to the *Apologia*, with its chime of proper names, still brings a moisture to our eyes. The triumphant tramp of Gibbon, the headlong imagery and Biblical fervor of Ruskin, the languid music of Walter Pater, each holds its separate charm, and the charm is not archaic.

Is such prose impossible any more? Certainly it is not. The heritage of the language is still ours, the birthright of our noble English tongue. Simply, we do not dare to let ourselves go. We seem tortured with the modern blight of self-consciousness; and while the cheaper magazines are almost blatant in their unblushing self-puffery, they are none the less cravenly submissive to what they deem popular demand, and turn their backs on literature, on style, as something abhorrent to a race which has been fed on the English Bible for three hundred years. Their ideal of a prose style now seems to consist of a series of staccato yips. It really cannot be described in any other way. The 'triumphantly intricate' sentence celebrated by Walter Pater would give many a modern editor a shiver of terror. He would visualize it as mowing down the circulation of the magazine like a machine gun. Rhythm and beauty of style can hardly be achieved by staccato yips. The modern magazine writer, trying to be rhetorically effective, trying to rise to the demands of heightened thought or emotional appeal, reminds one of that enthusiastic German tympanist who wrote an entire symphonic poem for kettledrums.

I read one of the autumn crop of new novels the other day. Curiously enough, it was written by a music critic who, in his reviews of music, is constantly insisting on the primal importance of melody and harmony, who is an arch foe of the modern programme school and the whole-tone scale of Debussy. But the prose of his novel was utterly devoid of these prized elements, melody and harmony. A heavy, or sometimes turgid, journalistic commonplaceness sat upon it. I will not be unfair and tear an illustration from some passage of rightly simple narration. I will take the closing sentences from one of the climactic chapters, when the mood had supposedly risen to intensity, and, if ever, the prose would have been justified in rising to reinforce the emotion.

'The house was aroused to extravagant demonstrations. Across the footlights it looked like a brilliantly realistic piece of acting, and the audience was astonished at the vigor of the hitherto cold Americano.

'But Nagy was not deceived. Crushed, dishevelled, breathless, she knew that her dominion over him was gone forever. She had tried to show him his soul and he had begun to see the light.'

Now, an ear attuned to the melodies of English prose must surely find this commonplace, and the closing sentence of all actually as harsh as the tonalities of Strauss or Debussy seem to the writer. Let us, even if a little unfairly, set it beside a passage from *Henry Esmond*, again a climactic passage, but one where the style is climactic, also, rising to the mood.

'"You will please, sir, to remember," he continued, "that our family hath ruined itself by fidelity to yours: that my grandfather spent his estate, and gave his blood and his son to die for your service; that my dear lord's grandfather (for lord you are now, Frank, by right and title too) died for the same cause; that my poor kinswoman, my father's second wife, after giving away her honor to your wicked perjured race, sent all her wealth to the King; and got in return that precious title that lies in ashes, and this inestimable yard of blue ribbon. I lay this at your feet and stamp upon it; I draw this sword, and break it and deny you; and had you completed the wrong you designed us, by Heaven I would have driven it through your heart, and no more pardoned you than your father pardoned Monmouth. Frank will do the same, won't you, cousin?"'

This justly famous passage, be it noted, is dialogue. To-day we especially do not dare to rise above a conversational level in dialogue. We should be accused of being 'unnatural.' Does no one speak beautifully any more, then, even in real life? Are the nerve-centres so shattered in the modern anatomy that no connection is established between emotions and the musical sense? Does an exquisite mood no longer reflect itself in our voice, in our vocabulary? Does no lover rise to eloquence in the presence of his Adored? If that is the case, surely we now speak unnaturally, and it should be the duty of literature to restore our health! Nor need such speech in fiction float clear away from solid ground. Notice how Thackeray in his closing sentence — 'Frank will do the same, won't you, cousin?' — anchors his rhetoric to the earth.

We are, let it be said again, in the grasp of realism, and realism but imperfectly understood. Just as our drama aims to reproduce exactly a 'solid' room upon the stage, and to set actors to talking therein the exact speech of every day, so our oratory, so-called, is the reproduction of a one-sided conversation, and our novels (when they are worthy of consideration) are reproductions of patiently accumulated details, set forth in impatiently assembled sentences. But all this does not of necessity constitute realism, because its effect is not of necessity the creation of illusion, however truthful the artist's purpose. Of what avail, in the drama, for example, are solid rooms and conversational vernacular if the characters do not come to life in our imaginations, so that we share their joys and sorrows? Of what effect are the realistic details of a novel, whether of incident or language, if we do not re-live its story as we read? Surely, the answer is plain, and therefore any literary devices which heighten the mood for us are perfectly justifiable weapons of the realist, even as they are of the romanticist. One of these devices is consciously wrought prose. For the present we plead for its employment on no higher ground than this of practical expediency.

But how, you may ask, — no, not you, dear reader, who understand, but some other chap, a poor dog of an author, perhaps, — can consciously wrought prose aid in the creation of illusion? How can it be more than pretty?

Let us turn for answer to Sir Thomas Browne, to 'The Garden of Cyrus', to the closing numbers : —

'Besides, Hippocrates hath spoke so little, and the oneirocritical masters have left such frigid interpretations from plants, that there is little encouragement to dream of paradise itself. Nor will the sweetest delight of gardens afford much comfort in sleep, wherein the dulness of that sense shakes hands with delectable odours; and though in the bed of Cleopatra, can hardly with any delight raise up the ghost of a rose.'

That is archaic, perhaps, and not without a certain taint of quaintness to modern ears. But how drowsy it is, how minor its harmonies, how subtly soothing its languid melody! It tells, surely, in what manner consciously wrought prose may aid in the creation of illusion. The mood of sleep was here to be evoked, and lo! it comes from the very music of the sentences, from the drowsy lullaby of selected syllables.

We might choose a quite different example, from a seemingly most unlikely source, from the plays of George Bernard Shaw. One hardly thinks of Mr. Shaw with a style, but rather with a stiletto. His prefaces have been too disputative, his plays too epigrammatic, for the cultivation of prose rhythms. Yet his prose is almost never without a certain crisp accuracy of conversational cadence; his ear almost never betrays him into sloppiness; and when the occasion demands, his style can rise to meet it. The truth is, Mr. Shaw is seldom emotional, so that his crisp accuracy of speech is most often the fitting garment for his thought. But in *John Bull's Other Island* his emotions are stirred, and when Larry Doyle breaks out into an impassioned description of Ireland the effect on the imagination of the heightened prose, when a good actor speaks it, is almost startling.

'No, no; the climate is different. Here, if the life is dull, you can be dull too, and no great harm done. (*Going off into a passionate dream.*) But your wits can't thicken in that soft moist air, on those white springy roads, in those misty rushes and brown bogs, on those hillsides of granite rocks and magenta heather. You 've no such colors in the sky, no such lure in the distances, no such sadness in the evenings. Oh, the dreaming! the dreaming! the torturing, heart-scalding, never-satisfying dreaming, dreaming, dreaming, dreaming! (*Savagely.*) No debauchery that ever coarsened and brutalized an Englishman can take the worth and usefulness out of him like that dreaming. An Irishman's imagination never lets him alone, never convinces him, never satisfies him; but it makes him so that he can't face reality nor deal with it nor handle it nor conquer it : he can only sneer at them that do, and (*bitterly, at Broadbent*) be "agreeable to strangers", like a good-for-nothing woman on the streets.'

This, to be sure, is prose to be spoken, not prose to be read. Different laws prevail, for different effects are sought. But the principle of cadence calculated to fit the mood, and by its melodic, or, as here, its percussive character to heighten the emotional appeal, remains the same.

But beyond the argument for cadenced prose as an aid to illusion, employed in the proper places, — that is, where intensity of imagery or feeling can benefit by it, — is the higher plea for sheer lingual beauty for its own sake. Shall realism preclude all other effects of artistic creation? Because the men on our streets, the women in our homes, talk sloppily, shall all our books be written in their idiom, all our stage characters reproduce their commonplaceness, nearly all our magazines and newspapers give no attention to the graces of style? I am pleading for no Newman of the news story, nor am I seeking to arm our muck-rakers with the pen of Sir Thomas Browne. I would not send Walter Pater to report a football game (though Stevenson could doubtless improve on most of the 'sporting editors'), nor ask that Emerson write our editorials. But there is a poor way, and there is a fine way, to write everything, and inevitably the man who has an ear for the rhythms of prose, who has been trained and encouraged to write his very best, will fit his style appropriately to his subject. He will not seek to cadence his sentences in bald narration or in exposition, but he will, nevertheless, keep them capable of natural and pleasant phrasing, he will avoid monotony, jarring syllables, false stress, and ugly or tripping terminations which throw the voice as one's feet are thrown by an unseen obstacle in the path. His paragraphs, too, will group naturally, as falls his thought. But when the subject he has in hand rises to invective, to exhortation, to the dignity of any passion or the sweep of any vision, then if his ear be tuned and his courage does not fail him he must inevitably write in cadenced periods, the effectiveness of his work depending on the adjustment of these cadences to the mood of the moment, on his skill as an artist in prose.

And just now the courage of our young men fails. The unrestrained abandonment of all art to realism, of every sort of printed page to bald colloquialism, has dulled the natural ear in all of us for comely prose, and made us deaf to more stately measures. The complete democratizing of literature has put the fear of plebeian ridicule in our hearts, and the wider a magazine's circulation, it would seem, the more harm it does to English prose, because in direct ratio to its sale are its pages given over to the Philistines, and the dignity and refinement of thought which could stimulate dignity and refinement of expression are unknown to its contributors, or kept carefully undisclosed.

I have often fancied, in penitential moments, a day of judgment for us who write, when we shall stand in flushed array before the Ultimate Critic and answer

the awful question, 'What have you done with your
language?' There shall be searchings of soul that morning, and searchings of forgotten pages of magazines and
'best sellers' and books of every sort, for the cadence that
may bring salvation. But many shall seek and few shall
find, and the goats shall be sorted out in droves, condemned
to an eternity of torture, none other than the everlasting
task of listening to their own prose read aloud.

'What have you done with your language?' It is a
solemn question for all of us, for you who speak as well
as for us who write. Our language is a priceless heritage.
It has been the ladder of life up which we climbed; with
it we have bridged the sundering flood that forever rolls
between man and man; through its aid have come to us
the treasures of the past, the world's store of experience;
by means of it our poets have wrought their measures,
our philosophers their dreams. Bit by bit, precious
mosaic after precious mosaic, the great body of English
literature has been built up, in verse and prose, the crown
of that division of language we call our own. Consciously
finding itself three centuries ago, our English prose blos-
somed at once into the solemn splendors of the King James
Bible and then into the long-drawn, ornate magnificence
of Sir Thomas Browne, never again till our day to lose
consciousness of its power, to forget its high and holy
task, the task of maintaining our language at full tide and
ministering to style and beauty. There were fluxes in
the fashions, naturally; little of Browne's music being
found in the almost conversational fluency (but not lax-
ness) of Addison, even as the suave Mr. Addison himself
has vanished in the tempestuous torrents of Carlyle.
But there always was an Addison, a Carlyle, a Newman,
a Walter Pater, whose work loomed large in popular regard, whose influence was mighty in shaping a taste for

prose style. Who now, we may ask, looking around us
in America, looms large in popular regard as a writer
of ample vision, amply and beautifully clothed in speech,
and whose influence is mighty in shaping a taste for prose
style? It is not enough to have the worthies of the past
upon our shelves. Each age must have its own inspiration.
Again we hear the solemn question, 'What have you done
with your language?' Only Ireland may answer, 'We
have our George Moore, and we had our Synge not long
ago — but we stoned his plays.'

We have stifled our language, we have debased it, we
have been afraid of it. But some day it will reassert
itself, for it is stronger than we, alike our overlord and
avatar. Deep in the soul of man dwells the lyric impulse,
and when his song cannot be the song of the poet it will
shape itself in rhythmic prose, that it may still be cadenced
and modulated to change with the changing thought and
sound an obligato to the moods of the author's spirit.
How wonderful has been our prose, — gravely and chastely
rich when Hooker wrote it, striding triumphant over the
pages of Gibbon on tireless feet, ringing like a trumpet from
Emerson's white house in Concord, modulated like soft
organ-music heard afar in Newman's lyric moods, clanging
and clamorous in Carlyle, in Walter Pater but as the oft
fall of water in a marble fountain while exquisite odors
flood the Roman twilight and late bees are murmurous,
a little of all, perhaps, in Stevenson! We, too, we little
fellows of to-day, could write as they wrote, consciously,
rhythmically, if we only cared, if we only dared. We ask
for the opportunity, the encouragement. Alas! that also
means a more liberal choice of graver subjects, and a
more extensive employment of the essay form. Milton
could hardly have been Miltonic on a lesser theme than
the Fall of the Angels, and Walter Pater wrote of the Mona

Lisa, not Lizzie Smith of Davenport, Iowa. It is doubtless of interest to learn about Lizzie, but she hardly inspires us to rhythmic prose.

ROUND COLUMBUS CIRCLE

From *The Romany Stain*

By CHRISTOPHER MORLEY

THE other evening as I was walking along Fifty-ninth Street I noticed a man buying a copy of *Variety* at a newsstand. Obedient to my theory that life deserves all possible scrutiny, I thought it would be interesting to follow him and see exactly what he did.

I chose my quarry not merely at random. People who read *Variety* are likely to be interesting because they are pretty sure to be connected, no matter how remotely, with that odd, unpredictable, and high-spirited race who call themselves "artists", or "professionals." He might be in vaudeville, or in burlesque, or in the world of "outdoor shows." He might be a "carnival man", or a cabaret performer, a dancer, an "equilibrist", a marimba bandsman, a "sensational perch artist", a "lightning change artist", a "jass baby", a saxophonist. He might be the manager of a picture house; he might be in the legitimate. He might even be one of my favourite pair of artists (of whom I think with affection: I have never seen them, but their professional card appears now and then in *Variety* — "Null and Void, The Dippy Daffy Duo").

So I followed him discreetly, to see what might happen.

At Columbus Circle he paused and looked about him rather as though he felt himself in a congenial element. The blue mildness of the night was bright with exciting

signs, the ancient one of the full moon seeming rather
pallid compared to the electric picture of Socony Oil
pouring from a can into a funnel.   There was a constant
curving flow of skittering taxis, especially the kind that
have slatted black panels abaft the windows: these look
like little closed shutters and give a sense of secrecy,
mystery, and vivid romance.   Upon all this my fugitive
gazed with a sort of affection; then he turned and stood a
minute before the window of Childs' where small gas
flames were as blue as violets under the griddle.   I supposed that perhaps he was hungry, for he gazed pensively,
but perhaps he was also thinking that the restaurant had
quaintly changed its sex since afternoon; for now it was
bustling with white-clad men instead of the laundered
ladies of a few hours ago.   He went on to an adjoining
florist's window, and here he studied the lilacs, orchids
(in their little individual test tubes), lilies of the valley,
forsythia, narcissus, daffodils, pussy-willows, sweet peas.
It was a very springlike window, I saw his eye fall upon the
deftly wrapped sheaves of paper inside the shop, where
bright colours glimmered through swathes of pale green
tissue.   These parcels were all addressed, ready to go out,
I supposed to very beautiful ladies.

He passed on (he had lit a pipe, by the way) by the Park
Theatre, and he cast an observant eye upon that, noting
that it was dark.   Perhaps he pondered the vicissitudes of
the show business.   The windows of several haberdashers,
all announcing their proximate retirement from traffic,
won declensions from his eye: there were some quite
lively shirts at $1.85 that seemed nearly to obtain his
suffrage.   But again I saw him lured by food.   A very
minute, narrow doggery, intensely masculine in aspect,
but with its courteous legend LADIES INVITED glossed
upon the pane, exhibited a fry of hamburger steak, liber-

ally besprinkled with onion slivers. These he gravely considered. But still he proceeded ; and still, in the phrase of Mr. Montague, I "committed myself to his vestiges."

It was the automobile business, next, that drew his attention. Those astonishing windows just south of the Circle plainly afforded him material for thought — places where, in great halls of baronial aspect, on Oriental rugs and marble floors, under little whispering galleries where the salesmen retire to their orisons, America's most shining triumphs are displayed. He was fascinated by the window of U. S. Rubber — where a single tire, mounted on a canary-coloured wheel, and an array of galoshes and arctics are gravely displayed under tall blue hangings and festoons of artificial flowers. Or the Goodrich window, where a huge flattened circlet has the space to itself on a crinkled wealth of purple-green shot silk. Amethystine lights shine through glazed screens behind this monstrous tire : drapes of imitation Spanish moss and enormous vases give the effect of a vaudeville stage set for some juggling act. The automobile business has learned all the tricks of Victorian stage *decor;* perhaps that was why my *Variety* reader was so thrilled. Another window, where the car comes bravely to the aid of the hard-pressed Church ("To Church in Their Chevrolet" — have you seen it?), is even more dramatic. Here the department store lends a hand also, for the modes worn by the figures are from Fifth Avenue. I was rather thrilled when I saw my fugitive halt also in front of the Dame Quickly showroom : a much more businesslike display, where the latest models of the Quickly family exhibit their modest and competent elegance.

But it was most interesting of all to find him striking off Broadway and entering the lobby of the Grenoble Hotel. He peered about the lobby as though he were expecting to meet someone; but I could n't help suspecting that this was chiefly for the benefit of the clerk at the desk; what he really wanted was a quiet place to sit down and read his *Variety*. At any rate, he occupied the resilient corner of a couch for some time, studiously conning the magazine. I should have liked to tell the clerk behind the counter the reason why the Grenoble is always a special place to me — it was there, I believe, that Rudyard Kipling lay dangerously ill twenty-five years ago. I wonder if the hotel register holds any record of that momentous incident.

Presently — after carefully scanning the columns which tell how much each play took in at the box-office last week: perhaps the only positively accurate gauge of New York theatrical tastes; you will learn with surprise, for instance, that one of the leading moneymakers is a show called "Abie's Irish Rose" — my subject folded up *Variety* and set forth again. Following, I was pleased to see him stop at Mr. Keyts's bookshop on Fifty-seventh Street; and even more surprised to note that the thing that seemed most to catch his eye was a fine photo of Henry James. He complimented the saleslady upon it, and he bought a book. It was a copy of Sherwood Anderson's *Winesburg, Ohio*, in the "Modern Library."

But it was plain that all this time the idea of food had been loitering agreeably in the back of his mind. I trailed him back to Columbus Circle, and there, to my amusement, he returned straight to the little hash-alley where he had admired the meat patties with onions. He went in and sat down at the tiny counter. "Hamburg steak," he said, "and put plenty of onions on it." And then, after a moment, "Coffee with plenty."

"It 's plenty of everything with you to-night," said the whitecoat, genially.

"Sure, everything but money," remarked this mysterious creature. He propped up his *Winesburg* against the
sugar basin and read while he ate.

At this point, fearing that my sleuthing might cause
him to become self-conscious, I went thoughtfully away.

THE TRUE PATRICK HENRY

BY BURGES JOHNSON

*Reprinted by permission from " The Window ", a maga-
zine published by students of the University of Colorado.*

IT is one of the perquisites of professoring that one may
travel far afield on a small income and charge up some of
the costs to Education, — or else to certain acquiescent
audiences that might spend their money more wisely,
though never more benevolently. (Here is an opening
sentence for you, my dear Editor, that violates all of the
rules.)

Wherefore it was that one of your last summer's faculty
became a peripatetic professor in the fall and rambled
over the Great Divide into the western valleys, in an
ancient car, accompanied by two of his natural guardians.

It is not for me to attempt to describe here the scenic
wonders of that trip. What you do not already know the
railway folders and the chambers-of-commerce bulletins
are quite willing to tell you, with a plethora of adjectives
that even a Boulder Dam might not control. But there
are two equally commonplace topics that I would touch
upon : one is the clear pure air, so clear that even the eye
of the mind seems to see further in it ; so pure that it has
a cleansing effect upon the spirit. And the other topic is
People, — human beings, — folks.

We took plenty of time to the business of using the air and meeting folks, over on the western slope. It is a country very easy to reach, though some of your eastern-slope garage men seemed to wish to create a different impression. For nearly four months we explored its highways and byways, skidding on some, bumping over others, and now and then gliding evenly along on the very edge of the world, with a fatalistic belief that our time had not yet come to topple off. From the top of Monarch Pass to the foot of Shiprock our patient car carried us, and in between lay Gunnison and Ouray and Silverton and Durango and Farmington, and hot springs and warm springs and clear cold nights and deep canyons and the high dizzy brink of Kingdom-Come. And all along the way we met pleasant folks.

Mind you, I am not in agreement with those professional westerners who noisily claim the West's exclusive pos-session of all human virtue, and then slap you on the back so that it hurts. Give me room enough for a swing, and secure footing, and a ready exit, and I can hurt any-body's back, without proving anything. Men's morals average about the same everywhere, as the records of credit bureaus and help-yourself-cafeterias prove; the point I wish to make is that where we journeyed you may see men a little more clearly, and after looking as sharply as you will, you find that they are all at least fifty-one per cent to the good.

It is not only the clearer air that enables one to see people more distinctly; it is the fact that there are fewer things to obstruct the vision. Just as one may not see trees because of the forest, one may not see men and women where there are crowds. In crowded neighbor-hoods, too, so many other things keep us from seeing our neighbors: theatres, and public receptions, and large churches, and organized charity, and trolley cars and policemen. And undoubtedly high white collars get in the way. It is easier to appraise Adam, when you can see Adam's apple.

Of course there are the same varieties of human nature in the sparsely settled country as anywhere else, but there are fewer of those social conditions that tend to turn the natural virtues sour. No, not every variety: the unctious and the puffy sorts are missing, — those that swell up and strut when the eyes of the multitude are upon them. You find such in politics and the Church, but not in sparsely settled country. Crooks we met there, of course; but a crook is more likeable when he is not a hypocrite, and hypocrisy thrives best among crowds. We met some ex-professional gamblers. I have known plenty of gamblers in more crowded neighborhoods, and they were not half so likeable because they played against men who did not know they were gambling. We met one old villain who was said to have two notches on the stock of his rifle, which by the way was his favorite weapon. He was a great improvement upon another old gentleman I know who must have at least a hundred similar notches on the stock of his bank-account, which is *his* favorite weapon.

But I did not mean to touch particularly upon odd specimens. I did mean to emphasize the fact, though it be trite, which was borne in upon me with new emphasis: that a cross-sectional view of folks, viewed close up, in a country where the viewing is unobstructed, strengthens and establishes one's optimism.

It was while I was living on the western slope that I picked up a book I had long ago been told I should read. "It tears the veil of hypocrisy from the features of war," it "exposes the cant of so-called patriotism"; in a word it tells us just how all the boys really behaved in France.

I read it, and to my surprise I remained calm — even mildly amused. I was once in France, and I saw there drunkenness and debauchery. I saw many other things also. As I pondered over the book there in the clear air of the western slope, I recalled a man who in my own college days had visited a great eastern university that I knew well, — and knew from the inside. He was a reverend gentleman of wide repute, but with a lecherous mind. He discovered that a young man might better be sent to Hell than to that university, and he proved it by data which was all true — as far as it went. Its weakness lay in the fact that he saw only those boys who were doing just what he was looking for; and the swirling crowd kept him from seeing even that clearly. I wish that old scavenger had not gone to his final reward. Because I should like to have him look about our world today, a generation later, and see how many lads of that day who were hell-bent in that very university are now doing fine clean work as men in the Church and professions and affairs. He guessed wrong, as it is now possible to prove. Undoubtedly he saw many of those boys doing things that later they deeply regretted; deeds that left scars. But he would have been less likely to guess wrong if he had met them singly, face to face, with time and room to talk or work or go fishing with each of them.

Another book I picked up on the western slope; there are several of its sort, some good, some bad; some written with an eye to the truth; some with half an eye for the truth, and an eye-and-a-half for the gate receipts. It told the "truth" about General Grant — or was it Jefferson, or Roosevelt, or Bishop Brooks? — I disremember. At any rate, it proceeded to prove that the long established and popular conception of its subject as a "great" man was unjustified; and it did so by overstressing that tithe of his annals which were most humanly unheroic.

The book would have disturbed me once, — but not now, out in that clear air. I could turn from it with a yawn, hunt up a most evilly profane friend I had lately discovered, and go fishing with him. I knew that he would restore my confidence in human kind. We could talk together hopefully of other men, and even indulge without shame in a little worship of the old heroes. In a land where you can see so easily how bad a man is, you more truly measure men's virtues.

This must surely be an essay, my dear Editor, because you can cut it off anywhere, to fit your pages. But Ernest Rhys says, in his definition of an essay, "it may preach, but it must never be a sermon." Then bang! another rule has gone flat, — and not a garage in sight.

"If this be reason," as Patrick Henry says, "make the least of it."

SUGGESTIONS FOR ESSAYS

Subjects suggested by some of the essays in the preceding collection. Students choosing one of these topics, or any kindred ones, may find their ideas stimulated by reading the essays cited, or may find therein sources of brief quotation or allusion.

"Self-Revelation"   "Man's Favorite Topic — Himself"
Montaigne: *A Preface;* Cowley: *Of Myself;* Morley: *Round Columbus Circle*

"My Favorite Books"   "Books to Keep"
Montaigne: *Of Books;* Bacon: *Of Studies;* Ruskin: *Of Kings' Treasuries;* Morris: *Comfortable Books*

"Authors That Bore Me"
Montaigne: *Of the Institution and Education of Children*

"Plagiarism"   "Whose thoughts am I thinking"
Montaigne: *Of the Institution and Education of Children;* Irving: *The Art of Book Making;* Stevenson: *A College Magazine*

"Traveling Companions"   "Solitude"
Bacon: *Of Travel;* Hazlitt: *On Going A Journey;* Thoreau: *Where I Lived*

"King Arthur and His Knights"
Caxton: *A Printer's Prologue*

"On Being in Debt"   "Poverty"
Chaucer: *Dame Prudence;* Ecclesiastes: *The Vanity of Riches;* Cowley: *Of Myself;* Ecclesiasticus: *A House of One's Own;* Lamb: *Old China*

"My Favorite Play"
Shakespeare: *Hamlet's Advice;* Eaton: *Confession in Prose*

"Vanity Cases"   "Girls"
T. T.: *Of Painting the Face;* Gosse: *The Whole Duty of Woman;* Holmes: *The Autocrat*

"Concerning Beards"
T. T.: *Of Painting the Face*

"College Professors"
Fuller: *The Good Schoolmaster*

"Studying"
Fuller: *The Good Schoolmaster*; Bacon: *Of Studies;* Montaigne: *Of the Institution and Education of Children*

"When Winter Goes"
Dekker: *Of Winter*

"Tact"
Theophrastus: *The Tactless Man*

"Bores"; "Wisdom of Silence"
Theophrastus: *The Bore;* Bible: *The Tongue;* Steele: *Jack Lizard;* Carlyle: *Symbols*

"Boarding Houses"
Ecclesiasticus: *A House of One's Own*

"Good Resolutions"
Bunyan: *The Slough of Despond*

"Interventions of Providence"
Defoe: *Robinson Crusoe*

"A New Medical Discovery"
Pope: *The Grand Elixir*

"Reformers"
Swift: *A Meditation upon a Broomstick*

"Political Bunkum"
Swift: *The Art of Political Lying*

"On Going to Church"
Addison: *Sir Roger at Church*

SUGGESTIONS FOR ESSAYS 317

"Witch Hunting"
Addison: *Witches*

"The Good Old Days"
Lamb: *Old China*

"Early Rising"
Lamb: *Popular Fallacies;* Hunt: *Getting up on Cold Mornings;* Chesterton: *On Lying in Bed*

"Borrowers"
Lamb: *The Two Races of Men*

"When I Was Very Young"
Thackeray: *Tunbridge Toys;* Beerbohm: *A Relic*

"Slumming"
Dickens: *Night Walks*

"Trees in the City"
Holmes: *The Autocrat*

"On Being in a Hurry"
Thoreau: *Where I Lived*

"Christmas Presents"
Emerson: *Gifts*

"Following a Flag"
Carlyle: *Symbols*

"The Passing Generation"
Gosse: *The Whole Duty of Woman*

"Adventures with a Glee Club"; — A Dramatic Troupe
Schauffler: *Fiddlers Errant*

"Writing for the Fun of It"
Stevenson: *A College Magazine;* Eaton: *A Confession in Prose*

"Realism"
Eaton: *A Confession in Prose;* Johnson: *The True Patrick Henry*